The Art of Computer Networking

We work with leading authors to develop the
strongest educational materials in computing,
bringing cutting-edge thinking and best
learning practice to a global market.

Under a range of well-known imprints, including
Prentice Hall, we craft high-quality print and
electronic publications which help readers to understand
and apply their content, whether studying or at work.

To find out more about the complete range of our
publishing, please visit us on the World Wide Web at:
www.pearsoned.co.uk

The Art of Computer Networking

Russell Bradford

PEARSON
Prentice
Hall

Harlow, England • London • New York • Boston • San Francisco • Toronto • Sydney • Singapore • Hong Kong
Tokyo • Seoul • Taipei • New Delhi • Cape Town • Madrid • Mexico City • Amsterdam • Munich • Paris • Milan

Pearson Education Limited
Edinburgh Gate
Harlow
Essex CM20 2JE
England

and Associated Companies throughout the world

Visit us on the World Wide Web at:
www.pearsoned.co.uk

First published 2007

ISBN: 978-0-321-30676-0

British Library Cataloguing-in-Publication Data
A catalogue record for this book is available from the British Library

10 9 8 7 6 5 4 3 2 1
11 10 09 08 07

Typeset in 10/12pt Times by 71
Printed and bound in the United States of America

The publisher's policy is to use paper manufactured from sustainable forests.

BRIEF CONTENTS

CONTENTS

PREFACE

This book, like so many, has grown from an undergraduate Networking course. Its current content is rather more than a single course could comfortably cover, though it is all relevant for an adventurer into the jungle of networks.

It is somewhat biased towards the Internet and the protocols the Internet uses, namely TCP/IP. Other network technologies are touched on more to give a flavour of alternatives and contrasts of approaches than to give a deep insight. In fact, to give a deep insight into any single aspect of networking is worth a book in its own right, so I have had to be somewhat selective in the topics covered. Though, in the end, the criterion of choice for inclusion is simple: this book contains the stuff I find interesting about networking. The intent is to provide a taster for many concepts, but with enough information for the reader to follow up and deepen their understanding. For the details, please refer to the various RFCs and standards documents that are listed in the margins.

RFC 2555

As is traditional, each chapter ends with some exercises. What is less traditional is their form: they are less of the 'write down everything you know', but more 'go and try this'. You are expected to find out things for yourself and experiment! You may need to read up and learn other things before you can tackle the problems directly: this is all part of the exercise. The best way of learning this kind of material is by direct experience. And quite often there might not be a single answer, or even a 'right' answer.

> Occasionally there are snippets of text like this one. These are bits and pieces that are not part of the main thrust of the text, or things that may only make sense later. Ignore at the first reading, if you wish.

For the structure of this book we follow the 'traditional' approach of tracking the layering models and move from the lowest (physical) to the highest (application). This goes against the current fashion for a top-down approach, but I feel this is better for the modern reader who has a lot of experience in using the Internet and knows where we are headed.

In the end, reality is not cleanly layered and both bottom-up and top-down approaches regularly trip up and have to refer forward or backward to justify their progress and I believe referring towards the familiar rather than towards the unknown is more comfortable.

A note on the title: *The Art of Computer Networks*. While this initially reflects Knuth's wonderful series on algorithms (if only we could all have such a clear insight!), I would also like to think we have some passing resemblance to Sun Tzu's *The Art of War*. We need both the lofty strategic overview and the eye for small detail if we want to win with networks.

One final comment on acronyms: the subject of networking has more than its fair share. Being techie-based, that is perhaps inevitable, but it can make the newcomer feel a little lost amongst the TLAs. For this I can only offer sympathy and note that most acronyms can be safely forgotten.

Remember, the Art is in the Details!

INTRODUCTION

1.1 What Is this Book about?

Many people will have used a network, be it the World Wide Web, email, or another of the utilities that are starting to worm their way into our everyday lives. Some aspects of networks will be familiar to many, such as clicking in a Web browser, or deleting spam from our inbox. There is a lot of (mostly) hidden technology that drives this phenomenon we call the Internet, and this book aims to give a passing familiarity with some of it.

A network is any means of connecting entities – usually computers – together so that they can communicate. The means of connection can be wire, optical fibre, radio, satellite, sound waves, string, semaphore or whatever, but the general idea is that we have channels capable of transmitting information between entities. Networks are useful for many reasons:

- Resource sharing. The 'traditional' reason for having a network is so I can use that big supercomputer 100 miles up the road. Or I can use the department's high-quality colour printer from the comfort of my office.

- Communication and collaboration. I can work with people on a different continent, sharing data, running experiments and writing papers. This includes video and voice conferencing and email.

- Information gathering. If I need information about the latest developments in CPU design, I can look through the Web or USENET.

- Reliability through replication. If my highly valuable database is replicated on another machine and if my machine crashes, then the data is safe. Note this is also a protection against malicious attack.

- Entertainment and commerce. From static content such as traditional newspapers and video on demand, to interactive applications like multi-player games or user participation quiz shows, and to the big wide world of consumerism that is inventing new and better ways to relieve us of our cash.

And much more, of course. The value of a network is that it enables entities to communicate. One of the original inventors of Ethernet coined *Metcalfe's law*:

> The value of a network expands exponentially as the number of users increases.

The Internet has proved this law many times over.

A network can be big or small: from a single piece of wire connecting two machines to the entirety of the Internet. And whenever you have more than one entity – be it computer or person – you have all the usual problems of communication: Are they mutually comprehensible? Do they share a common world view? Is their means of communication efficient, or even suitable for the purpose?

'Networks' is a huge subject. There are masses of intricate detail, some of which is very subtle and hard to understand. On the other hand the rewards of understanding even a small part of the subject can be substantial, both intellectually and financially.

Networks are big money at the moment – just look at how fast the Internet has grown – but most people do not realize networks have been around for a long time in many guises. Mention 'networks' and most only think of the Internet. We have:

- The telephone system. An ancient technology that represents a huge investment of money in systems and copper wire buried in the ground. The major problem to solve is how to make a connection from subscriber A to subscriber B; once this is made, relaying the conversation between them is relatively straightforward. The telephone network is now caught up in the Internet boom and is modernizing rapidly, with much investment in optical fibre and digital exchanges.

- The cell or mobile phone system. This is newer and still developing (the next generation of phones is just arriving). There is big investment in transmitter stations and radio wavelengths. Now A and B are moving about, the system must cope with that.

- TV and radio. These are one–many systems mostly, namely *broadcast* systems. The investment is in content, transmitters and relayers (e.g., satellites).

- Cable networks. TV again, but also telephone and data can be supplied via cable.

- Data networks. Examples are private-company nets and dial-up systems. Each has its own protocol, both in terms of hardware (voltages, number of wires, etc.) and in proprietary software. There have been many examples: DECNet, Microsoft, Novell IPX, AppleTalk, to name just a few.

- The Internet. Often confused with the World Wide Web, which is just one thing that the Internet serves. Actually email has been most important application in the development of the Internet. The Internet also enables data transfer, remote access, conference video, and many other services. The 'Internet' is actually a collection of smaller networks all connected together using a widely agreed protocol: the Internet Protocol (IP). The smaller networks are owned by companies or governments or individuals and may be themselves composed of even smaller networks. There is a strong hierarchical shape to the Internet, but there is no one in overall charge. Each group owns its own part of the Internet and they all agree on how to connect to the other parts: the Internet is a great collaborative effort. This is in contrast to the above proprietary systems where economics drives secrecy and isolation.

The success of the Internet at the expense of private, proprietary systems is due to the Internet being public, open, and that it uses standards from the hardware level on up.

There are technical groups to oversee the growth and development of the Internet, but these are generally non-profit. See Section 1.5.

It is often convenient to classify networks by their size. The three major divisions are

- LAN (Local Area Network). A network in a building or organization controlled by a single institution. The main requirements are for speed and responsiveness.

- MAN (Metropolitan Area Network). A city-wide network, used by many organizations. Problems to solve include accounting: who pays for what. When more than one organization is involved, this is sure to be a difficult problem. An example: the University of Bath is connected to the Bristol and West of England MAN (BWE MAN). The BWE MAN joins several local institutions in the west of England to the *Joint Academic Network* (JANET), the main academic network for the UK.

- WAN (Wide Area Network). Long haul, e.g., country-wide or between countries. Additional problems here are the (relatively) long delays as the data necessarily takes longer to get to its destination; there are protocol conversions between different parts of the network, since one country may use different hardware or software than another. JANET is a WAN used by the UK academic community.

There is much overlap between these classifications: in particular, 'WAN' is often taken to mean anything bigger than a LAN. Different technologies can be targeted at the problems of a particular size of network. For example, Ethernet is good (cheap and fast) for LANs but poor for WANs, where the more expensive ATM, say, is better suited.

Other classifications you may see include: community area network (CAN, p. 74), personal area network (PAN) and wireless personal area network (WPAN, p. 73), but the above three are the main ones technologically speaking.

Networks can be further classified as *broadband* or *narrowband*. The term 'broadband' (or *wideband*) means different things to different people. Technically, it means a communications medium that has a large number of frequencies available to transmit information, so many channels can use it simultaneously. This is in contrast to narrowband (or *voiceband*), which is just wide enough to carry a voice channel. Related is *baseband*, meaning a single channel network (like Ethernet). Lately, though, as networks have moved into the public consciousness and marketing has taken over, these terms are being used to indicate network speeds, so narrowband means 'up to 64Kb/s' or sometimes 'up to 56Kb/s', while broadband is anything faster. Sometimes even, narrowband simply means 'slow' and broadband 'fast'.

There are many standards that define the Internet. The principal players are the *Request for Comments* (RFC) documents for software and the *Institute of Electrical and Electronics Engineers* (IEEE) standards for hardware. RFCs, published by the *Internet Society* (ISOC), are at the heart of the Internet: if you want your machine to interoperate with the others on the Internet its software must follow what these documents say. In practice, many software vendors take liberties and diverge from the standards through either buggy implementation or attempts to gain commercial advantage. The general rule for implementing RFCs is

> be as close to the RFC as possible in what you do yourself, but be as liberal as possible regarding what you accept from others.

Following this maxim will enable the greatest interoperability throughout the Internet.

Marginally useful stuff Where appropriate to the matter being described, the number of an RFC or other standard will appear in the margin.

1.2   Other Resources

A primary source for those wishing to study the Internet protocols is Stevens' *TCP/IP Illustrated, Volume 1*. This is a bible of the IP, distilling down the RFCs and covering many aspects in practical detail.

There are a huge number of other books about, though beware of the 'IP for Windows' kind of books. They just tell you what buttons to click in which configuration tools, but give no understanding of what's really happening.

The Web is a good source of information: all the RFCs, various standards and an excess of discussion of Internet-related things are easily found.

Due to the rapid change in Internet technology, Stevens is a trifle out of date in places, but the majority of the content is still absolutely relevant. Of course, by the time you read this, it is absolutely certain that some of the content of this book is out of date. This is just a measure of how fast the Internet changes: protocols and applications are forever being tweaked, upgraded and improved. In fact, the only way to keep up with the Internet is to use it!

1.3   How Big Is a Megabyte?

There are several ways to measure things in the computer world and some people use the same words to mean different things.

For example, when describing memory, 1MB generally means 1 megabyte, which is $2^{20} = 1048576$ bytes. On the other hand, hard-disk manufacturers usually use 1MB to mean $10^6 = 1000000$ bytes. Thus you can't fit a megabyte of memory on a megabyte disk! And worse, sometimes the two systems are mixed: the 1.44MB floppy disk uses a megabyte of 1024000 bytes.

To try to disambiguate the confusion, there is an official International Electrotechnical Commission (IEC) standard that defines a megabyte as definitely 10^6 bytes and introduces a new unit, the *mebibyte*, that is definitely 2^{20} bytes. This takes the first two letters of the existing name and adds 'bi' for binary. Unfortunately, not many people are yet aware of this system and fewer still have adopted it.

Traditional measures are:

Traditional name	K kilo	M mega	G giga	T tera	P peta	E exa
Binary	$2^{10} =$ 1024	$2^{20} \approx$ 1.04×10^6	$2^{30} \approx$ 1.07×10^9	$2^{40} \approx$ 1.10×10^{12}	$2^{50} \approx$ 1.12×10^{15}	$2^{60} \approx$ 1.15×10^{18}
Decimal	1000	10^6	10^9	10^{12}	10^{15}	10^{18}

while IEC measures are:

IEC name	Ki kibi	Mi mebi	Gi gibi	Ti tebi	Pi pebi	Ei exbi
Value	2^{10}	2^{20}	2^{30}	2^{40}	2^{50}	2^{60}

We shall be using the traditional binary

b	bit	B	byte
M	mega	G	giga
K	kilo	s	second

so that 10Mb means 10 megabits and 10KB/s means 10 kilobytes per second, though sometimes when talking about data rates we shall be lazy and use Mb to mean Mb/s. For example, '10Mb Ethernet' should be '10Mb/s Ethernet', but the former is common usage.

Often in specifications and standards you will see the word 'octet'. This means 8 bits. This is used in preference to the usual term 'byte' as the word 'byte' historically and on some rare systems is used to denote a different number of bits, generally in the range of 4 to 10. We shall, however, be using 'byte' with the commonly accepted sense of 8 bits.

1.4 Internet History

The timeline of the Internet is very interesting and deserves a book of its own. The 'definitive' Internet history has been standardized and can be found at http://www.zakon.org/robert/internet/timeline/ and RFC 2235.

RFC 2235

What follows is a *very* sketchy history of the Internet. Much is omitted and much is simplified.

Executive summary: it's the fault of the Russians.

At the height of the Cold War, in 1958, the Soviets had just launched Sputnik. The Americans retaliated by founding the Advanced Research Projects Agency (ARPA, later to become the *Defense Advanced Research Projects Agency*, DARPA) to develop high technology for the military.

In the mid 1960s ARPA wanted a system to allow researchers to use each other's computers, which were still rare and very expensive. Its design was to be non-centralized to avoid single points of failure, specifically nuclear attacks. Simple telephone links between machines would be too vulnerable, as chopping one would split the network. ARPA moved to the idea of *packet switched* networks and multiple routes between hosts.

The telephone system is (or rather, used to be) based on *circuit switching*. This means that the objective is to provide an (electrical) circuit from A to B over which the conversation will be carried. This is like reserving the whole of the East Coast railway line to allow a single train to go from London to Edinburgh. A second train cannot use the line until the first has reached its destination and released the line. This is clearly wasteful of the track, but ensures the train gets to its destination in the best possible time.

The alternative is *packet switching*. The train is broken up into carriages and each is sent singly down the track. The big advantage is that several trains can share the same line: their carriages can be interleaved. Furthermore separate carriages of the same train can actually take different routes, as long as we reassemble them in the correct order at the destination. This gives us better use of the track bandwidth and resilience against leaves on the line.

In terms of data, packet switching is just this: chop the data up into manageable chunks or *packets* and route each packet individually. Compare this with circuit switching, where a dedicated line is set up for the transaction. We shall compare the pros and cons later.

The first ARPA net consisted of Interface Message Processors (IMPs) connected by transmission lines. These were multiply connected together in a redundant fashion for reliability. If one link was broken, packets could use an alternative route to their destination. The IMPs used *store and forward*: that is, they read an entire packet into their memory before sending it on. These were 24KB minicomputers connected by 56Kb telephone lines.

Note that, as is still true today, it was common for the Internet to use the existing telephone system to carry the signals.

In 1969 the network went live with four nodes: Stanford Research Institute, UCLA, UC Santa Barbara and the University of Utah (Figure 1.1). They specifically connected incompatible host computers to demonstrate the machine independence of their system. The protocol the network used was called *Network Control Protocol* (NCP). Very soon it was found that remote access of computers was not the main use of the system, but email and discussion groups. The social side of the Internet was starting to be recognized.

By the end of 1972 there were 30 or so hosts connected across the width of the USA. In 1973 University College London joined up, the first international connection.

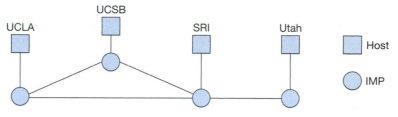

Figure 1.1 The original ARPANET.

The protocols the network used were under continuous development and by 1974 the *Transmission Control Protocol/Internet Protocol* (TCP/IP) emerged to replace NCP. As the operating system of choice at that time (Unix) had TCP/IP built in, it was easy for universities to join the ARPANET.

And many did. The year of 1979 saw the advent of USENET newsgroups: a logical progression from telephone dial-up bulletin boards and the discussion groups.

By the early 1980s there were hundreds then thousands of machines connected. It was becoming a little difficult to manage all the names and addresses for all the machines, so new protocols were developed to collect machines into groups called *domains* and have a non-centralized method of naming. This was the Domain Name System (DNS): the .com was born. In 1982 the word 'internet' was first used to describe a network of networks.

In the mid 1980s a high-speed successor to ARPANET was developed. The National Science Foundation (NSF) created the NFSNET *backbone* which was set up between the six NSF supercomputer sites and this provided major trunking between regional networks. This started with 56Kb telephone lines, but was soon upgraded to 448Kb fibre optic lines and then 1.5Mb lines in 1990. By the end of the 1980s, there were hundreds of thousands of hosts on the Internet.

In 1989–1990, the old ARPANET was decommissioned.

Soon big business started to be interested in the Internet phenomenon. They provided commercial IP networks and the network backbone was replaced by a commercially driven infrastructure.

This growth was fuelled by the uses people made of the networks. Mostly email, but other things, too. The popularity was helped by the use of a single open standard protocol to connect machines. It was non-proprietary and open so anyone could adopt it and implement it. Many other standards, e.g., OSF in the UK, IBM's mainframe network, BITNET, HEPNET (high-energy physics), SPAN (NASA), and so on, existed, but their reach was limited. The only protocol allowed on the Internet was IP and this ensured that (say) an IBM machine could talk to a DEC machine regardless of their internal workings. Slowly the other networks declined and machines and applications were converted to TCP/IP. Everybody started using the IP in their systems in preference to their own or bought-in protocols.

In 1992 the Internet hit 1 million hosts. There was general use in universities and a few companies, mainly for email. Ethernet at 10Mb/s emerged as the LAN technology of choice.

The invention of Gopher in 1991 was an early step towards a global information system. The University of Minnesota invented a system to simplify the fetching of files from remote machines with its 'go for' system. This presented the user with a list of files and directories and these could be linked to other Gopher systems anywhere else in the world. Gopher was popular for a while, being text based and thus suitable for the majority of terminals in use at the time. Gopher is still supported in the major Web browsers, though it is increasingly difficult to find a Gopher server still running.

However, it was the invention of the World Wide Web (WWW) in 1991 that really drove the second phase of growth of the Internet. Tim Berners-Lee at CERN (European Centre for Nuclear Research) needed a way to control the huge amounts of data (reports, pictures, programs, etc.) that were spread across the many participating countries. He invented the World Wide Web. It was similar to Gopher, but with a graphical point-and-click interface and the ability to display pictures (and later, sound and video). He and Marc Andreessen developed the Mosaic browser (1993), later to become Netscape.

This was a big breakthrough: point-and-click interfaces allow use by computer phobic people.

There was sudden massive growth as the Internet was recognized to have commercial value for delivering content via the WWW and the general public at home could use browsers to access it via modems. After several false starts (when it initially tried to market its own proprietary system) Microsoft fell into line and the Internet took off.

There was a huge growth in Internet Service Providers (ISPs), companies that connect you to the Internet, e.g., AOL. Similarly for companies selling over the WWW, billions of dollars were spent on and over the Internet. There was massive growth in infrastructure involving advances in optical fibre technology and processor power.

In the UK 'free' dial-up ISPs arrived (non-subscription services that were financed by a slice of the cost of the telephone call) and these boosted the expansion of the Internet into the home. Homes got affordable 'fast' modems which ran at 56Kb/s.

Internet companies went public and reaped billions. The 'dot com' boom reached its peak, with investors pouring money into anything that had .com attached, regardless of viability. Telecoms companies put billions into unproven technology.

Entertainment companies (generally TV, film, and music publishing) started taking an interest, mostly through fear of losing control of their dissemination of entertainment to a rag-bag of new companies over which they had no dominion.

Soon came the dot com crash: investors finally realized the emperor had no clothes and the overinvestment in technology caused the stock market to crash. Most Internet companies shrank, many died.

High-speed networks came to the home via the cable TV/telephone network, via *Asymmetric Digital Subscriber Line* (ADSL) and via many other methods. Out of the ashes of the dot com crash grew much more sustainable companies: home shopping using the Internet is now a multi-billion-dollar concern.

'Traditional' suppliers of telephony started to move their networks to Internet technology; TV and music companies nervously started to use the Internet to deliver (in particular, to sell) content.

The Internet is huge now. Who knows what is next?

1.5 Internet Management

The question of who oversees what in the Internet is a complex and sometimes contentious one. For technical issues the ISOC heads a group of committees, with input from national and international standards groups like the IEEE, the International Organization for Standardization (ISO), and the International Telecommunications Union (ITU) amongst others. These run relatively smoothly.

RFC 2031

On the other hand, managerial issues, like the control and selling of domain names, are fraught with discord between the parties involved, mainly due to the fact that large sums of money are concerned.

Roughly, the big players (Figure 1.2) are:

* Internet Society, ISOC. An international non-profit organization to foster the expansion of the Internet. It oversees and funds the other organizations, e.g., publishing RFCs for the IETF.

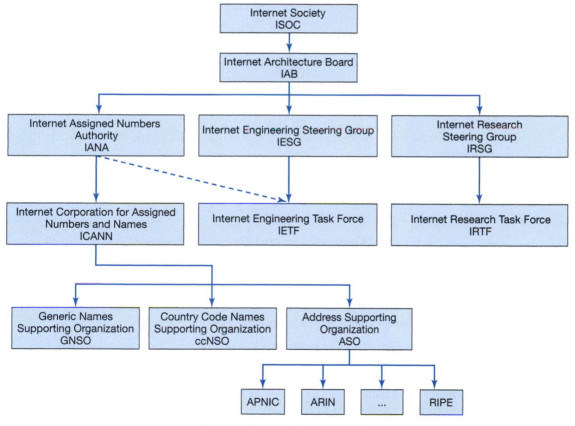

Figure 1.2 Internet organization.

- Internet Architecture Board, IAB. A technical committee to advise the ISOC. It has a long-term view of the Internet.

- Internet Engineering Task Force, IETF. The people who actually identify the problems and devise solutions and protocols to implement them. For example, through the *RFC Editor* they produce the RFCs. Decisions are made on 'rough consensus and working code', meaning that real code that implements a solution has more weight than fancy words describing solutions that do not yet exist.

- Internet Engineering Steering Group, IESG. A technical committee to oversee the IETF. It decides if the rough consensus of the IETF is good enough to become a real standard.

- Internet Research Task Force, IRTF. A group who are working on the future of the Internet, researching new ideas that may one day be useful.

- Internet Research Steering Group, IRSG. A committee to oversee the IRTF.

- Internet Assigned Numbers Authority, IANA. Keeps track of protocol details like TCP port numbers, ARP hardware types, and so on, for the IETF. Most importantly, it allocates DNS domain names and IP addresses.

- Internet Corporation for Assigned Names and Numbers, ICANN. Runs the commercial parts of IANA, namely domain names and IP addresses. ICANN oversees the DNS root name servers (p. 141). ICANN has three supporting organizations: ASO, ccNSO and GNSO.

- Address Supporting Organization, ASO. Deals with IP address allocation. This is divided into a number of regions that look after geographic areas:
  - Asia Pacific Network Information Centre, APNIC, for Japan and the Asia Pacific region.

  - American Registry for Internet Numbers, ARIN, for North America (not Mexico).

  - Réseaux IP Européens, RIPE, for Europe.

  - Latin American and Caribbean Network Information Centre, LACNIC, for South America, Mexico and the Caribbean.

  - AfriNIC, covering Africa, has just arrived.

- Country Code Names Supporting Organization, ccNSO. Deals with two-letter top-level country domain names, e.g., uk, jp and so on.

- Generic Names Supporting Organization, GNSO. Deals with non-country-specific domains, such as com and coop. See Chapter 8.

There is further delegation of domain names to hundreds of registrar companies that sell names and numbers to the final customer.

1.6 Exercises

Exercise 1.1 For each of the above committees find their Websites, determine their mission statements and write notes on their latest achievements.

Exercise 1.2 For your organization (university, company, or whatever) determine the administration of your computer network, e.g., who is responsible for new computer names, who is responsible for network security, and so on.

Exercise 1.3 Do some shopping: find out how you would buy a domain name of your own. Where is the cheapest place to buy? Don't forget to look at the terms and conditions of your purchase!

Exercise 1.4 Find some active Gopher sites. Compare the experience of using Gopher to that of using the WWW.

Exercise 1.5 Write an essay on what you see as the future of the Internet.

LAYERING MODELS

2

2.1   Introduction

Building a network is a very complicated problem. There are many things to be addressed:

- What hardware do we use? This includes things like cables and optical fibres right down to the design of plugs and sockets.

- How do we encode data bits on the hardware? What voltages, what speed? Do we want to use binary values or something more complicated?

- What standard of service do we wish to provide? Reliable, connectionless, stream oriented, packet switched? Is flow control included (to prevent a fast machine overwhelming a slow one)?

- What interface to the computer do we want? How do programmers actually use the network?

- What protocols should we use to connect applications? For example, how information is passed along the WWW?

The thing to note is that we have to have standards all the way from the lowest part of the hardware right up to the highest level of the software if every pair of machines in the world is to be able to communicate. If any part of the system fails to be standard, it is possible that communication will fail. This is clear when we try to plug a copper cable into an optical socket, but is also true if we use a Web server that does not produce standard HTML.

One way to approach this is to have one huge standard that fixes everything at every level. But this is not very flexible. Maybe we want to upgrade the hardware: do we have to rewrite our browser to accommodate the new standard?

2.2　The Seven Layer Model

The solution adopted is to decompose the big problem into several smaller problems and in 1983 a *layered* standard was proposed. Or, to be more precise, a *reference model* was proposed, the ISO Open Systems Interconnection (OSI) Reference Model. This is commonly known as the *OSI Seven Layer Model*. It describes several principles you should think about when approaching a standard for a network. It doesn't actually give a standard for a network itself (though there was one directly based on it as a separate standard).

OSI 7498

The principles involved were:

- a layer should be created where a different level of abstraction is needed;

- each layer should perform a well-defined function;

- the function of each layer should be chosen with an eye towards defining internationally standardized protocols;

- the layer boundaries should be chosen to minimize the information flow across the interfaces;

- the number of layers should be large enough that distinct functions need not be thrown together out of necessity and small enough that the architecture does not become unwieldy.

The magic number of layers was decided to be seven: this was felt to be just the right number. Here we describe the seven layers with their classical properties, though you should note that not everyone sticks hard and fast to this kind of division of behaviours.

2.2.1　The Physical Layer

Sometimes called the *PHY layer* or *layer 1*, this is the hardware layer and deals with the transmission of bits over a channel. Typical problems are what voltages (or change of voltages) or colour and intensity of light pulses should be used to signify a one and a zero; how long (in time) a bit should be; how many wires to use in a cable; what each wire is for. This is an electrical or optical or mechanical or other specification that transmits a continuous stream of bits (if we chose to use bits). Note that this layer might be radio or any other transmission medium rather than copper wire or optical fibre.

This layer is sometimes divided into two sublayers for extra flexibility:

1. Physical Media Dependent (PMD) sublayer for actual hardware like optical transceivers or copper wire. For example, 10Gb Ethernet has two kinds of optical transceiver for short- and long-range networks.
2. Physical Coding Sublayer (PCS) or Physical Layer Convergence Procedure (PLCP) sublayer is for how bits are encoded on the PMD. For example, 10Gb Ethernet uses a 64B/66B encoding (see Section 3.5).

2.2.2   The Data Link Layer

Sometimes called the *MAC layer* or *media access layer* or *layer 2*, this layer takes the physical medium and decides how to use it to provide a channel where there are no undetected errors of transmission. We can use a physical layer that is prone to errors (e.g., radio) as long as we can detect those errors and then we can do something about them.

Typically this is achieved by breaking the input data into *data frames*, and transmitting each frame individually. A frame is just a chunk of bytes which might be tens or thousands of bytes long. Some standards specify that *acknowledgement frames* should be returned from the receiver to the sender indicating successful receipt. If a frame is corrupted (lost or damaged), the data link layer could retransmit it or inform the next layer of the problem. A popular choice is to do nothing at all and let a higher layer figure out a remedy.

Another problem that can be addressed at this layer is *flow control*. Perhaps the sender is pumping out data faster than the receiver can currently cope with: some means of telling the sender to slow down must be employed. Similarly, when the receiver has caught up, it can inform the sender to speed up again.

2.2.3   The Network Layer

Also called *layer 3*, this is concerned with controlling the operation of the network, including the question of how to route a packet from source to destination. This might include the problem of congestion control: if too many packets are trying to use one line we might reroute some, or use flow control to slow some sources down.

We can also deal with internetwork problems at this layer. Perhaps a packet is routed from one network to another that has a smaller frame size so some action must be taken, such as breaking the frame into smaller frames or perhaps simply refusing to pass on the frame.

The network layer also deals with things like *accounting*: counting the number of bits sent by a user so we can bill them later.

2.2.4   The Transport Layer

This layer, *layer 4*, accepts arbitrary data from the next, the session layer, and arranges it into packets suitable for the network layer (*packetization*). Similarly, it receives packets from the network layer and reconfigures them in the correct order for the session layer (*depacketization*).

This layer can manage network connections, maybe sending one data stream out over several connections to improve throughput, or multiplexing several data streams over one connection to save money. This layer also provides the type of service available to the user: examples are reliable (error-free), order preserving, connection oriented or connectionless.

It would be natural to want all our data transmissions to be 100% perfect: the bits that arrive are exactly the bits that were sent. However, arranging this can be very difficult given the unpredictable nature of hardware. Techniques (e.g., acknowledgement frames) can be used to approach reliability, but there is a cost (e.g., an acknowledgement frame can reduce the time and space that is available for real data). Sometimes (see Section 9.3) we would rather not pay the cost, but instead allow for a margin of error in the data: transmission of audio is such a case, where slightly incorrect data is fine, but delayed data is not. In other cases (e.g., payroll data) we are happy to pay the overhead to get the 100% reliability.

Similarly, in a packet-oriented system, it may or may not be important that the packets containing the data arrive in the exact same order they were sent. Imposing order may cause extra expense that you might prefer not to pay in some applications.

A *connection-oriented* network is one where a path is made from the source to a destination and all data flows along this path. For example, when making a telephone call, a connection is set up before the data (the speech) can flow. In pre-digital days, telephone exchanges used to set up a physical copper path from caller to callee. A connection-oriented system is best when there needs to be good, smooth, uninterrupted flow of data.

In a *connectionless* network no connection is made and each packet is treated individually. This is like the postal system, where each letter is delivered individually. Two letters from the same source to the same destination could quite easily go via different routes and it is very possible that a later letter could be delivered before a letter posted earlier. A connectionless system is best when the data is small or irregular and you do not want the overhead of setting up a connection. Connection oriented is normally associated with circuit switching and connectionless with packet switching (Section 1.4).

TCP/IP is considered to be reliable, order preserving and connection oriented, though the connection path is more conceptual than real.

2.2.5   The Session Layer

Layer 5 allows the user to create a *session* between the source and destination. One example is a remote login session: you make the session by using `telnet` or `ssh` or whatever and this session persists until you log out, when the session is taken down. Sometimes a session can be very short, e.g., just long enough for an email or Web page to be transmitted.

This layer takes care of things like synchronization: if you have a large file to transmit that takes 2 hours and the network or the remote machine crashes after 1 hour, the session layer can reestablish the connection at the point it left off rather than starting again. The session persists even if the transport disappears for a while.

2.2.6   The Presentation Layer

The presentation layer, *layer 6*, is getting very close to the end user. It provides things that are commonly needed so we do not have to reimplement them in every application.

This includes stuff like standard encodings for characters (e.g., ASCII), integers (e.g., two's complement big endian) and floating point (e.g., IEEE), so that machines at either end can agree on how a stream of bits should actually be interpreted.

2.2.7 The Application Layer

Layer 7 is the top layer in this model. It contains the protocols that end users' applications need, like telnet to log into a machine, SMTP for email, HTTP for the WWW and so on.

Beyond the application layer are the programs that the user sees: a browser that uses HTTP or an emailer that uses SMTP to send email.

2.3 How the Layers Fit Together

In a pure implementation of the model each layer has contact only with the layers immediately above and below it (Figure 2.1).

Going downward, data in each layer is passed to the next below via *encapsulation*. This is just transforming the data in such a way that the layer below can cope with it transparently and in such a way that it can be untransformed back to the original data at the other end.

The transformation might:

- add an identifying header or trailer (or both);

- encode certain bit patterns that might otherwise be misinterpreted or mis-transmitted by the next layer (e.g., see p. 46);

- put items into a standard form, e.g., ensuring integers are in a universally recognized format (see Chapter 11);

- do some arbitrarily complex manipulation;

- do nothing at all!

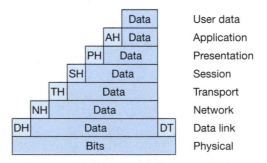

Figure 2.1 A possible OSI encapsulation.

This process starts when the user data from some program is passed to the application layer. This might add some stuff: for example, a standard email header on an email message.

This is passed to the presentation layer. As far as this layer is concerned, it just gets a bunch of bits from the application layer. It doesn't (or shouldn't) know that the first few bits are an application header. This layer may transform the data in some way (e.g., convert characters to a particular format) and may prepend its own header that contains useful information for the process that eventually unpacks the data.

And so on down through the layers. Each layer may perform any transform on the data and may prepend headers. Or a layer may do nothing at all: it all depends what you need to do for the job in hand. For example, the data link layer sometimes has a header and a trailer: this is so the start and end of a frame are clearly marked in the physical layer.

At the other end the receiving stack of layers unwraps and untransforms each layer appropriately. Sometimes the untransform is not successful: one example is matching between different character sets in the presentation layer since different character sets on different operating systems do not always contain representations of the same collection of characters (think of sending a message in Japanese to a European machine). In such cases the unwrapper just has to hope for the best.

2.4 Why Layers and Encapsulation?

The use of encapsulation seems wasteful: if the original data are small, then the packet on the wire could be mostly headers from the various layers. This is overhead that reduces the effective throughput of the transmission. Surely it is better to just put the data directly into the link layer?

The idea of using layers is for flexibility. Suppose we have a 10Mb network card in our machine and someone comes up with an improved 100Mb card. Because the physical layer is (almost) totally separate from the data link layer, we can just write a new standard for a 100Mb physical layer and slot it in where the old 10Mb one used to be. The upper layers do not even need to know the hardware has changed. Imagine having to rewrite every email program, Web browser and other application each time something changed in the network.

This is why we need to separate functionality carefully: the network layer and above should certainly know nothing about what hardware you are using.

In fact, the above example has happened several times: the Internet runs over (amongst many others), 10Mb Ethernet, 100Mb Ethernet, 1Gb Ethernet, 10Gb Ethernet, telephone lines (SLIP and PPP), radio. The user sitting at their terminal has no idea of what is going on beneath them.

In principle you could use carrier pigeons as the physical layer and your browser should work unchanged, apart from a slow-down, maybe.   RFC 1149

> Someone did actually implement this RFC, with real carrier pigeons! And someone else used drips of water as the physical layer in an 'H2O/IP' network. And bongos.

Figure 2.2 Tunnelling.

Indeed, encapsulation may not stop even at this, the physical layer. For example, there are physical limits on the size of an Ethernet (speed of light problems, p. 26), so how can we connect up an Ethernet that spans the Atlantic? One way we might do this is to *tunnel* the Ethernet traffic inside some other kind of network, ATM or SMDS, for example (Figure 2.2). These protocols can work over long distances.

We simply stuff an Ethernet packet into the ATM network and it pops out the other end to continue in its Ethernet world. The ATM protocol (itself a link layer protocol) is being used as a data link layer. In practice, things are more complicated of course and we tend to tunnel at the network layer level as this is more efficient.

An analogy for layering: suppose you are sending a present to a friend abroad, France say. You wrap the present securely ('encapsulate the present in brown paper'), you address the parcel correctly ('add a header'), and give it to the Post Office. The Post Office puts the parcel on a plane destined for France ('encapsulates it in the plane'). When the plane reaches France, the package is 'de-encapsulated' and it carries on in its journey. When it reaches its destination, your friend de-encapsulates the parcel to discover the present.

Someone once wrote software to tunnel TCP/IP over email. This allowed TCP connections through a firewall – but very slowly!

RFC 3093
RFC 1149
RFC 2549
RFC 2003

There is also a standard for tunnelling TCP/IP over HTTP and, of course, RFC 1149 (updated by RFC 2549) for IP over avian carriers.

There is even a standard for tunnelling IP in IP! This seemingly strange layering is useful for connecting remote networks, say two offices of the same company, into a single network using the Internet as the tunnel. Encryption is usually used in the tunnel to prevent private information being read on the public Internet. This is called a *Virtual Private Network* (VPN, Section 13.5.1). IP in IP is also used in Mobile IP (Section 6.11).

2.5   The Internet Model

The OSI model was very successful at getting people to concentrate on the specifics of a network implementation. However, implementations based directly on it were not popular, principally because they were complex and quite slow. By sticking too rigidly to the layers and following the principle of insulation between the layers it is difficult to get any real speed from an implementation.

Another model, the *TCP/IP Reference Model*, also called the *Internet Reference Model* and the *Department of Defense Four-Layer Model*, was developed by DARPA in the 1970s

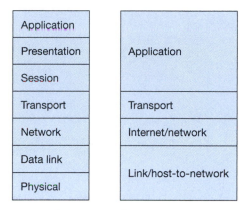

Figure 2.3 OSI vs. TCP/IP.

with the principles of the Internet in mind: namely, resilience to damage and flexibility of application.

This is a four layer model, in contrast to the OSI model's seven (Figure 2.3).

2.5.1 The Link Layer

Also known as the *host-to-network* layer, *data link* layer or *network access* layer.

This covers both the hardware of the OSI physical layer and the software in the OSI data link layer. The TCP/IP model does not say much about this layer as it recognizes that there can be many different types of hardware to send your packets across. This layer has to be capable only of sending and receiving IP packets.

2.5.2 The Network Layer

Also known as the *Internet* layer. This handles the movement of packets about the network, including routing. This layer defines a specific packet format and a protocol, the Internet Protocol (IP), to manipulate those packets (Figure 2.4).

2.5.3 The Transport Layer

Also known as the *host-to-host* layer. This is analogous to the OSI transport layer. It provides for a flow of data between source and destination. Two protocols are defined at this level, TCP and UDP.

The Transmission Control Protocol (TCP) is a reliable connection-oriented protocol that delivers a stream of bytes from source to destination. It chops the incoming byte stream into packets and passes them to the Internet layer. It copes with acknowledgement packets and resends packets if it thinks they have been lost. Going the other way, it receives

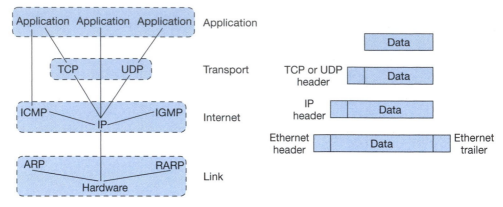

Figure 2.4 Internet Protocol.

packets and reassembles them into a continuous byte stream, sending acknowledgements for successfully received packets. Flow control is also handled here.

The User Datagram Protocol (UDP) is an unreliable, connectionless protocol for those cases where you do not want TCP's overhead or do not require its reliability. UDP is used for situations where fast delivery is preferred to accurate delivery, e.g., sound or video.

The world 'unreliable' is being used in a technical sense here as meaning 'not guaranteed reliable'. Many typical unreliable networks are actually pretty reliable these days.

Theoretically, TCP and UDP should not have to be layered on top of IP, but their specifications actually tie them into IP. This is breaking the principle of layering but TCP/IP was designed before the concept of layering was recognized as important.

> The TCP checksum includes some fields from the IP layer in a straightforward violation of the layering precept.

2.5.4 The Application Layer

The next layer is the application layer, which provides protocols like SMTP, FTP and telnet. This model does not have session or presentation layers.

Unfortunately, presentation *is* important so applications have to cope with presentation issues themselves, e.g., by using libraries like XDR (Chapter 11) to convert data to a machine-independent form. You can try to avoid the worst problems by sticking to a tightly restricted subset of values such as the ASCII character set. Even then occasional glitches do occur, such as Web pages generated by some tools which use fancy non-standard characters where simple characters were all that was required. This is due to these tools not following generally accepted standards. The result is Web pages that look fine on some browsers, but can be unreadable on other browsers.

The Internet model is somewhat more flexible than the OSI one. Applications can (in rare cases) use the network layer directly (IP and ICMP) rather than going through TCP or UDP. This appears to contradict the point of using layers, but (a) it is convenient and (b) since we are talking about IP we already know what the lower layers look like and they are unlikely to change often. We shall have to pay the price if there *is* a change: a case in point is the introduction of IPv6, the next version of the IP. For the overwhelming majority of cases applications do use TCP or UDP. This kind of pragmatism is common when the Internet is involved.

2.6 Models and Protocols

It is easy to confuse the OSI and Internet *models* with the OSI and Internet *protocols*. A model is a set of guidelines on how one should go about designing a network protocol. For example, it can say 'use a physical layer which will deal with voltages, frequencies, etc.'. The model does *not* say 'use copper wire and voltages of 5 V representing 1 bit'. That is a specific protocol implementation.

A model can have many implementations that fit it. For example, consider the following network: two plastic cups joined by a piece of string. The physical layer is the cups and string; the network layer is empty; the transport layer is saying 'over' at the end of each voice packet; the application layer is whatever we are talking about. This is a network implementation that fits the Internet model.

2.7 Comparing OSI and Internet Models

There is a rough correspondence between the two models, apart from the missing and merged layers (see Figure 2.3). And there are big differences.

The OSI model was developed *before* an implementation, whereas the Internet model was developed *after* TCP/IP was implemented and is more a description of what happened. OSI makes a clear distinction between the model and implementation, while the Internet is more fuzzy.

OSI is very general, whereas Internet is very specific. OSI is more flexible in that is it not tied to a specific protocol and is better able to adapt to changes in technology. On the other hand, the OSI model had many problems when it came to an implementation where it was found that the layers provided did not correspond well to reality. Extra sublayers were developed and the simplicity of the OSI model was lost.

As it turns out, TCP/IP has been widely successful, while the OSI model is relegated to books on networking. Many reasons for this have been given, but the major ones seem to be that the committee defining OSI took so long that TCP/IP was already widely established by the time the standard was published. Also, the standard was so complex that only poor implementations of OSI were made, while the simpler layering of TCP/IP was fairly easy to make run well. Seven is not a magic number and other proposals had more layers (splitting up several layers into smaller, easier ones), or fewer (in particular the Internet model). It appears that seven was chosen as IBM already had a seven layer protocol (Systems Network Architecture, SNA).

> It is important to realize that layering is there for structuring only. Layers must be followed for interoperability, but they need not be followed for implementation.

The TCP/IP model is not all-singing, all-dancing either, it does have problems. The specification is confused with the implementation; it is only really good for describing TCP/IP and no other protocol stack; the physical and data link layers are merged, making it hard to talk about (say) copper wire vs. fibre installations.

The OSI model is widely used; the OSI protocols are virtually never used. The Internet model is rarely used; the Internet protocols are extremely widespread. A compromise is used by Andrew Tanenbaum in his excellent book *Computer Networks*: split the link layer of the Internet model into a physical and data link layer:

1. Physical

2. Data link

3. Network

4. Transport

5. Application

This appears to be a good compromise in that it matches well with reality (i.e., TCP/IP) and is somewhat more flexible than the Internet model.

2.8   Exercises

Exercise 2.1 The link layer in Ethernet adds 18 bytes of header and trailer (Section 3.2). What does this mean for the maximum possible throughput of data for a 10Mb Ethernet? A 100Mb Ethernet? Does this align with real life throughput? Explain.

Exercise 2.2 The network layer in TCP/IP adds a 20 byte header (Section 6.1). What does this mean for the maximum possible throughput of TCP data for a 10Mb Ethernet? A 100Mb Ethernet? From your understanding of encapsulation, could this layer dispense with this header? Explain.

Exercise 2.3 A wireless network is described as being 11Mb, but when used can never seem to get more than half that. Explain why as (a) a network support officer, (b) a marketing officer.

Exercise 2.4 Find other examples of encapsulation in life.

Exercise 2.5 Compare and contrast the OSI model against the Internet model.

Exercise 2.6 In real implementations of the Internet model (and others) the layers are sometimes blurred to aid efficiency. Discuss the pros and cons of doing this.

Exercise 2.7 Read about the ISO implementation of the seven layer model (ISODE, actually just layers 4 to 7) and make notes on its main features.

ISO 8072
ISO 8073

Exercise 2.8 Consider broadcast TV. Classify its parts according to (a) the OSI and (b) the Internet models. Which is a better match?

Exercise 2.9 The IEEE split the OSI data link layer into a logical link control (LLC) sublayer and a media access control (MAC) sublayer. Read up on this and discuss how it fits in with the OSI and Internet models.

Exercise 2.10 Consider when layering goes wrong: find examples (e.g., on the Web) where insufficient attention has been paid to the presentation layer. Why do you think that people neglect the presentation layer?

THE PHYSICAL AND LINK LAYERS 1: ETHERNET

3.1 Introduction

We shall now look at each layer in turn, starting at the bottom: the link layer, including the physical layer. The link layer carries IP packets and *Address Resolution Protocol* (ARP) packets. ARP is generally considered as part of the link layer, while IP is above in the Internet layer.

There are many popular link layers used out there in the real world as there are many different kinds of problem that need addressing. For example, Ethernet is popular for LANs; PPP and ADSL are used for connecting end users to ISPs; ATM is used in WANs; wireless is used in all kinds of situations. In the next few chapters we shall be working our way through a selection of these protocols.

3.2 Ethernet

RFC 894

The Ethernet standard was defined in 1982 by DEC, Intel and Xerox. It uses a method called *Carrier Sense, Multiple Access with Collision Detection*, or CSMA/CD (see Section 3.3), and runs at 10Mb. That is, 10Mb/s is the signalling rate, namely the rate of the physical bits on the wire. The rate available to the user is less, as we shall see. Each host on an Ethernet (technically, each *interface*, as a host might well have more than one network interface) has a 48 bit address that uniquely identifies it.

RFC 1042
IEEE 802.3

A couple of years later the IEEE published another standard, 802.3, which is almost but not quite the same as Ethernet. It is sufficiently different that they do not interoperate, though you can have packets from both standards on the same wire without interference. Ethernet is by far more popular.

This being the link layer, we must define how bits are laid out on the wire.

An Ethernet *frame* (aka packet) starts with two 6 byte fields containing 48 bit *hardware addresses* (also known as a Media Access Control or MAC address): first destination, then source (Figure 3.1). Every Ethernet chip in the world has its own unique 48 bit hardware

Destination address	Source address	Type	Data	CRC
6	6	2	46–1500	4

Figure 3.1 Ethernet frame.

address burned in at the time of manufacture. For example, a typical address could be 0:20:48:40:2e:4d, written as a sequence of six hexadecimal numbers.

The top 22 bits of this 48 bit address identify the vendor of the Ethernet chip, while 24 bits form a serial number set by the vendor. One bit is used to indicate a broadcast or multicast (see Section 6.9.2) address and the last bit is used to indicate a 'locally administered address', where the address has been reassigned to fit some local policy.

Next in the frame is the 2 byte *type* field. This is a number that indicates what kind of data follows: for example, (hex) 0800 indicates an IP packet, while 0806 indicates an ARP packet (Section 5.4). These numbers are defined in RFC 1700 *et seq*. This allow the system to pass the data quickly to the relevant program in the next layer.

RFC 1700

Then comes the actual data. This can be up to 1500 bytes. Curiously, there is also a minimum size of 46 bytes. The reason for this will be explained shortly. If the data section would be less than 46 bytes, it is padded out with 0 bytes. Somehow the data field must itself encode how long its real data part is (which is somewhat against the spirit of layering).

Finally there is a 4 byte *checksum* (aka *cyclic redundancy check*, CRC). This is a simple function of all the bytes in the frame and is intended to catch errors in transmission. It is computed by the source host just before sending the frame. On receipt, the destination recomputes the checksum on what it got. If an error occurred in the transmission of the frame this should show up as a difference in the values of the received and computed values of the checksum. If this happens the packet is assumed corrupted and the frame is dropped. In Ethernet it is up to a higher layer to realize this has happened and to take corrective action.

One Ethernet address is special: all ones, or ff:ff:ff:ff:ff:ff. This is the broadcast address: the packet goes to all machines on the (local) network. One or more machines may choose to reply. This will later be seen to be useful when bootstrapping other parts of the IP.

3.3   CSMA/CD

The limitations on packet size are imposed on Ethernet because of physical considerations of the hardware. Ethernet is a shared medium (the *multiple access* in CSMA/CD), which is to say many machines are (at least conceptually) connected by a single piece of wire that they all use. If there is a signal on the wire, very soon it occupies *all* the wire: it's just way the electricity works. This single shared medium is called an Ethernet *collision domain*.

IEEE 802.3

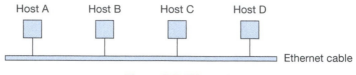

Figure 3.2 Ethernet.

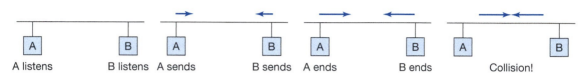

Figure 3.3 Collisions.

If host A in Figure 3.2 wishes to send a frame to host B, but C is already sending to D, then A must wait, since the shared cable is already occupied. Thus A listens on the wire (*carrier sense*) until C has finished and then attempts to send. However, B, say, might also be waiting to send to D, say. So A and B will start sending at the same time, both continuing to monitor the wire as they do so. Both A and B hear the frames clash (*collision detection*) and both stop transmitting immediately. They each wait for a small random time (they *back off*) and then start listening again. As the delay is random, one of the two will start before the other, thus resolving the clash.

This is why a packet has a minimum size: the speed of light in the wire. A packet has to be sufficiently large that all hosts on the network can see it before they decide to transmit. If very small packets are allowed, hosts can transmit a whole packet and not spot a collision further down the wire. See Figure 3.3.

CSMA/CD is very good for low usage of the shared medium, but performs poorly for high usage due to many collisions: more time is spent backing off from collisions than sending packets. If a host has to back off more than 16 times, the packet is simply dropped. The network is so heavily loaded that there is no point in trying anymore. Again, a higher layer will have to take remedial action as necessary. If collisions hit less than 5% of packets, the Ethernet is considered to be working normally. If more than 50%, though, you should consider breaking the network up into smaller pieces (Section 6.5).

3.4   Ethernet Hardware

The Ethernet standard includes the specification of the kind of cables needed. Originally, a thick coaxial cable was required, but over the years there have been many updates.

This is a selection of Ethernet cable types:

Name	Cable	Max segment	Speed	
10Base5	Thick coax	500 m	10Mb/s	'Thicknet', chunky yellow, vampire taps
10Base2	Thin coax	200 m	10Mb/s	'Cheapernet', 'thin ethernet', 'thinnet', actually 185 m max segment
10Base-T	Twisted pair	100 m	10Mb/s	Telephone wire, Cat 3 cable; 150 m on Cat 5
10Base-F	Fibre optic	2000 m	10Mb/s	Long distance
100Base-T4	Twisted pair	100m	100Mb/s	100Mb Ethernet on two telephone cables (Cat 3)
100Base-T	Twisted pair	100 m	100Mb/s	100Mb Ethernet, Cat 5 cable, aka 'fast Ethernet'
100Base-F	Fibre optic	2000 m	100Mb/s	Long distance
1000Base-T	Twisted pair	100 m	1Gb/s	Gigabit Ethernet, Cat 5 or Enhanced Cat 5

There are several others, including optical fibre gigabit. The *Max segment* is the longest allowable stretch of cable in a single unbroken section.

The most important aspect is the increase of speeds in the standards. The 100Mb and 1000Mb (aka Gigabit) Ethernet standards are more or less the same as the original standard (in terms of frames layout, CSMA/CD, etc.) but simply faster. There are one or two wrinkles, such as minimum frame size and the amount of time you listen for a collision, but mostly it just follows through.

In terms of deployment, 10Mb is currently in decline, 100Mb is very common, 1Gb is widespread, 10Gb is emerging and talks on 40Gb are progressing.

The original Ethernet, 10Base5, runs on a fat coaxial cable with *vampire taps* containing a *transceiver*. The taps are little boxes that bite into the Ether cable to make a connection. There is a minimum gap of 2.5 m between taps: Figure 3.4. The transceiver contains the electronics to do the collision detection. This supports a cable (up to 50 m long) to the host containing five twisted pairs of wires, with a large and unwieldy socket (AUI socket) on the end.

There are many rules governing 10Base5 that are necessary to ensure good function. A segment can be extended with up to a maximum of four *repeaters* (which simply amplify the electrical signal), therefore five segments (total length of 2460 m) can be connected together. Of the five segments only three can have devices attached (100 per segment). A total of 300 devices can be attached on a single thicknet broadcast domain. This is called the *5–4–3 rule*.

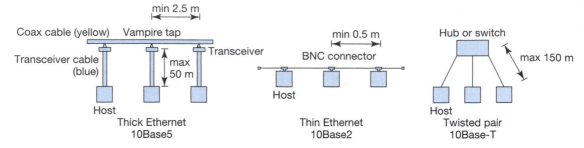

Figure 3.4 Wiring Ethernets.

However, 10Base5 is expensive, inflexible (physically as well as metaphorically), hard to install, and the AUI plugs have a tendency to fall out of their sockets; 10Base2 and 10Base-T are much simpler.

Thinnet, or 10Base2, uses simple coaxial cable, much like TV aerial cable. It plugs in using simple passive BNC (variously called *British Naval Connector, Bayonet Neill Concelman* or *Bayonet Nut Connector*) connectors (no vampire taps or transceivers needed). This is much cheaper and easier to lay around the building and to connect up. The necessary electronics are now on the interface card in the machine, not in a separate transceiver. The minimum gap between connections is 0.5 m and a segment can have up to 30 machines. The BNC plugs directly into the card in the computer with no intervening cable.

A segment can be extended with other segments using up to four repeaters, i.e., five segments in total. Two of these segments, however, cannot have hosts and can only be used for extending the length of the network (to 925 m). What this means is that three segments with a maximum of 30 stations on each can give you 90 devices on a thinnet broadcast domain.

Twisted pair connects in a very different way. Also known as *unshielded twisted pair* (UTP), this is literally a bunch of eight wires twisted together in four pairs: the twists help reduce electrical interference. This is essentially a bundle of high-quality telephone cables. On the ends are RJ45 (*Registered Jack*) plugs.

UTP has a standard classification into levels of quality according to the ability to transmit signals:

- Category 1: No performance criteria.

- Category 2: Rated to 1 MHz (used for telephone wiring).

- Category 3: Rated to 16 MHz (used for Ethernet 10Base-T).

- Category 4: Rated to 20 MHz (used for Token Ring, 10Base-T).

- Category 5: Rated to 100 MHz (used for 1000Base-T, 100Base-T, 10Base-T).

- Enhanced Category 5: Rated to 200 MHz (used for 1000Base-T, 100Base-T, 10Base-T).

- Category 6: Rated to 250 MHz (used for 1000Base-T).

Now 10Mb Ethernet requires the use of Cat 3 (or better) cable, whereas 100Mb needs Cat 5. You can run Gigabit Ethernet on *Enhanced Category 5*. This is good-quality Category 5 where you need to be really careful about making good, clean connections in the plugs and sockets and is rated to 200 MHz. Category 6 supports Gigabit with ease. The next category, Category 7 (600 MHz), is in the process of standardization.

Further, in an Ethernet, instead of a single backbone cable that all the machines connect to, each machine is wired to a central box. This can be a *hub* or a *switch*, both of which relay packets from one segment to another. The difference between them is the degree of intelligence in the forwarding.

A hub is ignorant of any protocol above the physical layer and simply echoes all packets onto all wires. This makes a hub-connected system look electrically like a 10Base2 or 5 Ethernet. It is a single *collision domain* as a packet from any host has the potential to collide with packets from all other hosts, regardless of their source and destination. The collision domain shares the 10Mb or 100Mb available bandwidth.

A switch understands a link layer protocol, e.g., Ethernet. It knows where each host is and is able to direct a packet down that single segment that has the right machine on the end rather than copying it to all the output wires. This means now that each output cable is a separate collision domain. There will only be a collision if two machines try to send to the same destination at the same instant; there will be no collision between machines sending packets to *different* machines at the same instant. Thus there is potentially 10/100Mb bandwidth available between each pair of machines simultaneously.

Often switches are even more cunning than this: they can *store and forward* packets. If a switch finds the output channel is busy it can store a packet in internal memory and forward it later when the channel is free. This means that each source–destination path is a separate collision domain. If this is happening we can do away with CSMA/CD completely, as there can be no collisions! If the output channel is exceptionally busy, the memory buffer can fill up and then the switch will just drop any more incoming packets until space becomes available. Recall that Ethernet CSMA/CD will itself drop packets after 16 tries, so this is not so bad as it seems. It is up to a higher layer protocol to discover the loss and take remedial action.

Incidentally, it is this point that is the major cause of lost packets in the modern Internet: being dropped through congestion en route causing buffers to overflow.

An alternative to store and forward is *cut through* switching. In this, the switch starts forwarding the frame before all of it has been read. This decreases the latency of the packets as they travel through but reduces the overall reliability as the switch might be forwarding a corrupt packet: it cannot know if a packet is corrupted until it has been completely read and the checksum computed.

Switches are more complicated (read 'expensive') than hubs, but give better total throughput and better efficiency under high load (few collisions). These days even switches are cheap and it is getting increasingly difficult (and pointless) to find a hub.

Hubs and switches (Figure 3.5) are also applicable to the other kinds of Ethernet, but are overwhelmingly associated with UTP.

If you have a switch and your hardware supports it, twisted pair can run *full duplex*, meaning that there can be 10/100Mb *to* the machine simultaneously with 10/100Mb *from* the machine. This is a total of 20/200Mb per pair of machines in flight at a time. This

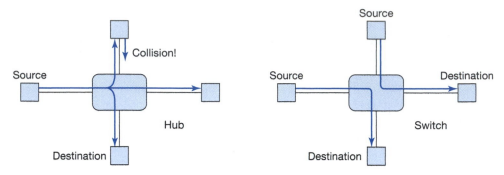

Figure 3.5 Hubs and switches.

is because there can be no collisions between inward and outward traffic as they are transported over different twisted pairs within the cable. The alternative is *half duplex*, where traffic can only go in one direction at a time. Typically, half-duplex Ethernet uses CSMA/CD while full-duplex Ethernet is switched and does not.

You can buy converters that connect together the different kinds of Ethernet cable, e.g., thinnet to twisted pair. Some network cards have more than one type of socket on them. Thicknet is virtually never seen these days, with thinnet only found in old installations and UTP being widely used, and Cat 5 (or better) UTP being used for all new installations.

> If you need to connect just two machines, you can do this with UTP without a hub or switch. Simply join them with a *crossed* cable: this has a pair of wires switched in the plug at one end – much cheaper than buying a switch.

3.4.1 Further and Faster

IEEE 802.3u
IEEE 802.3

Note that 100Base-T Ethernet (and above) is backwardly compatible with 10Base-T Ethernet if both hosts at the ends of a cable implement *auto-negotiation*. When the hosts are first connected they compare their abilities, which includes full or half duplex and speed of operation. This is done by encoding information in the initial signals that Ether interfaces exchange when they are connected. Having done this, they can agree on their optimal speed and duplex. A host that does not auto-negotiate can safely be assumed to be an old 10Mb Ethernet, though some interfaces are clever enough to analyse the signal they are reading and make an intelligent guess. Thus a switch can plug into 10Mb and 100Mb networks with equal ease knowing that it is using the best protocol for each of the hosts it is talking to.

Now 100Mb (and 10Mb) Ethernet actually only uses two of the four twisted pairs in a UTP cable: one pair for out and one pair for back. You are recommended not to use the other two pairs in a cable since the 100Base-T standard does not take into account possible electrical interference from those pairs. Even so, there are some manufacturers that sell 2-into-1 splitters so you can get two connections along a single cable.

That's not to say you can't use those spare wires for something else. The IEEE 802.3af IEEE 802.3af Power over Ethernet standard describes how to use them to deliver power: useful for supplying a networked device in a place without a handy power source. A good example is an Internet telephone. Powered Ethernet switches are starting to appear: these are being driven by the growth of interest in IP telephony, *Voice over IP* (VoIP, Section 12.11). Final specifications are not yet available, but the specification appears to be about 45 volts DC with a maximum current of at least 250 mA.

Gigabit Ethernet (802.3z) over copper (802.3ab) uses all four pairs with a different IEEE 802.3z
IEEE 802.3ab physical encoding of the bits (see Section 3.5) and transmits and receives simultaneously on all pairs of wires.

Gigabit will run over standard Cat 5 if you are lucky, though you should use *Enhanced Cat 5* (or Cat 6 or more) to be sure it will cleanly support the more exacting electrical signals.

The minimum Ethernet frame size of 64 bytes is required in Ethernet for the CSMA/CD method to work. At gigabit speeds, using the original 10Mb Ethernet's minimum packet size would imply a maximum cable length of 10 m: not very practical. A 512 byte limit would be more sensible, allowing a limit of 80 m. But Gigabit Ethernet does keep the 64 byte limit. Short packets are followed by a *carrier extension*, a special 'hold the wire' signal to fill up to the end of a 512 byte slot. CSMA/CD regards this as part of the packet and so holds off sending until it can be sure the wire is empty.

This means we might have 448 bytes of overhead on a small frame and so Gigabit Ethernet's performance on small packets would not be much better than 100Mb Ethernet. The theoretical limit works out at about 86Mb/s when sending 64 byte frames. As a partial fix for this, Gigabit Ethernet allows *packet bursting*, where several packets can be sent before relinquishing hold on the wire. If a host has several packets to send, it sends the first one normally (possibly including carrier extension). If that gets through safely, the host still has control and can send more packets (without the need for carrier extension) up to a limit of 8192 bytes in total. It must then release the medium. This decreases the overhead if we want to send many small packets.

All this complication means that for best performance Gigabit Ethernet really ought to be used in full-duplex mode on a switched network: then there is no need to worry about collisions and we can dispense with carrier extension and packet bursting. Notice, also, that a full-duplex connection will have no inherent distance limit (apart from electrical considerations).

Now 10Gb Ethernet is standard Ethernet with just three differences: IEEE 802.3ae

1. It runs over optical fibre connected with a *XAUI* (pronounced 'zowie') socket.

2. It is full duplex only and does not have half duplex and CSMA/CD.

3. It operates at 10Gb/s.

There is a proposal for 10Gb over twisted pair copper (10Gbase-T, using Cat 6A cable), but this may take some time to work through. Work on a 40Gb Ethernet standard has begun. Just think on that: 10Gb Ethernet is 1000 times as fast as the original Ethernet over a timescale of less than 20 years!

Why the 40Gb standard rather than the traditional 10-times-faster-than-the-previous? This is because previous Ethernet standards had borrowed physical specifications from existing technologies such as Fibre Channel and SONET (Section 4.5.2). There is no existing 100Gb/s protocol, so the IEEE 802.3 Committee has chosen the fastest available: 40Gb/s SONET OC-768. If you want more bandwidth you can aggregate several 40Gb links.

Current *dense wave division multiplexing* (DWDM) fibre technology allows 10Gb/s per wavelength and about 160 wavelengths per fibre. A modest bundle of 10 fibres could carry 16Tb/s. There's still lots of room for growth!

The designers and engineers of Ethernet are confident that it will get ever faster and more commonly used, driving out all other physical/link layer technologies. One of the more ambitious claims is that eventually even computer buses will be Ethernets connecting machine components (like video cards, sound cards, the processor, and memory) each of which has its own globally unique (IPv6) address. For example, the *Internet SCSI* (iSCSI) standard has been developed to adapt the popular SCSI bus protocol to run over TCP/IP (see Section 12.7).

3.5   Physical Encodings

We now look at the actual encodings of bits on the wire. The simplest encoding would be to use 0 V for a zero and a positive voltage 1 V, say, for a one. This has a number of problems:

- How can we distinguish between a free network (nobody transmitting) and some-body transmitting a stream of zeros? They look the same electrically.

- The sender and receiver need to be accurately synchronized to the starts and ends of bits, since with a long strings of ones or zeros they could drift out of step. This means that, for example, the sender might send 1000 ones, but the receiver could think that it was only 999 ones.

- A long stream of ones would be encoded as a steady 1 V on the wire, namely a DC voltage. This is something that gives electrical engineers great difficulties, as it is much easier to connect together equipment that has average voltage 0, e.g., an AC voltage.

- A similar problem happens with the lasers in an optical system: it is not too good to have continuous laser beams representing a stream of ones.

Engineers prefer an encoding where the average voltage is about zero. Thus they use encodings of the data stream that approximate this even if the data is all ones or all zeros.

So Ethernet and 802.3 use a *Manchester encoding* (Figure 3.6). This chops the time interval for a bit into two halves: a one is represented by a high voltage in the first half

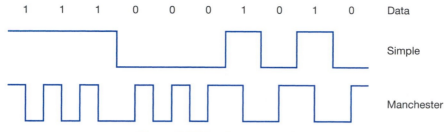

Figure 3.6 Manchester encoding.

and a low voltage in the second. A zero is represented by the reverse: a low voltage in the first half and a high voltage in the second. The actual voltages used are +0.85 V for high and −0.85 V for low. On average, the voltage is zero. There is an extra advantage that this signal is easy to synchronize with: a transition through zero is always the middle of a bit.

> Using 0.85 V is also a compromise. Smaller voltages require less power, but are more prone to interference from noise from the surrounding electrical environment.

There is one drawback. The bandwidth that the Manchester encoding requires is twice that of the simple encoding as the frequency of the signal is doubled. A 10Mb rate requires a 20 MHz signal. This is not so bad, but it is correspondingly worse with 100Mb and higher rates.

Cat 5 cable is rated to 100 MHz so we can't use Manchester encoding for 100Mb Ethernet. The encoding is more subtle. It uses a *4B/5B* system, meaning that four data bits are encoded into five physical bits. Thus four consecutive zero bits 0000 become the five bits 11110, say. Physical representations are called *symbols* and they need not be binary valued. A couple of extra 5B patterns are used for frame start and end, and one for 'idle network' (to maintain synchronization).

So far this has only made it worse in terms of bandwidth. But now the encoding uses a three level (ternary) electrical encoding called *MLT-3*. MLT-3 is like Manchester in that it encodes 1 bits by transitions, but now the transitions are cyclically from 0 to 1, then 1 to 0, then 0 to −1, then −1 to 0, then 0 to 1, and so on. A 0 bit is encoded by no transition. The 4B/5B translations are such that each five symbol chunk has at least two transitions in the MLT-3 signal, which helps synchronization and also minimizes DC current. So 0000, with no transitions, becomes five symbols 11110, which has four transitions.

An example is the byte value 15, or hexadecimal 0E. This is translated nibble by nibble by the 4B/5B encoding to 11110 and 11100. Figure 3.7 shows how these might be encoded in signal transitions. The actual encoding depends on where we happen to be in the current cycle.

This runs at 31.25 MHz giving a symbol rate of 125 Mbaud. This is because the fastest electrical cycle happens with a stream of all one symbols (IDLE) and then we get a complete cycle every four transitions (0 to 1 to 0 to −1 to 0), giving us four symbols

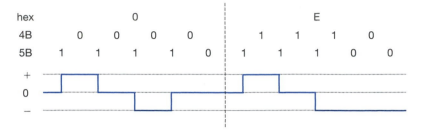

Figure 3.7 4B/5B and MLT-3.

	Data		Control
value	symbol	name	symbol
0000	11110	IDLE	11111
0001	01001	J	11000
0010	10100	K	10001
0011	10101	T	01101
0100	01010	R	00111
0101	01011	S	11001
0110	01110	QUIET	00000
0111	01111	HALT	00100
1000	10010		
1001	10011		
1010	10110		
1011	10111		
1100	11010		
1101	11011		
1110	11100		
1111	11101		

Figure 3.8 4B/5B encoding.

per cycle. Typically, though, we get frequencies of around 4/5 of this (25 MHz) as data symbols have four one symbols or fewer (Figure 3.8).

A *baud* is the number of symbols per second, where a symbol represents some chunk of information. A symbol might represent a bit, or 2 bits, or 2/3 of a bit, and so on; 100Mb Ethernet requires a symbol rate of 125 Mbaud (efficiency 80%) due to 4B/5B encoding. Here one symbol encodes 0.8 bits.

The frequency a signal runs at has other implications, in particular the amount of electrical interference it produces. A system running at 25 MHz is friendlier to the electrical environment than one running at 31.25 MHz.

Gigabit Ethernet over copper uses a much more sophisticated 8B/10B encoding invented by IBM for its Fibre Channel network. It runs over five electrical levels (± 2, ± 1, 0) over all four pairs of wires in the cable in both directions simultaneously. The encoding, PAM-5, gives us 2 bits per symbol: four levels to encode 00, 01, 10, and 11, and one for error correction. This runs at 125 Mbaud, as before, so we have 2 bits $\times$ 125 Mbaud $\times$ 4 pairs $= 1000$Mb/s in both directions simultaneously.

> Clever signal processing is required to disentangle the outward signal from the inward signal. The processors on a Gigabit Ethernet interface are about the complexity of a 486 microprocessor.
>
> The 8B/10B encoding is also used in the serial ATA (SATA) disk interface and Digital Audio Tape (DAT).

As previously mentioned, 10Gb Ethernet is primarily optical. Optical systems only use binary encodings: either the laser is on or off so they do not have the option of multiple level encodings.

3.6   An Alternative to Ethernet

Ethernet, while being the major contender for LANs, is not the only player. As a contrast, we take a quick look at an alternative, Token Ring (Figure 3.9).   RFC 1748
IEEE 802.5

Rather than have a shared segment of wire, we can have a circular network. Rings have been around for a long time (at least since 1972) and are well understood. They are really a collection of point-to-point links that happen to form a ring.

A packet circulates around the ring, being passed from one interface to the next until it reaches its destination. The ring is controlled by a special packet, called the *token*. When the ring is idle, this token circulates. If a host wants to transmit a frame it must wait until the token arrives. It removes the token and replaces it with its data packet, which continues round to the destination. The destination reads the packet. The packet continues

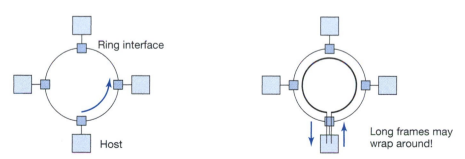

Figure 3.9 Token Ring.

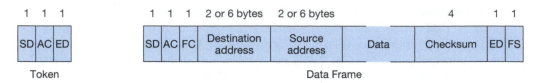

Figure 3.10 Token Ring frame.

around the ring until it reaches the source again, which removes the packet and replaces the token, thus releasing the network.

If many machines are waiting to send packets, the token will therefore be grabbed in a round-robin style, giving natural bandwidth sharing.

Token Ring runs at 4 or 16Mb (and lately, 100Mb and more) over UTP.

The token is 3 bytes long:

- Starting delimiter. A special pattern of electrical signals that does not correspond to a data byte (an invalid Manchester encoding).

- Access control. This byte contains the *token bit*, which is zero for a token and one for a data frame.

- An ending delimiter. Similar to the SD.

The data frame (Figure 3.10) is arbitrarily long:

- Starting delimiter.

- Access control.

- Frame control. This distinguishes a data frame from other kinds of frames which are used to control the network.

- Destination and source addresses. Six byte addresses as for 802.3/Ethernet, but a variant allows two byte addresses.

- The data. This can be of any length up to a maximum time limit, which is generally 10 ms, the *token-holding time*, which is 5000 bytes.

- A checksum.

- An ending delimiter.

- Frame status. Contains various status bits, in particular 'destination present and frame read successfully'. This is noted by the sender when the packet returns as a check that the packet was read by the destination.

Packets also have *priorities*. The AC field contains a priority value, as does the token. That packet can only be sent if the token has priority not greater than the priority of the packet. Similarly, a host can raise the priority of the next token by raising the priority of the current data frame.

Rings have several advantages over Ethernet:

1. Good bounds for time to access the network: Ethernet is non-deterministic as it may have to repeatedly back off and this is bad for real-time applications (such as machine control systems) where predictability is important.

2. Smooth degradation under high load: Ethernet gets very inefficient at high loads.

3. There is no practical limit on the size of the network.

4. There is no minimum packet size, thus reducing overhead.

5. Point-to-point links are cheap and easy to build.

On the other hand:

1. A ring is difficult to extend: you have to take the entire network down to add a machine, but with Ethernet you just plug in.

2. A broken interface is a big problem to everybody as it breaks the ring: with Ethernet you probably wouldn't notice.

3. There is a fixed large delay while you wait for the token: at low load the delay on Ethernet is virtually zero.

4. The details of Token Ring are quite complicated, involving the priorities of packets and means to monitor the liveness of the system (regenerating the token if it gets lost, etc.): Ethernet is relatively simple.

On the whole, though, the two use roughly the same technology and get roughly the same performance. In practice, Token Ring is rarely seen and Ethernet is seen everywhere.

3.7   Exercises

Exercise 3.1 CSMA/CD was developed from the ALOHA Protocol. Find out about ALOHA and discuss the differences between it and CSMA/CD.

Exercise 3.2 Compare and contrast

(a)   thick,
(b)   thin, and
(c)   twisted pair

Ethernet in terms of

(i)   physical properties,
(ii)   ease of installation, and
(iii) overall cost.

Exercise 3.3 Encode your name (in ASCII) in

    (a)   simple Manchester,

    (b)   4B/5B and MLT-3.

Estimate the time taken to transmit the symbols in (b) on a 100Mb Ethernet.

Exercise 3.4 Discover more about encoding schemes like 4B/5B and 8B/10B. What do other media (such as CD, DVD, digital TV, etc.) use?

Exercise 3.5 Token Ring has several desirable properties. List its advantages over Ethernet and discuss why Token Ring is not more popular in the marketplace.

THE PHYSICAL AND LINK LAYERS 2: GOING FURTHER

4

4.1   Introduction

It would be nice to have Ethernet to connect everybody's homes to the Internet, but few people have the right sort of cables connecting them and the right sort of equipment in their homes. Instead a lot of people use telephone lines to connect to the Internet via a *modem* which encodes data into audible tones that can safely traverse the telephone network. Modems have two good features: they work over existing telephone wires, which can be quite old and unreliable, and they do not require upgrading of equipment at the local telephone exchange, so there is no additional expense for the telephone company.

In this chapter we look at modems and other ways of squeezing data down the telephone line to the home, and widen our view to the technologies that WANs employ to move large volumes of data over long distances.

4.2   Modems

A modem does *mo*dulation and *dem*odulation. That is, it modulates digital information into analogue sounds and demodulates analogue sounds into digital information.

For historical and technical reasons telephone companies only transmit sounds in the range of about 300 Hz to 3300 Hz: this is why telephone calls have that recognizable 'telephone quality'. These frequencies capture just enough of the human voice to produce a recognizable sound. Frequencies outside this range are filtered out by the phone system and dropped.

This frequency limitation is quite a problem for a modem as it must restrict itself to using those frequencies for the analogue sounds it generates and so the data rate available via a standard telephone line is strictly limited, even though the cables themselves (often Cat 2) are capable of a much wider range of signals (see Section 4.8).

Note that modems are not limited to telephone lines and acoustic signalling. If you have cable, you might be able to connect via a cable modem which modulates and demodulates onto whatever medium the cable service runs.

There has been a long sequence of modem standards developed firstly by Bell Labs, then by the International Telephone and Telegraph Consultative Committee (CCITT), which became the International Telecommunications Union Telecommunications Sector (ITU-T), a United Nations body. These start at a lowly 300 baud (encoding 1 bit per baud, see p. 34) and go all the way to 56Kb/s.

The ITU has produced very many modem standards, each backwardly compatible with the previous one in the sense that, say, a V.32 modem will be able to communicate with a V.22 modem at V.22 speeds, but can communicate with another V.32 at full speed. When modems first connect they go through a *training* phase where they determine the standard(s) supported by the other end of the connection and the state of the line between them. On a noisy line modems will use a lower data rate for greater reliability.

Standards highlights include:

V.21	300b/s
V.22	600 and 1200b/s
V.22bis	2400b/s
V.32	4800 and 9600b/s
V.32bis	7200, 12K, and 14.4Kb/s
V.34	28.8Kb/s
V.42	better error correction
V.42bis	data compression
V.44	better data compression
V.90	56Kb/s downstream, 33.6Kb/s upstream
V.92	56Kb/s downstream, 48Kb/s upstream

V.42bis

V.44

Not all V standards introduce new speeds, some introduce extra facilities like error correction and data compression. Compression is particularly useful as V.42bis can compress at a ratio of up to 4 to 1 (dependent on the source data), so potentially quadrupling the effective data rate. Similarly V.44 can compress up to 6 to 1. Other error-correction and compression standards exist, in particular the *Microcom Networking Protocols* (MNPs) are popular.

There are three ways to encode data in an analogue tone (Figure 4.1):

1. Amplitude modulation (AM). Values are encoded by the amplitude of the signal. For example, a large signal is a one, while a small signal is a zero.

2. Frequency modulation (FM). Values are encoded by the frequency of the signal. For example, a frequency higher than the norm is a one, while a frequency lower than the norm is a zero.

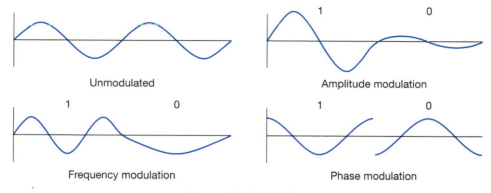

| Unmodulated | Amplitude modulation |
| Frequency modulation | Phase modulation |

Figure 4.1 Modulation.

3. Phase modulation (PM). Values are encoded by the phase of the signal. For example, a signal that reaches its peak slightly earlier than the norm is a one, while a signal that reaches its peak slightly later than the norm is a zero.

AM and FM should be familiar from radio.

Of course, just as with Ethernet encodings, all these can be extended to encode more than 1 bit per baud. For example, multiple frequencies can be used to encode multiple bits in a single cycle. The trade-off is that as more bits are encoded and more frequencies are used it becomes harder to distinguish exactly which frequency is being transmitted, particularly in the presence of noise.

In more advanced encodings, more than one of the above three can be used simultaneously. A popular combination is to combine amplitude and phase modulation in *quadrature amplitude modulation* (QAM). For example, QAM16 uses eight phases and two amplitudes to encode $3 + 1 = 4$ bits per baud. The various combinations of phase and amplitude form a pattern called a *constellation* (Figure 4.2).

Other variants encode more bits, and *trellis-coded modulation* (TCM) incorporates error-checking bits into the scheme.

> When digital terrestrial TV first appeared in the UK it used a QAM64 (6 bits per baud) encoding to transmit data. Governmental regulations on limiting the amount of interference with existing analogue broadcasts meant that only low-power transmitters could be used and it turned out that many homes could not get a reliable signal. The encoding was dropped to QAM16 (4 bits per baud) which increased the robustness of the signal received at the cost of a reduced bandwidth and therefore fewer TV channels.

A classical setup is to have modems at both ends: at home and at the ISP, so only an analogue signal is transmitted on the telephone network. As telecom equipment has now become digital there are digital-to-analogue (D/A) and analogue-to-digital (A/D) converters in the telephone exchanges to transform the voice signal into digital information. This is then carried digitally over the telephone company's network. In this situation we are

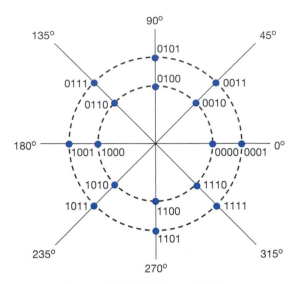

Figure 4.2 QAM16 constellation.

successively converting from D to A (home modem); A to D (exchange modem); D to A (remote exchange modem); and A to D (ISP modem). Moreover, each conversion between digital and analogue formats introduces noise and thereby reduces available bandwidth.

V.90   The V.90 standard recognizes the fact that both telephone companies and ISPs want digital data and so some of the conversions are a waste of time. Instead the ISPs can connect digitally directly to the telecom provider giving a digital path all the way to the local exchange (Figure 4.3). When converting digital to analogue we can get the maximum possible theoretical signalling rate of a telephone line of 56Kb/s. When converting from analogue to digital, noise limits us to a maximum of 33.6Kb/s. Thus a V.90 modem

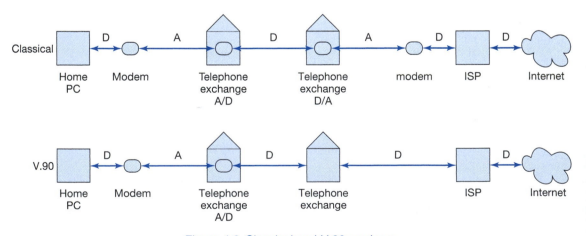

Figure 4.3 Classical and V.90 modems.

is asymmetric: we can get 56Kb/s downstream (towards the user), but only 33.6Kb/s upstream (away from the user). This asymmetry is not a real problem when you consider how most networks are used: some even consider it an advantage. A user types in a few characters or does a few clicks of the mouse. This becomes a small chunk of data to be sent out along the lower bandwidth link. The return data, e.g., a Web page, is much larger and returns along the faster link. Users generate little data but expect big replies and this matches the asymmetry.

The 56Kb/s is a nominal value: in practice it is limited to no more than 53Kb/s since a higher rate causes too much interference in nearby cables.

V.92 is V.90 plus a few changes:

V.92

- The upstream rate is improved to 48Kb/s.

- The initial setup connection time is reduced by half as it saves the state of the line from the previous connection and reuses it rather than redetermining it every time.

- There is a 'call-waiting' feature that can suspend the connection for a while to let you make a voice call and then reconnect immediately.

It is not expected that there will be any radical improvements in acoustic modems since (a) they already go as fast as theory and regulations allow and (b) newer, faster technologies such as ADSL (Section 4.8) are taking over.

4.3 ISDN

A voice channel is allocated 4 kHz of bandwidth in the telephone system. When a voice signal is filtered down to 300–3300 Hz this fits nicely with a bit of safety either side. Then, in early telephone systems, calls were *frequency shifted* and *multiplexed* onto a single wire. That is, analogue gadgets would raise the pitch of a call and bundle it onto a wire with other calls. The calls would be separated by filtering and then readjusting the frequencies at the destination. If you were to listen in on such a system you would hear a normal voice plus one or more chipmunk-sounding conversations of ever-increasing squeakiness.

Modern digital systems sample the filtered signal at 8 kHz, i.e., a sample every 125 μs. Each sample is 8 bits, so the data rate is 64Kb/s (note, as is standard with ISDN, here we use 'K' to mean 1000).

A long-established digital connection method is *Integrated Services Digital Network* (ISDN), sometimes called a *midband* technology as it sits between the speeds of narrowband modems and broadband ADSL. As telephone companies started moving to digital technologies in the 1970s, it was felt there was a need to take services like voice, fax and data and *integrate* then into a single unified service. Several devices can share a single connection; for example, it could be used to transmit (digitized) voice at the same time as data.

ISDN (Figure 4.4) uses all available bandwidth in the voice channel – and more – to get a full 64Kb/s data rate. It can get this rate as it uses a fully digital path from home to

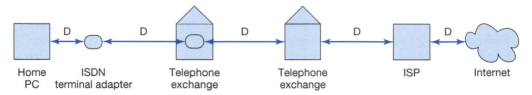

Figure 4.4 ISDN.

ISP and no acoustic modems are involved. In the home (or office or wherever) there is an encoder that produces a digital signal on the wire rather than an acoustic signal. This encoder is confusingly called an 'ISDN modem' or 'digital modem' by analogy with the analogue modem, but is more properly called a *terminal adapter*. As ISDN requires extra hardware both at home and in the local exchange, telephone companies like to charge special rates for the use of ISDN.

ITU-T I.100
et seq ISDN was developed by the CCITT (now the ITU-T) in the I-Series (ISDN Series) and G-Series (Digital Systems and Networks) of standards.

ITU-T G.700
et seq
ANSI T1.601 Physically, four voltages on the wire are used: ± 0.833 V and ± 2.5 V, so giving 2 bits per baud. A variety of encodings are used: North America uses one called 2B1Q while Europe uses 4B3T. The encodings run at 80Kbaud, so giving a data rate of 160Kb/s. This requires frequencies up to 80 KHz, more than the usual 3300 Hz for a voice channel, and may require removal of filters from the telephone line when ISDN is installed.

An ISDN frame is divided into three parts (Figure 4.5):

1. A sync field to introduce the frame.

2. A data and control field.

3. A maintenance field, containing flags, CRCs and the like.

The 'data and control' is 12 repetitions of 18 bit sections, each of which is subdivided into 8 bits of B_1, 8 bits of B_2 and 2 bits of D. The B_i are data channels while the D is control information. Thus we get B_i rates of 64Kb/s each and a D rate of 16Kb/s for a total of 144Kb/s. The frame overhead takes this up to the 160Kb/s. The control channel ITU-T Q.700
et seq D is specified in the ITU Q-Series of documents and controls various aspects of the connection management such as startup and teardown. The D channel is always active while the B channels are activated as needed.

Frames are collected together and sent in a *superframe* of eight frames totalling 1920 bits.

The above is the *Basic Rate Interface* (BRI). There is also a *Primary Rate Interface* (PRI) comprising 30 B channels plus one 64Kb/s D channel for a total of 1984Kb/s. In North America this becomes 23 B channels plus one 64Kb/s D channel for a total

Sync	Data + control	Maintenance
18 bits	216 bits	6 bits

Figure 4.5 ISDN frame.

of 1536Kb/s. PRI is used by big companies with larger data requirements and generally connects directly into the company's own telephone system.

To get the BRI electrical limitations require you to be within 5.5 km (3.5 miles) of the local telephone exchange, though this distance can be increased with the use of ISDN repeaters. The two B channels in BRI can both be used either for (digitized) voice or data (or fax, or anything else), and each will have its own telephone number. A typical arrangement is to have one voice and one data channel, but by using *Bandwidth ON Demand Interoperability Network Group* (BONDING, also called *channel bonding*) the two B channels can be joined to form a single 128Kb/s data channel.

ISDN has been fairly popular (despite its price) in Europe as it is relatively easy to install the terminal adapters both in the home and in the exchange. For example, you can buy ISDN cards that plug directly into PCs and many telephone exchanges have ISDN equipment ready. Furthermore, the B channels map easily onto the existing digital telephone channels in the telephone exchange. An additional advantage is a fast connect time: as the D channel is always active it enables new connections to be made in about 2 seconds instead of the 30–60 seconds for an acoustic modem. On the other hand, ISDN is rapidly disappearing, being replaced by the faster and more flexible ADSL (Section 4.8).

A derivative product is 'midband' ISDN, or *Always On/Dynamic ISDN* (AO/DI). This is designed to be an 'always on' connection without the expense of introducing new ADSL hardware. It is a standard ISDN $2B + D$ setup but 9600b/s of the D is used as a low rate data channel while the rest of the capacity is used for control, as before. This data rate is enough for lightweight stuff like email notification, but if more bandwidth is needed then one or more of the 64Kb/s B channels will automatically be switched on as required. What's more, the addition (and deletion when the data rate drops) of B channels is nearly instant. If both B channels are being used and a telephone (voice) call is initiated on that line, then one B channel automatically reverts to voice and the data rate drops from 128Kb/s to 64Kb/s.

4.4   SLIP and PPP

To use IP over ISDN or acoustic modems we need to use a link layer protocol. There are two common link layer standards for encapsulation of IP (and other) packets over telephone lines: SLIP and PPP. SLIP was common until PPP was developed and took over as the protocol of choice.

RFC 1618

4.4.1   SLIP

Serial Line IP, or SLIP, is a simple encapsulation for IP over serial lines. It is a *point-to-point* protocol, meaning it is designed to connect just two machines together.

RFC 1055

A frame is very simple (Figure 4.6): the data is terminated by a byte containing the hex value c0, called END. Often, implementations will start the frame with c0, too, just to be sure.

Figure 4.6 SLIP frame.

This means we can't have bytes with the value c0 inside the frame as they would be interpreted as the end of a frame. To get around this, SLIP uses *byte stuffing*. If we need to transmit a c0 it is replaced by two bytes db dc. In this context the character db is called ESC. Now to prevent the misinterpretation of a db that happens to be followed by a dc in the original data, we must stuff db, too. To send a value of db, we replace this by two bytes db dd. This causes a minor expansion of data, but not much.

Thus the byte stream 00 c0 db 01 gets transmitted in a frame as

c0 00 db dc db dd 01 c0

When reading the frame at the destination it is a simple matter to replace any occurrence of db dc by c0 and db dd by db to recover the original data. (This is a non-trivial example of encapsulation, Section 2.4.)

There is no defined limit on the frame size, but it is suggested that you should be able to cope with frames at least 1006 bytes long, though many implementations use 296 bytes (which accommodates 40 bytes of TCP/IP header plus 256 bytes of data). This is because 1006 is too large a frame: at 9600b/s it would take about 1 second to transmit a full frame. Suppose we are copying a large file across the network which results in a continuous stream of full frames. If we want to have an interactive login session at the same time we will have to wait about 0.5 s on average for the current frame to finish before the packet containing our keystrokes can get through; similarly for the response from the other end. Empirically, an interactive response time of more than 100–200 ms is felt by users to be too long. Reducing the frame to 296 bytes is a good compromise between interactive response and bulk data throughput. For modern machines with faster modems, 576 bytes or more is the size of choice. For example, on a 56K modem you may want to increase the frame to 1500 bytes.

> More importantly, the larger packet size reduces the amount of IP fragmentation. Most DNS packets can fit inside 576 bytes.

SLIP works, but it has problems.

1. The ends must have pre-agreed IP addresses: there is no mechanism for one end to tell the other its address.

2. No type field. SLIP only supports IP.

3. No checksum. Essential on noisy telephone lines to spot data corruption.

4. No authentication. Needed on dial-up lines to check on who is trying to connect.

Telephone lines are slow (4 kHz or 56Kb/s maximum), so any opportunities to improve throughput are welcome. TCP/IP has a large overhead of 40 bytes or more of header per packet (see Section 9.4) and typically you send many packets with nearly identical headers. A variant of SLIP, *compressed* SLIP (CSLIP), takes advantage of this repetition. RFC 1144 Instead of sending a full header, Van Jacobson devised a scheme that only sends the small differences and which reduces the average overhead to about 3 bytes. This greatly improves throughput, particularly in interactive traffic when there are many small packets. Van Jacobson also investigated compressing UDP/IP and IP separately but found the gains not to be worth the effort. Note that this is in complete disregard of layering and ties CSLIP to TCP/IP, but the benefits are too large to ignore.

4.4.2 PPP

The *Point-to-Point Protocol* was designed to fix the deficiencies of SLIP. There are three parts:

1. A framing for packets on a serial link, including error correction.

2. A *link control protocol* (LCP) for bringing up links, configuring them, and taking them down again.

3. A set of *network control protocols* (NCPs) to negotiate network layer options that are specific to the network layer.

RFC 1331 defines the encapsulation and RFC 1332 defines the NCP for IP. RFC 1331
RFC 1332
A frame starts (and ends) with the byte 7e (Figure 4.7). The next two bytes are *address* (always ff) and *control* (always 03). Next is the *protocol* field in 2 bytes. This tells us what protocol the data field contains (cf. the Ethernet protocol field, Section 3.2). IP has value 0021. The NCP for IP has value 8021. Two bytes for a checksum of the frame (the address, control, protocol and data fields) and 7e to end.

There are up to 1500 bytes in the data field, but this maximum can be negotiated. As for SLIP, they must be escaped, but this time using 7d:

*   7e → 7d 5e

*   7d → 7d 5d

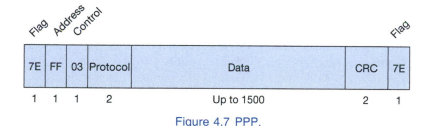

Figure 4.7 PPP.

- x, where $x < 20$ (hex) $\rightarrow$ 7d $[x + 20]$. So 01 becomes 7d 21. This is done as some modems interpret values < 20 specially.

Connections can negotiate extra things via the NCP, like header compression (as in CSLIP). PPP is much better than SLIP and should always be used in preference.

RFC 2364
RFC 2516

PPP was originally designed to be used as a link layer over telephone lines, but its flexibility and authentication abilities have resulted in its being used as an intermediate layer in other ways. Two popular uses are PPPoA, where PPP is layered over ATM (Section 4.6), and PPPoE, where PPP is layered over Ethernet. It seems strange at first sight to have IP layered over PPPoE over Ethernet rather than directly over Ethernet, but the NCPs that PPP provides are very useful in managing access control, billing and level of service, things that are very important to ISPs.

RFC 1990

A variant called *Multilink PPP* (MP) takes two or more connections and presents them as a single link. This is like ISDN channel bonding (p. 45) but works wherever PPP works. So if your ISP supports MP and you have multiple telephone lines you can get a correspondingly faster connection (presumably for a correspondingly larger fee!).

4.5   The T and E Hierarchies and SONET/SDH

In early long-distance telephone systems voice channels were frequency shifted and multiplexed onto a single line (Section 4.3). This meant that many conversations could simultaneously use a single expensive long-distance cable. The only problem is getting a signal to travel that far: amplifiers help somewhat, but an amplifier magnifies the noise on the line as well as the signal, so there are limitations on what can be done.

4.5.1   T and E

Moving to digital lines is a great improvement. Rather than direct amplification a digital repeater reads and reconstructs the original bitstream and then regenerates a pure new signal to send onwards. In this way, with enough repeaters, a digital signal can travel arbitrarily large distances. Another advantage, of course, is that digital carriers can take both voice and data. One of the original digital long-distance carriers was T1.

ANSI
T1.403-1999

Recall that a digital voice channel is an 8 bit sample every 125 μs, giving the $8 \times 8000 = 64$Kb/s rate of a normal telephone line (Section 4.3). A T1 link is 24 of these channels plus a 1 bit frame, making 193 bits every 125 μs, or 1.544Mb/s (here M is 1000000). If this is not enough, four T1 channels can be joined to form a T2 at 6.312Mb/s (slightly more than 4×1.544 due to tricks with the framing). This is repeated:

T carrier	Transmission rate (Mb/s)	Voice channels
T1	1.544	24
T2	6.312	96
T3	44.736	672
T4	274.176	4032

The T hierarchy is used in North America, Australasia and Japan. In Europe, South America, Africa and elsewhere a similar E hierarchy exists. An E1 is 30 64Kb/s data channels plus two 64Kb/s control channels, or 2.048Mb/s.

ITU-T G.701

E carrier	Transmission rate (Mb/s)	Voice channels
E1	2.048	30
E2	8.448	120
E3	34.368	480
E4	139.264	1920
E5	565.148	7680

Compare the E1 and T1 rates to the ISDN PRI (p. 44). The similarity is not a coincidence, as E1 is often delivered as ISDN $30B + 2D$ and T1 as $23B + D$.

If a company wishes to get a dedicated high-rate connection to the Internet it leases a T (or E) line from a telephone company. Costs, even for T1, tend to be quite high, but before the advent of DSL technologies (such as ADSL) there was no cheaper alternative.

4.5.2 SONET/SDH

The next stage is the introduction of optical networks. First came ANSI's *Synchronous Optical Network* (SONET), which the ITU took up and extended to the *Synchronous Digital Hierarchy* (SDH). Technically, SONET and SDH are different but the difference is so slight the two standards are generally lumped together and called SONET/SDH. This new standard has the advantage that it can mediate between the incompatible T and E hierarchies.

ANSI T1.105
ITU-T G.707

The rates are given as *optical carrier* (OC) levels in ANSI-speak (and *Synchronous Transport Signal* or STS levels for the equivalent electrical speeds); they become *Synchronous Transport Modules* (STMs) in ITU-parlance.

Common data rates are

OC/STS level	STM level	Transmission rate (Mb/s)	Voice channels
1	–	51.84	672
3	1	155.52	2016
12	4	622.08	8064
48	16	2488.32	32256
192	64	9953.28	129024
768	256	39813.12	516096

OC-9, OC-18, OC-24, OC-36, OC-96 also exist but are rarely implemented. There is a glimmer of OC-3072 (159Gb/s) for the future, but larger rates can also be attained by bundling together multiple OC-768s.

RFC 2615
ISO 3309
IP can be layered over SONET via ATM (Section 4.6), but this involves a *cell tax*, the overhead incurred when breaking a data stream into ATM cells (ATM calls frame cells). More efficient is to use PPP (Section 4.4.2) and the *High-Level Data Link Control* (HDLC) Protocol. IP traffic is encapsulated by PPP which is framed by HDLC (just a few bytes overhead) which is carried over SONET. This has significantly lower overhead than using ATM but loses ATM's support for Quality of Service (QoS) guarantees, something that is set to become more and more vital as sound and video services gain in importance.

Optical fibre links have immense capacity: with current technology a single fibre can carry 10Tb/s!

4.6   ATM

Asynchronous Transfer Mode is a link layer protocol that was designed to be fast and flexible. It is packet based, though packets are called *cells* in the ATM world and the technique is called *cell switching*. Cell delivery is not guaranteed, but order is. Thus, if packets A and B are sent in that order, and if both packets arrive, then they will arrive in that order.

A cell is of fixed length: 53 bytes (Figure 4.8). A fixed size was chosen as this makes ATM hardware much easier to design and build and therefore faster to run. This particular length was chosen as a compromise between large packets for low overhead and small packets for flexibility in carrying bursty traffic, like speech and video. Of the 53 bytes, 48 are data bytes while 5 bytes are ATM header.

ATM runs at 155Mb and 622Mb and is moving into the gigabit arena. It is packet based, but it is also connection oriented. Making a connection involves setting up a path between source and destination and then the same path is used for all the packets in this connection.

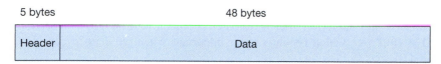

Figure 4.8 ATM cell.

These data rates might seem familiar. For example, OC-3 is the same speed as 155Mb/s ATM and OC-12 is the same as 622Mb/s ATM. The reason for this is that ATM was originally designed to run over SONET.

ITU-T I.432

ATM makes a big fuss over *Quality of Service* (QoS). You can define certain levels of service, e.g., a guaranteed minimum bandwidth or a guaranteed maximum packet delay, and ATM can ensure these levels will be maintained. Furthermore, different charges for different levels of service can be made. ATM grew from the telecom organizations, so we can understand the preoccupation with connections, quality and charging.

ATM was designed to be used at all levels, from LAN to WAN, but is most successful in the WAN sector. Some LANs run over ATM, but it is very expensive (cost of hardware) and Ethernet is dominant there. This is because Ethernet is well understood and hardware and software are widely available, while the IP-to-ATM layer interface is quite complex and hard to implement.

> For example, ATM provides a point-to-point connection that does not fit well with IP's support for broadcast.

On the other hand, ATM is a very good long-distance carrier and it has been used widely for large-bandwidth long-distance connections. For example, it is popular for links across the Atlantic.

There are a few standards for how to split data into ATM cells, the most useful being *ATM Adaption Layer 5* (AAL5) (Figure 4.9). There is no header but a trailer instead. It pads the end of a packet to a length that is 47 mod 48 and a single byte information field (currently unused) finishes that cell. The next cell starts with a single padding byte to align the next two fields (recall that the ATM header is 5 bytes long). These fields are a 2 byte length and a 4 byte CRC. A bit in the ATM header indicates that this is the last cell for the packet and the length field allows us to find the end of the packet within the previous cell. Note that this relies on the in-order transmission of cells to work. The maximum payload is $2^{16} - 1 = 65535$ bytes, but RFC 2225 recommends 9180 bytes as this matches the SMDS MTU (RFC 1209).

ITU-T I.363

RFC 2225
RFC 1209

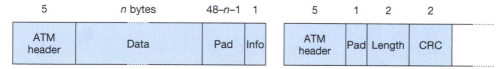

Figure 4.9 AAL5.

RFC 2684
RFC 2364

Packets are layered over AAL5 using RFC 2684, which can multiplex several IP (or other) streams into one ATM stream. Another approach is to layer PPP (Section 4.4.2) over ATM (PPPoA), which becomes more important when we start to consider ADSL (Section 4.8).

ATM has enjoyed a considerable run of success, with a large amount of deployment in WANs and other networks, but currently *Multiprotocol Label Switching* (MPLS) is making inroads into its territory.

> ATM bears a family resemblance to *Switched Multimegabit Data Service* (SMDS), a service popular in the early 1990s and devised by Bellcore. It also uses a 53 byte cell but runs at 56Kb/s to 34Mb/s (T3).

4.7 MPLS

RFC 3031

The next contender for the link layer is *Multiprotocol Label Switching* (MPLS). This was designed when it was decided that technology had advanced sufficiently so that the assumptions on the capabilities of technology that drove the design of ATM (leading to a small cell size amongst other things) no longer apply. So, for example, MPLS allows large packets, in particular 1500 bytes to be compatible with Ethernet. Another feature is that MPLS can carry link layer protocols, not just the network layer, so it can be used to transport Ethernet, ATM and even MPLS itself (see below) as well as IP.

The format of MPLS is very simple: at its heart is a 20 bit *label* (Figure 4.10). Switching in MPLS routers is based entirely on this label and so can be very fast and is independent of the higher layer protocol the packet is encapsulating. This is particularly important when the higher layer protocol has a complicated addressing mechanism, IP being a case in point. Label switching can be implemented cheaply in very fast hardware.

The label tells MPLS which *forwarding equivalence class* (FEC) a packet is in, which allows MPLS to treat all packets in the same FEC to the same QoS, apply traffic management, and so on. Again, this simplifies things immensely, which leads to cheaper and faster implementations.

As mentioned, MPLS can encapsulate itself: this leads to a *stack* of labels.

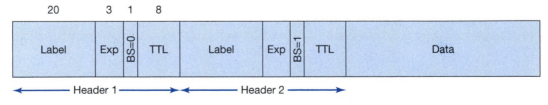

Figure 4.10 MPLS header stack.

The 32 bit header contains

- Label: 20 bits.

- Exp: 3 bits reserved for future experimental use.

- BS: a flag bit to indicate the bottom of the stack of labels.

- TTL: 8 bits of *time to live*. This is an integer that counts down by one each time the packet passes through a router and if it reaches zero the packet is discarded by the router. This prevents misconfigured routing loops sending packets round in circles forever and jamming up the network. Eventually such packets will disappear. See Section 6.2.8 for more on TTLs.

MPLS label stacks are useful for VPNs (Section 13.5.1). They allow management of routes in hierarchies and effectively extend the 20 bit label to an arbitrary range.

Like ATM, MPLS is packet based, but the FECs allow it to be regarded as connection oriented, too. Unlike ATM, the larger packet size in MPLS (as large as the physical layer allows) means that MPLS has less overhead and so is more efficient for layering IP and the like. Note that AAL5 over ATM requires that even the smallest data packet will require two ATM cells.

A major user of MPLS is British Telecommunications's *21st Century Network* (21CN) project that aims to replace BT's mixed technology communications and other networks with a single, simple IP-based network. The ability of MPLS to carry network layer protocols means that the transition will be relatively straightforward and easy to control.

4.8   ADSL

We conclude with another way of squeezing more data down the telephone line to the home or business: *Asymmetric Digital Subscriber Line* (ADSL). This is currently the standard way of connecting homes to the Internet and has overtaken traditional modems in popularity.

ANSI T1.413
Issue 2

Analogue modems are limited to 56Kb/s: this number is the maximum speed you can get from a standard analogue telephone line. This is because the telephone system filters out all frequencies apart from a 3 kHz chunk centred about the human voice (Section 4.2). Thus a traditional modem, which converts the data into sounds to be transmitted down the telephone line, is limited by this.

ADSL (one of a series of DSL standards, collectively called xDSL) tries to use the maximum available bandwidth the line provides. This means you can't use the existing hardware in the telephone exchange, but must replace it with a specific ADSL box. Similarly, the user must have an ADSL interface.

A certain amount of bandwidth is available on the telephone wire. This varies according to the quality of the wire, the length of the wire, the quality of the splices in the wire, local electrical interference, and many other things. The *asymmetric* in ADSL refers to the

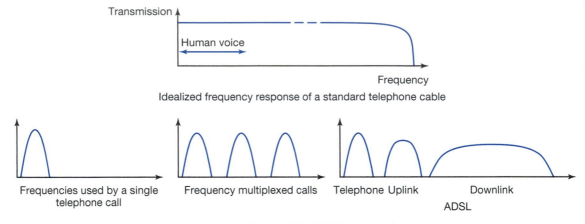

Transmission

Human voice

Frequency

Idealized frequency response of a standard telephone cable

Frequencies used by a single telephone call

Frequency multiplexed calls

Telephone Uplink   Downlink

ADSL

Figure 4.11 ADSL.

non-symmetric splitting of this bandwidth into *uplink* (towards the Internet) and *downlink* (towards the user) parts (Figure 4.11). For example, you might get 256Kb uplink and 2Mb downlink speeds, though these numbers vary widely. And you keep the 4 kHz channel for your telephone on top of that. The ADSL connection is permanently on, so there is no need to dial up an ISP.

As with V.90 modems (p. 42), this asymmetry is in the appropriate direction for the home user who needs more bandwidth from the Internet than to the Internet. On the other hand, this makes ADSL less popular for businesses who need to have a decent amount of bandwidth to send data outwards to customers.

Sometimes ADSL implementations overlap the upstream and downstream frequencies and rely on clever signal processing to separate the signals of the sending and receiving streams (called *echo cancellation*). This increases the bandwidth a little at the cost of extra complexity.

ANSI T1.413
Issue 2 ADSL is often encoded using *Discrete Multi Tone* (DMT). This splits the available frequency range (0 Hz to 1.104 MHz) into 256 channels of 4 kHz (Figure 4.12). Channels

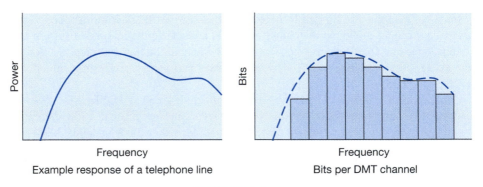

Power

Frequency

Example response of a telephone line

Bits

Frequency

Bits per DMT channel

Figure 4.12 DMT.

1–6 are not used by ADSL but are reserved for the speech channel, the *Plain Old Telephone Service* (POTS), though only the first channel is actually used. Channels 7–38 are upstream, while the rest are downstream.

Each channel encodes as many bits as noise on the line allows: this can be from 0 to maybe 15 bits/Hz. If a channel is particularly noisy (e.g., interference from nearby fluorescent lighting) it can only transmit a few bits per hertz. Neighbouring channels that are outside the range of the interference can transmit at full capacity. In this way we make the most of what the copper allows, working around the non-uniform transmissions along the wire.

An alternative encoding is *Carrierless Amplitude Phase* (CAP), but DMT seems to have won the market and CAP is rarely seen. CAP simply divides the frequency range into 25–160 kHz for upstream, 240 kHz–1.104 MHz for downstream and 0 Hz–4 kHz for POTS.

Both DMT and CAP use *Quadrature Amplitude Modulation* (QAM) to transform bits into signals. This uses the amplitude and the phase of the signal to encode bits (see p. 41).

As the distance between ADSL modems increases, the noise on the line between them gets greater, simply due to the increased amount of copper and the increased number of noise sources the line goes near. Thus the available bandwidth decreases. This means that ADSL has a limit on how far apart modems can be separated and still get a reasonable throughput: in practice this means there is a limit on how far a customer can be from the telephone exchange and still get an ADSL service. Note that this is the distance the cable travels, not as the crow flies, and this can be much larger than you think as telecom companies route their cables in strange ways. Commercial ADSL suppliers put a limit of about 5 to 6 km (3 to 3.5 miles) to get a decent data rate under the understanding that the bandwidth at these distances may not be as large as for shorter distances: a variant called *Rate Adaptive Digital Subscriber Line* (RADSL) tests the line upon connection and establishes the optimum rate.

Data is transmitted in *superframes* containing 69 ADSL frames. Frame 69 is for synchronization, the rest contain data. An ADSL frame contains two kinds of data: *fast data* and *interleaved data*. The fast section is used for time-sensitive data such as audio and can contain forward error correction bits. The interleaved section has purely user data. It is called 'interleaved' as the data bits are mixed about into an interleaved order which is intended to help against errors.

The *fast byte* has several uses: in frames 1, 34 and 35 it contains administrative flags; in frame 0 it contains a CRC; it can be used to signal to the other end that a CRC error occurred; and so on (Figure 4.13).

Many ISPs use ADSL as a layer to support ATM, so then we can have IP over PPP over ATM over ADSL. Using ATM also fits in well with the equipment at the telephone exchange: several ADSL lines plug into a *Digital Subscriber Line Access Multiplexer* (DSLAM) which converts DSL streams into (typically) ATM. This is particularly useful if an ATM layer is already there. Since ATM is used by many telephone companies for their internal data networks (Figure 4.14), this all ties together nicely.

ADSL is defined in the ANSI T1.413 Issue 2 standard together with ITU standards G.DMT and G.Lite. The G.DMT standard, also known as G.922.1 and *full rate ADSL*, allows 8Mb/s downstream and 960Kb/s upstream. G.Lite, also known as G.922.2 or

ANSI T1.413
Issue 2
ITU-T G.DMT
ITU-T G.Lite

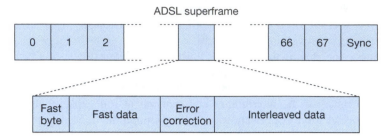

Figure 4.13 ADSL frames.

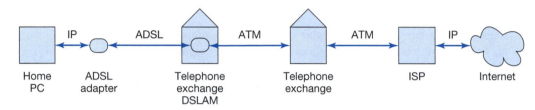

Figure 4.14 ADSL and ATM.

Universal ADSL, is a lower rate (1.5Mb/s downstream and 512Kb/s upstream) variant designed for the home market. Its advantage is that it does not require a splitter (filter) to be installed on the line to separate out the voice and data frequencies.

> A common method of delivery of ADSL to the home is to use a modem that plugs into the USB port on a computer. This means that an application, e.g., a Web browser, will be implemented using HTML over HTTP over TCP over IP over PPP over AAL5 over ATM over ADSL over USB over copper!

ADSL/RADSL is not the end of the story for DSL. There is a pantheon of other DSLs, mostly of the high-rate, low-distance variety. Included are:

ITU-T
G.DMT.bis
ITU-T
G.Lite.bis

• ADSL2. Defined in G.DMT.bis/G.922.3 for full rate and G.Lite.bis/G.922.4 for splitterless. This is backwardly compatible with standard ADSL but has better signaling and noise control; 50Kb/s more bandwidth; 180 m more reach; fast setup times; low-power modes to save energy when no data is being transmitted; channel bonding to bind together multiple streams into a single higher rate stream.

ITU-T
G.922.5

• ADSL2+/G.922.5. An extension to ADSL2 that doubles the data rate for short distances by increasing the frequency range used to 2.2 MHz. It should deliver 24Mb/s over short (perhaps 300 m) distances, dropping to 8Mb/s at about 3 km.

ANSI TR 28

• *High Rate* DSL (HDSL). Symmetric 1.544Mb/s. Maximum 3.5 km, over two twisted pairs.

- *Symmetric* DSL (SDSL). Symmetric bandwidth up and downstream at 1.544Mb/s. Over one twisted pair, 3 km. ETSI TS 101 524-1

- *Very High Rate* DSL (VDSL). Up to 26Mb/s downstream, 6.4Mb/s upstream, 300 m. Good for *fibre to the kerb* (Section 5.3). ETSI TS 101 270

- VDSL2, the successor to VDSL. This has the potential of symmetric 100Mb/s at up to 350 m. Up to about 2 km, this should beat ADSL2+ by 2 to 6Mb/s, tailing off to match ADSL2+ performance at longer distances. ITU-T G.993.2

- ISDN DSL (IDSL). Symmetric 144Kb/s. Uses ISDN equipment in a DSL way. Differences from ISDN are: always on, no voice capability and no *D* channel. A maximum distance of about 5.4 km. ANSI T1.601

More developments include the *Next Generation DSL*, variously called *Second Generation DSL*, *Etherloop*, and *Ethernet over POTS*. It takes elements from both Ethernet and DSL, promising combined speech and data at high data rates over distances comparable to ADSL.

Features of Etherloop include:

- Speeds of 10Mb/s at 1 km; 4Mb/s at 2 km; 2.5Mb/s at 2.5 km; 2Mb/s at 3.5 km; 1Mb/s at 4.5 km; dropping to 500Kb/s at 6 km.

- A half-duplex transmission scheme (ADSL is full duplex) is used which reduces interference to and from neighbouring cables and interference induced by things like wiring splices. This means that Etherloop can operate over lower quality cabling than ADSL.

- Etherloop transmits in packets, rather than continuously like the DSLs. When not transmitting it monitors the wire and adapts its transmission strategy to ensure it is causing the least possible interference with other wires in the cable bundle.

- It uses the range 30 kHz to 3 MHz (approximately) divided into about 12 over-lapping bands, using one at a time and hopping between bands when necessary to avoid interference.

- It uses a *Quadrature Phase Shift Keying* (QPSK, see p. 63) and QAM encoding on the wire for a 1.667Mbaud symbol rate. The number of bits encoded per symbol varies with distance.

- It is point to point only, so avoiding CSMA collision issues.

- It is symmetric: the full bandwidth available can be used in either direction (but not both simultaneously!).

- It has robust checksums and packet redelivery.

- Being based on Ethernet, it has good compatibility with existing systems (efficient encapsulation) and is relatively cheap to build.

Etherloop is starting to make an appearance connecting schools and hotels as a cheap alternative to a leased line. There is a possibility it may be adopted as part of the IEEE 802.3ah standard in a variant named 100BaseCu that peaks at 100Mb/s.

Many other physical/link layers exist: in particular, wireless links are becoming increasingly popular.

4.9   Exercises

Exercise 4.1 Trace the history of telephone modems, from the earliest system until V.92. Explain why modems stop at V.92.

Exercise 4.2 Show in detail how the message 'Hello {world}' would be transmitted in

   (a)   a SLIP
   (b)   a PPP (use protocol field 0000)

frame.

Exercise 4.3 The T and E hierarchies have (historically) been very important in the expansion of data networks. Read up on their history and development.

Exercise 4.4 Frame Relay, ATM and MPLS are direct competitors in the market. For various scenarios (a multi-site company, an ISP, a telecoms provider, etc.) discuss and compare them as solutions.

Exercise 4.5 ADSL is just one of several DSL standards. Write notes on as many of the others as you can find.

THE PHYSICAL AND LINK LAYERS 3: WIRELESS AND BEYOND

5

5.1   Introduction

The problem with wired networks is the wires: in LANs the wires get underfoot and in WANs they cost a lot to install (digging holes to install cables is expensive!). And in both they tie a machine to a particular location. It would be so much better to be connected to a network without all those irritating cables everywhere: this is the purpose of wireless networks, to free the machine physically.

There are already many extensive wireless networks about, namely the cellular telephone networks. Current Second Generation systems were not designed with data transmission as a primary concern, so it is not surprising that they do not support data terribly well. The emergent 3G networks are supposed to address this problem, but they are taking their time getting off the ground.

In Europe, all things wireless are overseen by the European Telecommunications Standards Institute (ETSI), while the USA has the Federal Communications Commission (FCC). Similar organizations exist in other regions. These are governmental bodies set up to manage the airwaves, allocating various bandwidths to various purposes and ensuring minimal interference between all the competing concerns for parts of the spectrum. Any wireless standard *must* be passed by these bodies before it can be deployed.

Wireless networks are used for WANs, LANs, and so on, just like wired networks, and we start by concentrating on wireless LANs (WLANs), in particular wireless Ethernet. We shall then widen our view to look at wireless WANs (WWANs), finishing with some general considerations about the link layer, both economic and technical.

5.2   Wireless Ethernet

The 802.11 group of standards deals with wireless Ethernet. In principle, this is just the CSMA/CD protocol run over radio waves rather than copper, but naturally there are many problems unique to wireless networks. These problems include:

IEEE 802.11

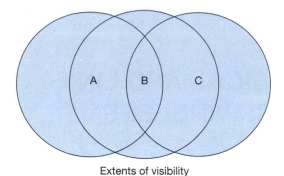

Extents of visibility

Figure 5.1 Visibility in wireless networks.

- Wireless networks generally have fairly high error rates due to electrically noisy environments, signal reflections, and so on.

- This means the bandwidth you get is heavily dependent on the circumstances of your environment and distance between hosts.

- Wireless networks generate electrical interference themselves.

- The allowed transmission power is usually kept quite low by the spectrum management bodies to reduce interference so the range achievable is often limited.

- If workstation A can 'see' B (i.e., B's transmissions reach as far as A) and B can see C (Figure 5.1), then C can't necessarily see A, so A may not be aware if there is a collision of its packets to B with packets from C to B.

- As packets are being broadcast, wireless networks are intrinsically insecure, so that extra care needs to be taken over security and authentication.

A technique known as 'war driving' involves driving about your neighbourhood with a wireless networked PC until you chance upon the signal from some unsecured system. Then you have free access to the Internet! Note that using a network without permission is illegal in the UK and probably elsewhere. Studies have shown that there are indeed many available networks out there. A similar trick works with cordless telephones.

The name 'war driving' is derived from the older 'war dialling' from the times when companies often had modems for their employees to dial in and use. A cracker would try every phone number in the company's telephone directory until they chanced upon a modem. This modem often had unrestricted access to the company's computer system.

War driving may seem like a victimless crime, but there have been reports of people using unsecured wireless networks as points to send millions of spam emails. This can rebound back badly on the innocent owner of the network, who might get blacklisted as a spammer.

There are several parts to the standard. Of principal interest are 802.11, 802.11a, 802.11b and 802.11g. The first, 802.11, also contains a specification for infrared wireless transmissions, but this doesn't seem to have been taken up by manufacturers with such great enthusiasm. Other parts include 802.11c for bridging between networks; 802.11d for harmonization of the standards between countries, in particular with regard to use of frequencies; 802.11e for aspects of QoS; 802.11f for communication between access points to support roaming; 802.11h for spectrum management (dynamic channel selection) for 802.11a in regions such as Europe that have particularly exacting requirements on the use of frequencies; 802.11i for updates to security.

IEEE 802.11c
IEEE 802.11d
IEEE 802.11e
IEEE 802.11f
IEEE 802.11h
IEEE 802.11i

5.2.1   802.11

The 802.11 and 802.11b standards were designed for LANs and operate in the 2.4 GHz waveband. The original 802.11 runs at 1Mb/s or 2Mb/s (i.e., a maximum of 1Mb/s and 2Mb/s, respectively), while 802.11b upgrades this to include 5.5Mb/s and 11Mb/s. Machines can be up to 100 m (300 feet) apart indoors and up to 300 m (1000 feet) outdoors. You might hear 802.11b being called 'Wi-Fi' or even 'AirPort'.

IEEE 802.11
IEEE 802.11b

The 2.4 GHz waveband is an unlicensed (i.e., you do not need a licence to transmit using these frequencies at low power) section of the radio spectrum that is allocated for industrial, scientific and medical (ISM) purposes.

'Wi-Fi' is actually a certificate of interoperability given to manufacturers whose equipment demonstrably works with that of other manufacturers. This is administered by the Wi-Fi Alliance (formerly the Wireless Ethernet Compatibility Alliance, WECA), a not-for-profit consortium of interested companies. Knowing that their wireless systems will work together whoever they bought them from is clearly a benefit to consumers.

5.2.2   Spread Spectrum

The bits are not transmitted over a simple single frequency as if it were a radio station. This is because there is a great deal of electrical noise in the 2.4 GHz frequency band that must be overcome; in particular, microwave ovens radiate in this band. Instead, the signal is spread over many frequencies within the range using a variety of techniques collectively called *spread spectrum* transmission. It is also called *wideband*, in contrast to *narrowband* which uses a single frequency to transmit data.

Two popular ways of doing this are *frequency hopping spread spectrum* (FHSS) and *direct sequence spread spectrum* (DSSS).

FHSS hops amongst frequencies in a pseudo-random fashion spending a little time transmitting at a given frequency before moving on to the next. In 802.11 it generally uses 79 1 MHz channels (fewer in certain countries). It hops every 400 ms or less (i.e., 2.5 hops or more per second) and the minimum hop size is 6 MHz or more. These numbers can vary, but the regulatory body of the country will set the limits that compliant implementations must remain within.

A hopping pattern covers all the available channels before repeating itself and there are 78 hop patterns to choose from. Note that the hopping patterns are well known and specified in the 802.11 standard.

An additional benefit is that multiple machines on the same network can each have (just about) the full 1 or 2Mb/s bandwidth: as one transmission hops about its subfrequencies it only rarely clashes with a second transmission also hopping about on a different pattern.

A 1 bit is encoded as a signal at a frequency slightly higher than the current hop frequency, while a 0 bit is slightly lower. This provides a 1Mb/s data rate. A 2MB/s rate is achieved by having four transmit frequencies, two above and two below the current hop. This encodes the bit pairs 00, 01, 10 and 11.

> FHSS was developed about 50 years ago by the military for secure wireless communication. If the hopping patterns are properly (pseudo-)random and kept secret, this make interception of a signal that much harder. Another advantage is that SS spreads the transmission power thinly over a large frequency range rather than having a big spike of power at one frequency. This is then harder to detect and itself causes less interference to other electrical systems.
>
> Some modern SS techniques use picosecond timing and produce a signal that is indistinguishable from the background noise more than a few metres away from the transmitter, but nevertheless can be picked up and decoded several kilometres away!
>
> Of the several possible available ISM frequencies that 802.11 might have chosen, the 2.4 GHz band was picked since (a) the wavelength allows small portable antennas to be used, e.g., in PCMCIA cards, and (b) the frequency was the highest that could at that time be easily generated by a cheap, mass-produced system. Higher frequencies mean more bandwidth, though they take more power and go through walls less well.
>
> The fact that microwave ovens use 2.4 GHz is a pragmatic choice and has nothing to do with resonant frequencies of water molecules. The value was originally chosen because (a) it would not interfere with the then existing communications systems and (b) waves of that frequency penetrate food sufficiently well that it will be cooked all the way through and not so well that they would pass straight through without heating the food. Most microwave ovens leak so little microwave radiation that their effect on 802.11 is pretty small.

DSSS is the alternative convergence sublayer specified by the 802.11 standard. This uses a *chipping code* (also called a *spreading code*), where a single bit is spread into a sequence of 10 to 20 *chips*. A chip is also a 1 or a 0, thus a 1 bit might be encoded as 01001000111 and a 0 bit as 10110111000 (a *Barker sequence*). The number of chips used in the code is called the *processing gain* (more accurately, the *spreading ratio*, but the subtleties need not worry us here). What is the point of doing this, as we are now sending 11 chips where we were previously sending just 1 bit? The answer is:

- A much greater resilience to noise: a few chips can be corrupted through interference and we can still recognize the original bit sent.

- The signal looks much like random noise even when a long stream of, say, 1 bits is transmitted. This spreads the power of transmission rather than having a very prominent spike in the power spectrum.

The necessary bandwidth is regained by using a larger chunk of the spectrum at once: a fixed 22 MHz for DSSS vs. a hopping 1 MHz for FHSS.

A variety of ways of encoding the chips are used, depending on the bandwidth needed:

- At 1Mb/s, *Differential Binary Phase Shift Keying* (DBPSK) using a process gain 11 chipping code, transmitted at 11 million chips per second. This uses phase shifts of the signal to encode ones and zeros.

- At 2Mb/s, *Differential Quadrature Phase Shift Keying* (DQPSK). As DBPSK, but with four possible phase shifts to encode 2 bits per symbol.

- At 5.5Mb/s in 802.11b, *Complementary Code Keying* (CCK). Based on DQPSK, but with varying spreading codes to encode more bits per symbol. Two bits are sent as phase shifts and 2 bits are communicated by the choice of one of four possible spreading codes.

- At 11Mb/s with CCK. Now 2 bits are sent as phase shifts and 6 bits are communicated by the choice of one of 64 possible spreading codes.

The allocated frequency range is split into up to 14 overlapping channels of 22 MHz each centered about specified frequencies. The number of channels actually available to the user depends on the country (Figure 5.2). In Japan you get all 14. In most of Europe ETSI allows 13 channels, while in other countries, such as the USA and Canada (FCC), France and Spain, fewer channels are available due to local licensing restrictions.

Channel	Frequency (GHz)	USA/Can	Fra	Spa	Eur	Jap
1	2.412	•			•	•
2	2.417	•			•	•
3	2.422	•			•	•
4	2.427	•			•	•
5	2.432	•			•	•
6	2.437	•			•	•
7	2.442	•			•	•
8	2.447	•			•	•
9	2.452	•			•	•
10	2.457	•	•	•	•	•
11	2.462	•	•	•	•	•
12	2.467		•		•	•
13	2.472		•		•	•
14	2.484					•

Figure 5.2 Available channels in a few countries.

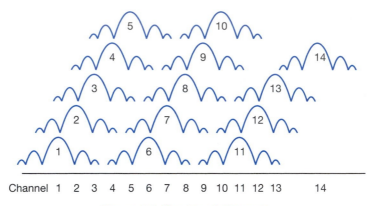

Channel 1 2 3 4 5 6 7 8 9 10 11 12 13 14

Figure 5.3 Overlap of channels.

The multiplicity of channels allows wireless networks to exist side by side, though you should not use adjacent channels on physically close networks as each channel overlaps its neighbours somewhat (Figure 5.3). Rough recommendations are as follows (though individual circumstances may vary): you should separate channels by at least 2 (e.g., use channels 1 and 4) to reduce interference, while separating by 4 should have no interference at all. This separation would permit up to three collocated networks, using channels 1, 6 and 11: thus, practically speaking, 802.11 has 3 channels, not 14. If the networks are not physically close together you have more leeway. You can separate channels by 1 (e.g., use channels 1 and 3) if the networks are about 40 m or more apart. Over 100 m, the nominal range of the signal, you can use neighbouring channels and of course you can reuse frequencies when the separation is sufficiently large that there is no interference.

> The power distribution of the signal is mostly close to the given frequency but has smaller low-power lobes on either side in a $(\sin x/x)^2$ waveform. For widely separated frequencies only the lobes overlap, so giving less interference. Alternatively, as the physical distance increases the lower power lobes fade away first, thus allowing closer frequencies.
>
> In practice it seems that the interference between channels separated by 3 (e.g., channels 1 and 5) is less than 1%, and this may be perfectly acceptable, particularly if you need more than the usual three collocated channels.

What are the relative strengths and weaknesses of FHSS and DSSS?

- DSSS has better immunity to noise.

- DSSS has less latency as you do not have a pause while the channel hops.

- DSSS supplies a larger per-network bandwidth of 11Mb/s, while FHSS can't do more than 2Mb/s.

- FHSS allows 26 networks to coexist, while DSSS allows just 3.

- FHSS has an aggregate bandwidth of 52Mb/s: 26 networks × 2Mb/s; DSSS has an aggregate bandwidth of 33Mb/s: 3 networks × 11MB/s.

- FHSS uses less power and so is better for portable devices.

- FHSS is cheaper to build.

- FHSS degrades more gracefully under heavy load.

Whatever the arguments, there are very few implementations of FHSS and DSSS has overwhelmingly taken the market.

The 802.11 standard employs *Carrier Sense, Multiple Access, Collision Avoidance* (CSMA/CA), which is similar to CSMA/CD, but is complicated by the fact that you can't always determine if there was a collision: your own signal can swamp everybody else's so you can't always detect them when they transmit at the same time as you, or the collision might happen outside the range you can hear.

CSMA/CA starts by listening for a signal (carrier sense). If the channel is free it sends its packet. If the channel is busy, the protocol waits until the current transmission ends and starts a *contention period*. This is a random interval of time that the host must wait before attempting to send. If the channel is still free at the end, send the packet. If several hosts are waiting to send, the one that had the shortest contention would get to send. Since the periods are of random length this means that every host has an equal chance of winning on average.

Additional features are added to CSMA/CA to make the system more robust. If the packet is safely received, the destination sends an acknowledgement (ACK) signal back. If the source doesn't get the ACK, it starts over and resends the packet. To help against the visibility problem, 802.11 has optional RTS/CTS *handshaking* (Figure 5.4). Before sending a packet the source host sends a *request to send* (RTS) frame. If the destination is happy with this (it is not already busy receiving data from some other host that the first couldn't see), it replies with a *clear to send* (CTS) frame. On getting this, the source sends its packet. Every other host in range of the destination will also see the CTS even if they didn't see the RTS and they will know they cannot transmit yet. Furthermore, the RTS and CTS contain the length of the desired transmission, so a third host knows how long it has to wait before transmitting.

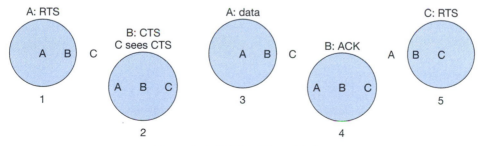

Figure 5.4 RTS/CTS handshake.

All this overhead means that 802.11 has a fairly large latency compared to, say, wired Ethernet, though it is possible to turn off RTS/CTS to gain a little speed. The alternatives are:

- RTS/CTS always. Preferable on large or busy networks.

- RTS/CTS never. Good on small or lightly loaded networks where each host can see all the others.

- RTS/CTS on large packets only. A compromise that reduces the relatively large overhead for small packets.

The 802.11 standard allows for an alternative to CSMA/CA that guarantees an upper limit on the time it takes before a frame can be sent. This is good for sending video streams and the like. In this method the access point polls each client and a client can only send when it gets polled. No manufacturer seems to have implemented this.

Modern 802.11 network cards implement a *microwave oven mode* where they try to work around the bursts of radiation that leak from the typical microwave oven. Typically this can involve fragmenting packets into smaller parts so that only small chunks of data get blasted by microwaves. These chunks can then be retransmitted.

Although 802.11b is nominally 11Mb/s and 802.11g is nominally 54Mb/s, this is actually the *signalling rate*, not the data rate the user sees. The signalling rate is the raw bit rate over the airwaves, but a lot of that bandwidth is consumed in overheads in CSMA/CA and elsewhere. Realistically speaking, you can only expect to get about 3 to 4Mb/s from 802.11b and about 20Mb/s from 11g. This means that 11b is not really fast enough for bandwidth-intensive applications like streaming video, but is plenty for general working (on the other hand, some modern compressing video codecs can supply DVD quality at 1Mb/s). An 802.11 frame can contain up to 2312 data bytes: increasing the MTU (p. 89) for the wireless interface can improve bulk throughput a little.

IEEE 802.11e   The 802.11e standard adds QoS to the 802.11 standards, providing multimedia support, additional security and improving performance in a noisy environment. This uses *packet bursting* (also known as *frame bursting*), which is running several frames together to decrease the average overhead of each packet and thus increase throughput. This applies to all of 802.11a, b and g. Hardware tested as being interoperable to (a certain subset of) 802.11e by the Wi-Fi Alliance gets to wear the 'Wi-Fi Multimedia' (WMM) label on the box.

5.2.3   802.11a and 802.11g

IEEE 802.11a   The 802.11a standard is designed for the user with high bandwidth demands and operates in the 5 GHz *Unlicensed National Information Infrastructure* (UNII) band. It uses a different encoding (*Orthogonal Frequency Division Multiplexing*, OFDM). This is similar in character to a chipping code, but the codes are carefully chosen so that a 1 bit from one source is distinguishable from a 1 bit from another source even if both are transmitted at the same time on the same frequency. This gives better error resilience and even allows channels to overlap somewhat with no degradation.

The standard specifies various rates from 6Mb/s up to a nominal 54Mb/s. It works over a shorter physical range than 802.11b/g, but for a given power and distance between machines it has a higher bandwidth. The expected realistic bandwidth from an 802.11a network tops out at around 22 to 26Mb/s over a short distance.

The 802.11g standard is backwardly compatible with 802.11b (it uses the 2.4GHz band and will interoperate with 802.11b at 11Mb/s or slower), but provides up to a signalling rate of 54Mb/s over distances comparable to 802.11b by using OFDM for its faster rates. The data rate is similar to 802.11a in a 802.11g-only environment, but can drop somewhat in a mixed 802.11b and 11g environment as the 802.11g standard is required to be friendly to 802.11b transmissions. IEEE 802.11g

How do 802.11a and 802.11g compare?

- They have the same bandwidth and both use OFDM.

- The signal from 802.11a is more lossy than 802.11g and will barely pass through walls: an 802.11a transmitter might have trouble covering an average-sized home while 802.11g normally has no problem.

- The higher frequency of 802.11a requires more power, so is less suitable for portable devices.

- On the other hand, the 5 GHz part of the spectrum is much less crowded than the free-for-all 2.4 GHz band and so is much less likely to get interference.

- You can only have a limited number of 802.11g networks physically close to each other (just as 802.11b) but 802.11a allows as many as 12 or more to operate together without mutual interference.

The Wi-Fi Alliance also tests 802.11a and 802.11g equipment for interoperability.

The 802.11a channels are not all identical: typically there are differing restrictions on the maximum transmission power allowed. This might vary from 4 W for one channel to 200 mW for another. This must be taken into account when planning an 802.11a network. In the UK, the current limits are

Band A 5.150–5.350 GHz	200 mW	unlicensed
Band B 5.470–5.725 GHz	1 W	unlicensed
Band C 5.725–5.850 GHz	2 W	licence required

The 802.11b/g transmitters (2.400–2.4835 GHz) are unlicensed and allowed 100 mW. Other countries have different regulations.

The 802.11j standard is a variant of 802.11a that takes Japanese regulations on power and frequency bands into account. IEEE 802.11j

In the marketplace 802.11g has won over 802.11a. Even though 802.11a hardware was out in the marketplace for about a year before 802.11g hit the streets, it appears that the backward compatibility of 11g with 11b has played to its advantage as there were already a huge number of 11b products installed. It has been suggested that 11a may gain acceptance in business environments where the extra aggregate bandwidth is useful, while 11g may be more popular in homes because of its backward compatibility and lower price. Perhaps, as more and more 11b/g devices appear, people will migrate to the less cluttered frequencies of 11a. More likely is that 11a will remain a minor player as both it and 11g are overtaken by new technology.

5.2.4   Wireless Networks

Wireless networks come in a variety of shapes and sizes (Figure 5.5). The 802.11 networks can be arranged in a point-to-point (aka *Ad-Hoc* or *Independent Basic Service Set* (IBSS) mode) configuration, where each machine can see the others and they contact their peers directly. Alternatively, they can be in a hub configuration where a central machine routes traffic (also called *infrastructure* or *Basic Service Set* (BSS) mode). This can work over a physically wider area than point-to-point, but requires the purchase of a hub called an *access point* (AP). APs usually have an Ethernet connection so they can bridge between wired and wireless.

There is also *Extended Service Set* (ESS) mode where you have multiple access points connected by (say) a wired Ethernet. In this setup you can *roam* between access points. This is the same as cellular telephone networks where your machine can transfer between transmitters as you physically move about. An ESS can cover an area as large as you like, subject to the usual limitations on the wired part.

Being a broadcast medium, wireless networks are particularly vulnerable to eavesdropping. Thus some kind of security mechanism is required, the very least being encryption of the data before it is transmitted. So, to prevent casual snooping of the signal, 802.11 employs *Wired Equivalent Privacy* (WEP) which uses the RC4 encryption algorithm with

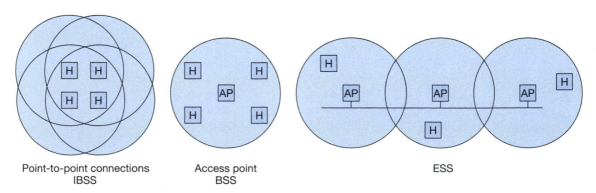

Point-to-point connections
IBSS

Access point
BSS

ESS

Figure 5.5 Coverage of wireless networks.

40 or 128 bit keys. Both ends of a transmission share a secret key which is used to encrypt the traffic before it goes out on the airwaves.

The choice of key sizes was due to the restrictions at the time the standard was drafted on exporting strong encryption systems from the USA. The 40 bit version could be exported, while the 128 bit version was for domestic US use. These restrictions have since disappeared, but their legacy lives on: manufacturers like to charge more for the 128 bit version even though there is no physical difference.

Now 40 bit security is better than no security, but it is not beyond the bounds of feasibility to go through and try all $2^{40} \approx 1.1 \times 10^{12}$ possible keys one by one. Furthermore, as people often use secret keys that are five character ASCII strings, this reduces the search space to about $2^{30} \approx 1.1 \times 10^{9}$ keys, or even fewer by using dictionary attacks.

If brute force is too much effort for you, it turns out that the WEP algorithm itself is breakable with a little ingenuity: after collecting a modest amount of traffic the system can be broken.

A little more on WEP encryption is needed here. The RC4 algorithm natively uses up to 2048 bits of key and when we have a smaller key it is merely repeated as many times as necessary to fill up the space. The 40 bit WEP variant is actually 40 secret bits plus 24 bits of *initialization vector* (IV) making 64 key bits in total. The IV is a value that is changed for each packet sent so that identical source packets won't end up as identical encrypted packets. This helps to conceal, for example, large blocks of zero data that would otherwise be recognizable as repeating blocks of encrypted data. The IV is sent in the clear (i.e., unencrypted) along with the encrypted data so the destination can construct the decoding key. Some implementations start with an IV of all zeros and increment it in some simple fashion, others choose it at random.

The 128 bit variant is actually 104 bits of secret key plus 24 bits of IV again, so this too is not as secure as it sounds.

The weakness of WEP is due to the shortness of the IV. The security of this encryption method depends on a key never being repeated, but there are only $2^{24} = 16777216$ different keys based on a given secret key, one per IV. A single link running at 11Mb/s will use all the keys within an hour. Multiple links, typically all using the same base key, will repeat proportionally faster. The reuse of IVs (e.g., by all machines starting with an IV of zero) adds to the problem. Even choosing IVs at random does not help, since the Birthday Paradox implies there will be a 50% chance of a repetition after only $2^{12} = 4096$ IVs.

To cap it all, many installations do not even bother to enable WEP!

Things are actually even worse than might be expected: a *reinjection attack* can decode blocks of data given even only small amounts of intercepted traffic.

Despite its problems you should always use WEP but further encrypt traffic yourself in a higher layer, e.g., using IPSec (Section 13.5.2) or ssh (p. 232).

A replacement for WEP, the *Temporal Key Integrity Protocol* (TKIP) has been developed to address the WEP problem. This preprocesses the secret key, stirring in the IV and the address of the sender (to prevent IV repetition amongst hosts producing the same encryption key), and outputs the key to be used. It also changes the secret key every 10000 packets to combat the IV Birthday Paradox problem.

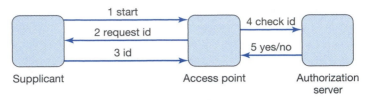

Figure 5.6 Port-Based Network Access Control.

The flipside of secrecy is the question of authority: should that machine be allowed to connect to this access point? Clearly, you can't allow any machine that comes along to tap into your network, so there needs to be some sort of access control. Currently, authorization in 802.11 is weak to non-existent: knowledge of the shared WEP secret key is generally taken as authorization to use the network. Some APs also check the hardware address on the packets to see if they are in its list of approved numbers. Unfortunately, many chips these days have software reconfigurable hardware addresses, so this is not much of a security improvement.

IEEE 802.1X
RFC 3748
RFC 2716

The IEEE 802.1X Port-Based Network Access Control standard fills just this gap. In this, 802.1X takes an existing protocol, the Extensible Authentication Protocol (EAP), which was designed for PPP (Section 4.4.2), and applies it to networks (wireless or otherwise).

When a host first contacts the access point the AP refuses to accept any traffic but 802.1X requests (Figure 5.6). This prevents casual usage of the AP. The host (called a *supplicant*) sends a 'EAP-start' message and the AP replies with a 'EAP-request identity'. The host responds with an identity packet. The AP can now choose to authenticate this identity in any way it likes: passing the identity to a dedicated authentication server is a popular choice. Authentication methods like *Remote Authentication Dial In User Service*

RFC 2865
RFC 1510

(RADIUS, normally used by ISPs to authenticate dial-in customers) and Kerberos are supported. If the authentication server is happy with the identity, it will then instruct the AP to accept all traffic (in particular IP) from the host. Use of cryptography ensures that identities cannot be spoofed.

Additionally, 802.1X agrees a new different WEP key for each host, thus addressing the key reuse problem.

This kind of authentication can also be used in ad hoc networks. As there is no central point of authority, machines can simply mutually authenticate in pairs.

> There have been claims recently that the 802.1X standard is flawed and can be subverted. For example, a hacker can send a 'session close' packet to a client and then take over its session with the AP. The original client would immediately renegotiate a new session with the AP so the user would not necessarily notice anything had happened. The AP thinks that the old connection is still fine and the hacker can use it.
>
> Note that '802.11x' means 'any 802.11' standard: this often gets confused with 802.1X.

The IEEE 802.11i Enhanced Security standard upgrades the RC4-TKIP of 802.1X to AES-CCMP (Advanced Encryption Algorithm-Counter-Mode/CBC-MAC) as part of a complete security framework for wireless networks. IEEE 802.11i

An interim standard has been published by the Wi-Fi Alliance. Called 'Wi-Fi Protected Access' (WPA) it aims to bridge the gap between WEP and the newly appeared 802.11i. In essence WPA is just a cut-down 802.11i using the parts that can be implemented on existing hardware: an important feature of WPA is that it will only require software and firmware upgrades to implement, so the many millions of units already deployed can take advantage of WPA. The full 802.11i requires features such as the Advanced Encryption Standard (AES) which may well need new hardware to be practicable.

In the long term the Wi-Fi Alliance will require a full 802.11i implementation for a system to be certified Wi-Fi compliant, but in the meantime just WPA will be required. To maintain recognizability 802.11i will be marketed as 'WPA2'.

EAP typically uses a central authentication server like RADIUS, which is overkill for a small office or home network. So WPA has a special Home/SOHO (Small Office/Home Office) mode. This is just a simple shared-key authentication mechanism where a user enters their password and it is verified directly. This password is used both to authenticate the user and to initialize the process of TKIP key rotation.

5.2.5 Other Wireless

Wireless data networks, once rare, are now popping up everywhere.

Personal and Local Area Networks

Bluetooth (named after a tenth century Danish Viking king of Scandinavia) is another wireless technology rather akin to 802.11b, but is designed for short-range point-to-point connections between appliances like TVs, fridges and telephones. It has a range of just 10 m, uses frequency hopping (up to 1600 times a second over 79 1 MHz channels), delivers about 1Mb/s, but uses much less power than 802.11b. Up to eight devices can be linked together in a *piconet*. Up to 10 piconets can overlap in a *scatternet*. Perhaps it's better not to think of Bluetooth as a wireless LAN, but rather as a wireless cable (sometimes it is said to be a wireless USB). Running IP over Bluetooth requires an intermediate layer, such as PPP (Section 4.4.2). IEEE 802.15.1

In fact, there is also a nascent Wireless USB (WUSB) standard. It has a target bandwidth of 480Mb/s (the same as wired USB 2.0) and will use ultra wideband radio (p. 74) over at least 10 m. Just as with normal USB, this is not a symmetric system, but has a master host that initiates all transfers to the devices in a point-to-point manner. Unlike normal USB, whose tree structure of devices does not make sense in a wireless setting, WUSB has a hub-and-spoke connection architecture: the master as the hub, and the devices around it. The idea is for WUSB to be compatible with USB and to be able to plug one into the other. There is also a plan to support the analogue of the USB On-the-Go, namely a peer-to-peer rather than master–slave system.

Next, there is HomeRF. Or, more accurately, there *was* HomeRF as the HomeRF consortium of companies has now disbanded. This group developed the *Shared Wireless Access Protocol* (SWAP) wireless standard. It gives FHSS rates of 1.6Mb/s (version 1.0) and 10Mb/s (version 2.0) over a distance of a 'typical home and yard'. An 40Mb/s version (version 3.0) never appeared. The distinguishing feature of HomeRF is that it also supplies six voice channels simultaneously with 127 data channels and is aimed at the 'wireless home'. The drive is towards low cost, so that a large part of HomeRF is software based, enabling the hardware to be very cheap.

IEEE 802.15.4 Yet another technology is IEEE 802.15.4 and its application-oriented extension Zigbee (apparently named after the zigzag dance patterns that bees use to communicate) which is designed with ultra-low-power consumption in mind. It is intended for a device to run for six months to two years on just a pair of AA batteries. In the 2.4 GHz band it provides 250Kb/s, but it also can operate at 868 MHz (Europe) at 20Kb/s and 915 MHz (North America) at 40Kb/s. The range is in the region of 30 m and the data rate is slower than 802.11 and Bluetooth, but the power consumption is significantly lower. A network can have up to 255 nodes and up to 100 networks can be collocated. Applications include things like home and industrial control, and Zigbee proponents predict a typical home may eventually incorporate perhaps 150 Zigbee devices.

All of 802.11b, Bluetooth, Home RF, Zigbee and some cordless telephones (and microwave ovens!) use the 2.4 GHz band, meaning that there is potential for contention and interference in these networks. The performance of a network will suffer if there is one of the others nearby. Some practical experiments have implied that Bluetooth and 802.11b seem to have minimal mutual interference under normal conditions.

IEEE 802.15.2

IEEE 802.15 IEEE 802.15 covers these very short-distance *personal area networks* (PANs). As well as Bluetooth, these standards consider kinds of high-data-rate (802.15.3) and low-data-rate, low-power (802.15.4) *wireless personal area networks* (WPANs).

IEEE 802.15.3/3a

IEEE 802.15.4

IEEE 802.11h IEEE 802.11h is looking into how networks can limit the amount they interfere with each other through spectrum management. For example, an AP could detect another transmission in the area and reduce its output power to try to limit interference (*Transmit Power Control*, TPC). Alternatively, it could automatically choose a different frequency (*Dynamic Frequency Selection*, DFS).

IEEE 802.11n In development is the IEEE 802.11n High Throughput Wireless standard. This will increase data rates over 11g by several techniques: by increasing the raw signalling speed; by reducing the overheads so that actual data rates are closer to the raw speeds; by allowing the simultaneous use of multiple channels. By using multiple antennas each sending and receiving multiple signals (*multiple input, multiple output*, MIMO) we get *spacial multiplexing*, allowing a larger data rate to be squeezed into a given radio space. The original goal was at least 100Mb/s of real throughput, but it seems that 540Mb/s may be achievable using a raw rate of 600Mb/s. The standard is expected to be ratified sometime in 2006, but already some early (non-certified) hardware is on sale, getting 300Mb/s throughput.

Metropolitan and Wide Area Networks

The IEEE 802.16 standard is for a broadband wireless MAN. Developed from the ETSI HiperMan standard, it operates over frequencies in the 10 to 66 GHz range (with subsequent extension to 2 to 11 GHz in 802.16a) and is designed for the *last mile* problem (see Section 5.3), namely the infrastructure required to get data from a public network to the home. The bandwidth available will be dependent on local regulations on the transmission power and the number of channels allowed in the above spectrum, but it should support from 2Mb/s to 155Mb/s per channel and should stretch to a 50 km (30 mile) range. IEEE 802.16

It uses *Demand Assignment Multiple Access–Time Division Multiple Access* (DAMA-TDMA), an adaptive version of *Time Division Multiple Access* (TDMA) which shares the available bandwidth amongst several users by chopping the channel into small time slots and fitting frames into one or more time slots. The standard is divided into three parts: IEEE 802.16.1 uses 10–66 GHz; 802.16.2 uses 2–11 GHz; 802.16.3 uses the licence-exempt 5–6 GHz. IEEE 802.16.3 will be backward compatible with Bluetooth, but deliver up to 20Mb/s.

The WiMAX (*World Interoperability for Microwave Access*) group tests for conformance with 802.16.

Thus there are three main groups standardizing wireless networks:

802.15	WPAN
802.11	WLAN
802.16	WMAN

Several other groups exist, such as IEEE 802.22 for Wireless Regional Networks (WRAN), which is poised to use the gaps in the spectrum that will be released when analogue TV is decommissioned. IEEE 802.22

Another variant, IEEE 802.16e Mobile Wireless MAN, is for mobile technologies, thus potentially competing with 802.11 in both sales and frequencies; 802.16e is predicted to appear in laptops in 2006 or 2007. IEEE 802.16e

A related standard, IEEE 802.20, Mobile Broadband Wireless Access (MBWA), also deals with metropolitan area mobile wireless, but with the emphasis on the case of a large number of users moving rapidly, up to 250 km/h. IEEE 802.20

HiperLan, another standard developed by ETSI, has dedicated spectrum (5.1 to 5.3 GHz) and provides five channels of 23.5Mb/s. It uses a variant of CSMA/CA and has link layer retransmissions. Designed for ad-hoc-style networks (no central control), it includes a protocol to forward packets between hosts if the source and destination are out of reach. Unfortunately, its complexity means that HiperLan has not been successful. Recently, though, the idea of forwarding has reemerged in the draft standard IEEE 802.1w, an adjunct to 802.11 Ad-Hoc mode, and in IEEE 802.1s Mesh Networking. IEEE 802.1w
IEEE 802.1s

HiperLanII is quite different from HiperLan, being designed for a managed infrastructure. Also from ETSI, it uses OFDM over 5.4 to 5.7 GHz with multiple data rates up to 54Mb/s. Using TDMA to share bandwidth it is essentially a wireless ATM (see Section 4.6). Indeed, ATM frames fit directly into HiperLanII time slots.

Around the corner is ultra-wideband (UWB), another form of spread spectrum with origins in the 1950s. Using an extremely short pulse (a *monocycle*, perhaps a nanosecond or less in duration) rather than a continuous signal (the *carrier*) to represent a bit, it spreads its transmission power over a range from near 0 Hz to a few gigahertz. Since the power is spread so thinly, the claim is that it does not interfere with other signals in that range (or rather, not unless there is a large number of transmitters). Plus, it has the benefits of being difficult to detect or jam. It promises high bandwidth at very low power: some developers claim 40Mb/s at 1/10000 the power of a conventional wireless network.

Wireless networks are assisting in the development of MANs and WANs since some people are looking at using wireless technologies like 802.11 to connect street-wide and larger collections of machines together in a *community area network* (CAN). In a commercial counterpart, some new companies are creating wireless 'hot spots', where they are licensing bandwidth from many wireless ISPs, bringing them together under a single brand name and reselling the bandwidth as a roaming service.

Cellular-Telephone-Based Systems

More emergent technologies build on the infrastructure provided by the mobile cell phone system. The *Global System for Mobile Communications* (GSM) is a TDMA system that shares bandwidth amongst users by using multiple time slots. It provides a data service (alongside its voice service) by using *circuit-switched data* (CSD). As its name implies, this is a circuit-based method that requires dedicated channels. This gives bandwidths of only 9.6Kb/s to 14.4Kb/s and so is not very suitable for modern Internet usage. Variants, such as *high-speed circuit-switched data* (HSCSD), take the rate up to 38.4Kb/s or even 57.6Kb/s, but the limitation here is that higher data rates require multiple time slots being dedicated to a single user, something that service providers regard as not economic.

GSM is a *second generation* (2G) system, where analogue cellular was retrospectively named *first generation* (1G).

The *General Packet Radio Service* (GPRS) delivers more. It is a connectionless (always on, so dial-up is not needed) packet-based system that has a theoretical maximum of 171.2Kb/s. A little background on GSM is in order. A GSM channel is divided into eight TDMA slots which are shared amongst several users. The 171.2Kb/s rate represents a single user taking all eight slots (running at 21.4Kb/s each) which is unlikely to be allowed by the service provider. A bandwidth of 85.6Kb/s is more typical in practice, using four downstream slots and one upstream slot.

> In fact, GPRS is not reliant on GSM and is also compatible with the TDMA systems used in North America: this was part of its design.
>
> On frequencies: GSM is used throughout the world on four different frequency bands. Europe, and many other areas of the world, use GSM on 900 MHz and 1800 MHz. European phones are mostly dual band for this reason and so work over much of the world. Some networks in the Americas use GSM on 1900 MHz and a few in South and Central America use 850 MHz.

Tri-band (900 MHz, 1800 MHz, 1900 MHz) and quad-band phones are becoming more common.

GSM enhanced with GPRS is often called a 2.5G cellular system.

A packet system makes a much more efficient use of bandwidth in a TDMA environment than the circuits used in CSD. That is not to say that CSD is dead: as GPRS sends packets over multiple channels this decreases reliability and causes variable latency of packets, both a problem if you want a good-quality video stream. Here, the fixed circuits of HSCSD can be an advantage.

Adding a better modulation technique, *Enhanced Data rates for GSM Evolution* (EDGE), triples the data rate of GPRS to 384Kb/s (using all eight slots, running at 48Kb/s each). EDGE is also used by the *Third Generation GSM* (3GSM) network, the new successor to GSM.

The phrase 'Third Generation' covers a multitude of technologies including: ITU-T M.1457

- EDGE.

- *Universal Mobile Telephone System* (UMTS), which uses *Wideband CDMA* (WCDMA), a variant of CDMA. CDMA is based on a chipping code (p. 62) system, while 'wide' really ought to be 'wider', as WCDMA channels are simply wider than previously used. UMTS is backward compatible with GSM in the sense that a UMTS phone can transparently hand off to a GSM cell (though it is not compatible in any other sense).

- A competitor to UMTS is CDMA2000, developed to be compatible with existing North American systems.

The important point is that these protocols were developed in the knowledge that data transmission would be an important application so they are designed to

- have data rates of 384Kb/s and maybe even 2Mb/s;

- be 'always on', i.e., permanently connected;

- be global, supporting transparent roaming between terrestrial and satellite systems;

- support multimedia well, e.g., streaming video.

The pace of development in this area is such that this section is guaranteed to be out of date by the time you read it!

In the future, maybe around 2010, expect Fourth Generation Networks, probably via a 3.5G stepping stone. Current rumours are that it should be IPv6 based and run at 100Mb/s.

There were, of course, radio networks even before 1G.

For recognizability, the acronym 3GSM has been adopted by companies selling 3G (Third Generation) UMTS.

Satellite

Some cellular wireless systems, such as GSM, can be adapted to satellite transmission. This has the potential of worldwide coverage at the cost of increased packet latency: the time it takes a packet to travel to and from a geosynchronous satellite is quite noticeable. It is better to use lower orbit satellites such as those employed by the Iridium and Globalstar telephone networks. Notice how the cellular technology is being used: now the cells are moving too! More solutions are discussed in the last mile problem, below.

In a few years' time, the Internet will be globally accessible at substantial data rates: did you want to watch that movie at the top of Mount Everest?

5.3 The Last Mile Problem

Also called the *first mile* problem since some people regard 'last mile' as too downbeat.

The biggest problem of delivering universal Internet access is the *last mile problem*. You may have a fancy infrastructure of multiple gigabit networks covering every city in the country but how do you get connectivity to where it is needed, i.e., businesses and particularly homes? The last mile problem is the question of how to bridge those last few metres and connect thousands or millions of users to your network, ideally with high-bandwidth links. The difficulty is primarily the cost of making those millions of connections.

IEEE 802.3ah

Many potential solutions are being tried:

1. Fibre to the Home (FTTH), also called Fibre to the Premises (FTTP). Connect each customer with new fibre (or copper). This gives many megabits of bandwidth (perhaps several megabits over copper, depending on the length of the cable), but is typically too expensive as it requires digging up every street in the country.

2. Fibre to the Kerb (FTTK), also called Fibre to the Node (FTTN) and Fibre to the Cabinet (FTTC). Cable up every *street*, and then you only need short copper connections from the telecoms street cabinet to the home. Short lengths of copper can support tens of megabit data rates. This is cheaper, but still a lot of new fibre must be laid.

3. Use existing infrastructure. This can be:
   (a) Existing copper connections, namely the telephone local loop. The *local loop* is the wire that connects a home to the local exchange. The ADSL solution is strong but has problems with limited reach: ADSL has strict distance limitations and not everybody is close enough to their local telephone exchange for ADSL to work. On the other hand this is relatively cheap and has quite decent bandwidth. When developments like BT's IP-based 21st Century Network (21CN, p. 53) are rolled out, this will aid the reach of IP into the home;

(b)   The cable TV network: very good connections, but not everyone has cable. The Data Over Cable Service Interface Specifications (DOCSIS) standard covers the cable TV (CATV) solution;

(c)   Other means, e.g., put data down electricity power cables. This is under development, but has problems in that it causes radio interference and currently has limited bandwidth. The HomePlug Powerline Alliance gives a standard for 200Mb *within* the home; they also have ideas for the last mile.

4. Long-range wireless. This uses city-wide radio networks, such as WiMAX (p. 73). It is fairly expensive to build the transmitters, but it is still cheaper than digging up roads. For example, some companies are selling 2Mb/s symmetric connections using the 3.5 GHz band. There has been some resistance over placement of transmitters through environmental concerns and worries about the effects of radio transmission on health. One response has been to put the transmitters on tethered balloons that float 1.5 km above ground!

5. Short-range wireless. Taking the idea of the Internet regarded as a collection of machines that forward data to each other, *mesh wireless* (see p. 73) has every home wireless point being a router that relays packets to the next access point until the packets reach the neighbourhood Internet connection (perhaps an FTTN). There are questions of security of data as it moves from node to node and also of dynamically changing routes as home owners turn their machines on and off. This also needs a critical mass of people taking part before it is effective.

6. Short-range wireless, again. In this scenario the short-range transmitters are within street lamp posts. Data is delivered to the lamp post by whatever means (ADSL, fibre, satellite links, etc.) and then radio links relay the data into the nearby houses. Part of the scheme is to have local caching of Web pages within the lamp post to improve response times and to decrease external bandwidth requirements. This idea is a spin-off of a UK Highways Agency proposal to monitor cars and their movements and manage traffic flow.

7. Satellite (Figure 5.7). This can be
    (a)   one way: have a satellite receiver in the home. Traffic toward the user comes via the satellite, while traffic away from the user goes via a telephone line. This gives asymmetric bandwidth, but as with ADSL the asymmetry is in the favour of the home user (and out of the favour of a business that supplies content). This is very expensive to set up (i.e., put up a satellite) and has somewhat larger network latencies than some people like, as the signal has to travel the 35800 km (22300 miles, approx 1/10 s each way) to and from the satellite. It is good for remote areas that are uneconomic to connect using other technologies and has an extensive coverage of the country;

    (b)   two way: have a satellite receiver and transmitter in the home. Now it is just like a wireless network and has symmetric bandwidth so is more suitable for businesses that want to supply content. It is still expensive and has a large

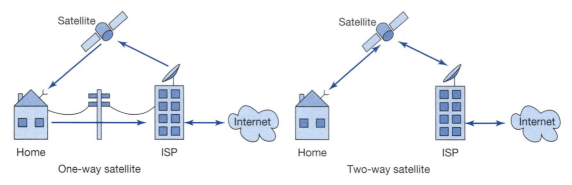

Figure 5.7 Satellite connections.

latency, but is now free even from the need to have a telephone connection and so suitable for very remote areas and undeveloped countries.

The last mile is primarily an economic problem, but has technological influences. The fact that so many differing solutions are appearing is an indication that the problem has not really been solved satisfactorily.

5.4 ARP

RFC 826   We now consider the *Address Resolution Protocol* here as it is often considered to be part of the link layer. It forms part of the IP and exists to solve one very specific problem: the gap between physical layer (e.g., Ethernet 6 byte) addresses and network layer (e.g., IP 4 byte) addresses. This problem does not exist if we are using, say, PPP, as this has no physical layer addresses.

Every machine on the Internet has at least one 32 bit (4 byte) IP address. It is unique to that machine (disregarding some considerations that will become clear later) and so identifies that machine on the Internet. There is a useful convention in writing IP addresses intended for human consumption: the 4 bytes are written as a *dotted quad* of decimal values. Thus the address

00000001000000100000001100000100

is written as 1.2.3.4. IP addresses are chosen by the local network administrator to suit the local network. On the other hand, Ethernet addresses are chosen by the interface chip manufacturer. Of course, a machine's IP address bears no relation to its Ethernet address. The Internet layer uses IP addresses exclusively, as it knows nothing about the link layer. IP addresses are separate for precisely this reason: so that IP can run over many different link layers.

The difficulty arises when the IP layer wants to send a packet over (say) Ethernet. It knows the destination's IP address, whereas to build the Ethernet frame we require the

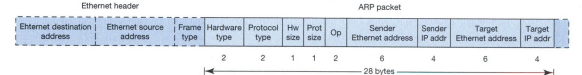

Figure 5.8 ARP packet.

destination's Ethernet address. Thus we need to find which Ethernet address corresponds to which IP address. This is done by ARP.

To determine the Ether address for an IP address, the source machine broadcasts an *ARP request* packet (Figure 5.8) using Ethernet address ff:ff:ff:ff:ff:ff (see p. 25). All machines on the (local) network read the packet and the target machine recognizes that the packet is a request for its address. It responds with an *ARP reply* containing its hardware address (the other machines do nothing). The source machine reads this reply and extracts the Ethernet address. The source machine can now use that Ethernet address to construct and send data packets to the intended target.

This packet is embedded in an Ethernet frame, of course. The frame type for ARP packets is 0806.

The packet is, in more detail:

- Hardware type. This is 1 for an Ethernet address.

- Protocol type. This is 0800 for an IP address.

- Hardware size, protocol size. The number of bytes each of these kinds of addresses occupies. This is 6 for Ethernet and 4 for IP.

- Op. This is 1 for an ARP request and 2 for an ARP reply.

- Address fields. The hardware and protocol addresses for the source and target.

In an ARP request the target hardware address is not filled in; after all, that is what we are trying to find out. In an ARP reply, the target is the original sender and the sender hardware address field contains the information we are interested in.

Of course it would be stupid and a waste of network bandwidth to have an ARP for every packet sent, so instead a cache of mappings from IP to Ethernet addresses is kept by each host. Entries in this cache time out and are removed after 20 minutes, typically. The next packet will require a fresh ARP.

If no machine on the network has the requested address, or that machine is down, no reply will be forthcoming. If this is so and an ARP reply is not received after a couple of seconds, an error message will be sent to the application trying to make the IP connection. The user might see a message like 'no such host', or 'host unreachable'.

Use the Unix command
`arp -a`
to look at the cache.

Sometimes it is useful to broadcast an ARP reply even when nobody has asked for it. For example, when a new machine has joined the network or an existing machine has changed its IP address for some reason (see p. 114). This is called a *gratuitous ARP*. All machines on the network are free to read any ARP reply and update their caches to reflect the given address association. This is most important in order to break old associations that are no longer valid but where the old association is still cached. Otherwise hosts might try to send packets to the wrong hardware address.

The ARP can be used in situations other than Ethernet and IP as it has parameterized fields and so can be used to associate pairs of any types of addresses, but it is by far most associated with Ethernet.

5.4.1 Bridging

There is a clever trick with ARP that can be used to extend networks: for example, making an Ethernet span a distance larger than the specifications allow, or joining a wireless network to a wired network so they appear to be a single network.

To do this we need a *bridge*. This is just a machine with two network interfaces, one on each network (Figure 5.9). If host h1 wishes to send to host h2 it must determine its hardware address. So it does an ARP broadcast for h2. The bridge sees this request and answers on behalf of h2 (it does a *proxy* ARP), but it answers with its *own* address b1.

Now h1 sends the data to what it believes is the address of h2, but is actually b1. The bridge reads the packet, recognizes that it is destined for h2 and forwards it to the other network where it is safely received by h2. Note that the forwarded packet will have the source hardware address b2 and destination hardware address h2.

If h2 replies it either (a) uses the hardware address it got from the original packet, namely b2, or (b) does an ARP, when the bridge again proxies for h1 with its own address b2. In either case, the data packet is delivered to the bridge, which forwards it to h1.

All this is very transparent to h1 and h2 who think that they are on the same network. Thus this is sometimes called *transparent* bridging. Notice that if h1 is communicating with both h2 and h3 the ARP cache on h1 will show that h2 and h3 apparently have the same Ethernet address, namely b1. This is not a problem.

This works very well for joining a pair of networks, but is less suitable for larger collections of networks, in particular when there are multiple routes between hosts. In IEEE 802.1d that case a more sophisticated method as given in the IEEE 802.1d Ethernet Bridging standard can be employed.

Figure 5.9 Proxy ARP.

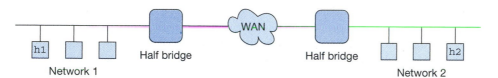

Figure 5.10 Remote bridging.

Bridging is also used to connect networks that are widely separated, e.g., over a WAN, so again they appear as a single network. This is called *remote bridging* (compare with tunnelling, Section 2.4) (Figure 5.10). For example, RFC1220 discusses remote bridging over PPP. The two endpoints of the PPP bridge are called *half bridges*.

IEEE 802.1g
RFC 1220

Remote bridging is similar in principle to local bridging, but now such bridges must address the problems of how to encapsulate or perhaps even directly convert between disparate link layers of the LAN and the WAN, coping with the differences in speed and packet sizes of the networks and so on.

Another variant is 802.1q *virtual bridging*. This allows more than one network to run traffic over a single physical network. It is normally engaged in switches and routers rather than end hosts.

IEEE 802.1q

Here is an example of how 802.1q might be used, see Figure 5.11. Suppose a company has two sites, Site 1 and Site 2, that are physically separate. There is a single dedicated link connecting the sites. The management want to run two separate LANs, A and B, but there are hosts for both A and B at both sites. The cost of installing a second link between the two sites to connect the two parts of each LAN is prohibitive.

What management can do is use 802.1q *tagging*. A frame from LAN A, say, arrives at the switch in site 1. The switch knows to route the frame across the remote link. It places an 802.1q *tag* on the frame: this is essentially an extra 4 byte link layer header containing a *virtual LAN* (VLAN) identifier (VID), which is just a small (12 bit) integer. The Ether-type field (p. 25) changes from 0800 for Ethernet to 8100 to indicate a tagged frame. The switch in site 2 receives the tagged frame and sees which VLAN to route to. It removes the tag and passes on the frame.

The strength of the tagging scheme is that it generalizes well to more complicated virtual LANs and allows multiple networks to share infrastructure; this can save a lot of money.

Figure 5.11 802.1q virtual LANs.

Bridging is useful, but shouldn't be taken too far. It is not the solution to making large networks. As the network gets bigger there will be more and more traffic travelling on it. In particular, broadcast traffic becomes a nuisance: just think of the number of ARP broadcasts alone! If you have a large network it can be better to split it into several separate subnetworks. See Section 6.5.

5.4.2 Reverse ARP

RFC 903

Reverse ARP, or RARP, solves the opposite problem to ARP: given a hardware address, find the IP address. This might happen when a diskless machine is booting and needs to find its IP address and only has its Ethernet address to go by. Alternatively, a domestic device such as a refrigerator may make a RARP request when it boots to find its IP address on the home network.

RARP is almost identical to ARP, but has frame type 8035 and op numbers 3 for a RARP request and 4 for a RARP reply. A server machine on the local network assigned to deal with the RARP service will read these packets and reply appropriately.

RARP is simple, but is limited by the fact that a hardware broadcast only goes to the local network: it is not passed between networks. The reason for this limitation on hardware broadcast is that it is not a good idea to pass on broadcasts arbitrarily, or else every broadcast will spread across the entire Internet! So some machine on the local network must be prepared to reply to a RARP, which may be inconvenient for large, multiply subnetted networks. More general solutions to the address finding problem exist: see DHCP (Section 6.10)

5.5   Exercises

Exercise 5.1 Spread spectrum wireless has an interesting and surprising history. Read up on this.

Exercise 5.2 IEEE 802.11b has rapidly been supplanted by 802.11g. At the time of writing, 802.11g with WEP security is the strongest widespread wireless system, commercially speaking, with WPA starting to be supported. What is the current system of choice at the time of reading?

Exercise 5.3 Take a walk around your neighbourhood with your wireless-enabled laptop. How many wireless networks can you find? How many are unprotected? *Don't try to use them without permission.*

Exercise 5.4 Write a review of last mile technologies. Which do you think is the most suitable for the lab/department/house you are in? Explain.

Exercise 5.5 Look into the various ways cellular telephone operators are providing data access to your mobile phone. Make sure you compare data rates and costs.

Exercise 5.6 Investigate the Ethernet addresses of the machines on your local network. Are there any security issues with ARP?

THE INTERNET/NETWORK LAYER: IP

6

6.1 Introduction

We now turn to look at the next layer in the IP: the Internet layer. This is the basis the Internet is built upon: a reasonably simple protocol that provides a foundation for the more complicated higher layers. The IP we describe is actually the fourth incarnation: IP version 4 (IPv4). We shall talk about IPv6 much later (see Section 6.8).

RFC 791

This layer provides a best-effort, connectionless, unreliable packet protocol. This combination was chosen as it represents a lowest common denominator of network properties and it relies the least on functionality of the link layer. Thus IP can run on top of mostly any link layer, be it reliable or not.

The basic design of the IP is a cooperative system. For a packet to get to its destination it is handed on from one network to the next, hop by hop.

The nodes in the networks have various names according to their function (Figure 6.1).

- Host. A computer that you actually use to do some work.

- Gateway. A machine that connects two networks.

- Router. A machine whose primary function is to decide where a packet goes next.

These are by no means mutually exclusive and you use a term to indicate how you are thinking of a component at the time. Gateways and routers can be hosts, though dedicated routing hardware is popular. Gateways do routing, though usually trivial. It is a basic precept of the Internet that an individual packet does not know how to get from source to destination: it is the routers' job to figure this out and it can be a very complicated business. See Section 6.3 and Chapter 7 for a full discussion.

The IP layer breaks the data stream into packets, often called *datagrams* in the context of IP, and prepends a header to each packet. A packet (including header) can be as large as 64KB, but is usually around 1500 bytes (this is only because much IP runs over Ethernet and Ethernet has this limit).

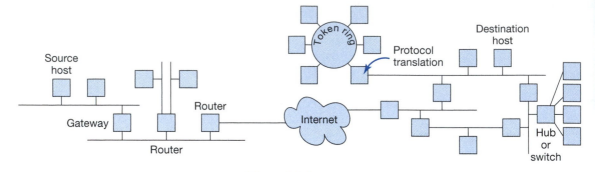

Figure 6.1 Internet.

We have the three words *frame*, *packet* and *datagram* all meaning roughly the same thing: a chunk of data. Later we shall add *segment*. The only difference between them is the emphasis we want to put on the chunk: for example, frames are typically at the link level while datagrams are at the transport level.

As IP runs over many different kinds of hardware, immediately we are faced with the problem of different link layers having different properties, in particular maximum packet size. What happens when a big packet hits a network with a smaller maximum limit? The IP deals with this by *fragmentation*: a single packet is subdivided by a router into several smaller packets. See Section 6.2.5 and the following for details. It is the destination's problem to glue the fragments back together.

6.2   IP Headers

We shall now deal with each field in the header in turn. The header and data are transmitted in *big endian* format, i.e., left to right, top to bottom, in Figure 6.2.

6.2.1   Version

This four bit field contains the version number, 4. The latest version of IP, which is being introduced very slowly, has version number 6. This field is used to aid such a transition.

6.2.2   Header Length

The header can vary in length: there are some optional fields later. So we need to be able to find where the header ends and the data starts: how should we distinguish between a header field and data that might just happen to look like a header field? An easy way is to supply the header length. This is given as the number of 32 bit words and is generally 5, which is the minimum length of the header (no optional fields).

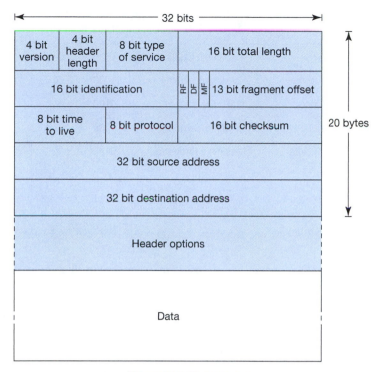

Figure 6.2 IP datagram.

This four bit field has maximum value 15, or 60 bytes, so we can have up to 40 bytes of options.

6.2.3 Type of Service

The ToS field allows us to tell a router how the datagram should be treated in terms of speed and reliability. For some data streams speed is more important than 100% reliability. Voice is a good example of this since the human ear is somewhat forgiving of losses. On the other hand, when we are transmitting data files (such as bank balances) and accuracy is paramount, we are willing to sacrifice a little speed for improved reliability.

RFC 1349
RFC 2474
RFC 1700

Four bits are used (Figure 6.3). Setting a bit indicates to routers that this packet should be treated in a particular way (if possible):

1. Minimize delay: do not hang on to this packet longer than necessary and maybe prioritize it over others.
2. Maximize throughput: not quite the same as minimizing delay as, say, collecting up a few packets and sending them off in a big burst may be more bandwidth efficient.
3. Maximize reliability: try not to drop this packet if the router is becoming overloaded (congested) with traffic; drop some other packet first.

Application	TOS	Value	Section
Telnet	Minimize delay	1000	12.2
FTP control	Minimize delay	1000	12.3
FTP data	Maximize throughput	0100	
SMPT control	Minimize delay	1000	12.4
SMPT data	Maximize throughput	0100	
ICMP	None	0000	6.12
NNTP (news)	Minimize cost	0001	12.12

Figure 6.3 A few of the recommended values for the TOS field.

4. Minimize cost: this is a packet where cost is more important than delay or reliability, so this packet might be delayed while others are prioritized.

A router is free to ignore this field, but it is becoming increasingly important as network providers want to charge different rates for different levels of service.

RFC 3168   Bits 6 and 7 of the TOS field are used in an *Explicit Congestion Notification* (ECN) mechanism (see section 10.6.3). If ECN is not supported by the sending host these bits should be set to zero.

RFC 2474   As TOS was only ever weakly taken up in real implementations, RFC 2474 refines and renames this field to be the *Differentiated Services* Field (DS Field) and the TOS bits to be the *Differentiated Services Code Point* (DSCP). Similarly for the corresponding field, Traffic Class, in IPv6 (p. 102). Care is taken to ensure those combinations of TOS bits that *are* actually used have the same interpretation as a DSCP, while new interpretations are supplied for those that were unused.

6.2.4   Total Length

This is the total datagram length, including the header, in bytes. A 16 bit field gives us a maximum size of 65535 bytes. This is tolerable to most people at the moment, but is too small for those who like to push big data about, and will be much too small in the near future as gigabit networks become more common.

Datagram size is important as we have several overheads in using packets:

- time overhead spent in splitting data into packets, adding headers, and then removing headers and reassembling the data stream at the other end;

- bandwidth overhead in that we are using 20 bytes for the header and not for data.

A bigger packet means better amortization of overheads. In the limit, with an infinite packet size (more familiarly described as a connection-oriented system), the overheads are minimized. But then we have the problems of a connection-oriented system.

6.2.5 Identification

This is an integer that is unique to each IP datagram, often incrementing by one for each successive datagram sent. It is used to reassemble a datagram if it gets fragmented. When a datagram is fragmented, it is split up into several smaller datagrams, each with copies of the original IP header (a few fields are changed, e.g., the total length). The identification field serves to group together fragments that came from a single datagram. A fragment is a datagram in its own right and can be fragmented itself. More details of fragmentation are given in Section 6.2.7.

6.2.6 Flags

Three bits are used as flags. Or rather, two are used and one is reserved:

1. RF. Reserved for later use. Unlikely ever to be used since the advent of IPv6.

2. DF. *Don't Fragment*. If the destination is incapable of reassembling fragments this bit is set to inform the routers on the path to the destination not to fragment. This might involve the routers choosing a slower path that does not fragment, or if this is impossible they might drop the datagram and return an error message to the sender. All machines are required to be capable of accepting datagrams of size 576 bytes.

    > In detail, all machines are required to be capable of *accepting* datagrams of size 576 bytes, either whole or in fragments. They must be able to forward datagrams of size 68 bytes without fragmentation (60 bytes for the largest IP header plus 8 bytes of fragment data).

    RFC 791

3. MF. *More Fragments*. All fragments except the last have this set.

6.2.7 Fragment Offset

As a datagram travels hop by hop across routers to its destination, it might hit an interface in a router that has a maximum packet size smaller than its own. In this case the datagram might be fragmented. The fragment offset is an integer that locates the current

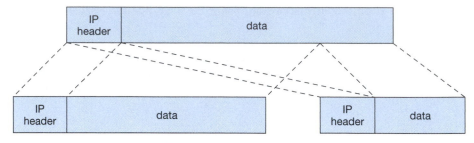

Figure 6.4 IP fragmentation.

fragment within the current datagram: note that the individual fragments may arrive at the destination out of order as they might take different routes to get there, so we need some way of reassembling the parts in the correct order. The value is a byte offset for position of the fragment, divided by 8. This means two things: (a) 13 bits is enough to cover the 16 bit range of possible offsets; and (b) each fragment (other than the last) must be a multiple of 8 bytes long.

Each fragment is a chunk of the original datagram data with a copy of the original IP header (Figure 6.4) and the various fragmentation and length fields set appropriately. When the fragment with MF not set is received, the destination can use the fragment offset plus fragment length to determine the size of the original datagram.

Fragmentation is a difficult issue and this is not a perfect solution as it causes a drop in efficiency:

- Performing fragmentation in a router slows down the processing of a datagram immensely: unmolested segments can be sent on much more quickly.

- There is extra overhead as more headers are being used for a given amount of data.

- There is extra overhead as more segments are traversing the network.

- The greater the number of fragments flying about, the greater the probability one will be lost or corrupted.

- If a single fragment is lost, the entire datagram must be retransmitted, which is a huge waste of bandwidth.

If the DF flag (see above) is set, then a router must not do fragmentation. If it cannot find any way of avoiding fragmentation, then the router will just drop the packet and return a 'fragmentation needed but DF set' message back to the sender (see Section 6.12). The sender can then choose to pick a smaller datagram size and resend.

Fragments can get lost, so destinations clear out fragments for an incomplete datagram after a suitable time, e.g., 30 seconds after the arrival of the first fragment (i.e., the fragment that *arrived* first). If they didn't do this memory would eventually fill with fragments for incomplete datagrams. Also, see Section 13.2.3 for why this is a good strategy. Well-behaved implementations return a 'timeout during fragment reassembly' message to inform the sender there is a problem.

A further wrinkle is that the rules say that if the initial fragment is lost (the fragment with offset 0) an ICMP need not be generated. This is because only that fragment contains the information (e.g., a UDP or TCP header) that will allow the sender's operating system to identify the connection that the data belongs to. An ICMP message is useless clutter if the host can't actually do anything with it.

Much better is the approach of IPv6, where a datagram is never fragmented en route. In IPv6, if a router realizes a datagram is too large for the next hop, it simply drops the datagram and sends an error message back to the source. The source can then resend smaller datagrams. This considerably reduces the complexity of the job routers have to do and consequently speeds up routing. And, just as important, the loss of a single packet will be recovered by the retransmission of that single packet, not the whole datagram that the packet was a fragment of.

Fortunately, even with IPv4, most of the time fragmentation is not required, and furthermore hosts are able to determine packet sizes by *MTU discovery*. The *MTU (Maximum Transmission Unit)* is the largest packet size a host or network can transmit (technically, it is the largest size an interface can send, but the term tends to be used in the more general sense). The *path* MTU is the smallest MTU on the path from source to destination, so if we send a packet of this size or less we know it will never be fragmented. The path MTU can be determined by sending variously sized packets with the DF flag set and watching for errors returned. When an unfragmented packet gets to the destination we have a lower bound for the MTU. Note that this is only an approximation, as we are trying to measure a dynamic system: in each probe the packet may take a different route that has a different path MTU! See Section 10.10 for details on path MTUs.

```
Find the MTU of an interface by
ifconfig -a
or
netstat -i
```

The *MRU (Maximum Receive Unit)* is an analogous value for the largest packet that an interface can accept. It is sometimes configurable independently of the MTU, e.g., in PPP connections.

6.2.8   Time to Live

This is a counter that is used to limit the lifetime of a datagram. If the routers get confused or are badly configured, a datagram may bounce back and forth or travel around in circles indefinitely. Eventually the network will be filled with lost datagrams and the real ones will not be able to push through the crowds.

The *TTL (Time to Live)* counter is designed to stop this. The TTL starts off at some value, say 64 or 32. Each time the datagram goes through a router its TTL is decremented. If the value ever gets to zero, the router must drop the datagram and send an error message back to the source. This will stop lost and misdirected packets: eventually the TTL in such a datagram will reach zero and it will be dropped.

The 8 bit field limits us to a maximum TTL of 255, but currently there appears to be no valid path in the Internet that is that long. The length of the longest path is called the *width* of the Internet.

> The width of the Internet goes up and down all the time. It goes up when new networks are attached, but it goes down when new links are installed or traffic is tunnelled over ATM, say, that connects previously distant networks. The IP regards a tunnel as a single hop, no matter how long or complex the ATM route might happen to be.
>
> The average length of a path in the Internet is measured to be somewhere near 20. The width is uncertain, but definitely over 32.

Originally this field was supposed to measure time in seconds: a router was supposed to decrement the field for each second it was queued in the router. In practice no one did this, but just decremented the TTL on each hop. The Internet is like this. What happens out there in the real world is important, not what the standards say. On the whole, though, most people try to follow the standards.

6.2.9   Protocol

RFC 1700 This connects the IP layer to the transport layer. This field contains a number that tells us what transport system software to pass the datagram on to. For example, UDP is 17 and TCP is 6.

6.2.10   Header Checksum

As in the Ethernet layer, this is a simple function of all the bytes in the header. If the checksum is bad, the datagram is silently dropped. It is up to a higher layer to detect a missing datagram and request retransmission: recall that IP is not guaranteed to be reliable.

This is not a perfect system as an error could arise in the checksum and nowhere else, meaning that an otherwise good datagram is dropped; or several errors in the header could combine and cancel themselves out; and so on. More sophisticated checksums could be more robust, but would be more time consuming to compute or require a larger field. Note that the TTL changes in each router, so the router must recompute and update the

RFC 1624 checksum on each hop, though this can be done quite efficiently.

6.2.11   Source and Destination Addresses

These are 32 bit numbers that uniquely determine the source and destination machines on the Internet. That is, each machine on the Internet has a different IP address. This gives us a maximum of 4294967296 machines on the Internet: actually fewer addresses are available since some are reserved for special purposes. This is not really enough. We discuss IP addresses in detail below.

> Note that computers don't have addresses, *interfaces* do. Though we are usually lax and talk about 'the address' of a host, it is important to note that we really mean the address of its interface. We are usually a bit more careful when the host has more than one interface.

We again gloss over the fact that IP addresses are not really unique: see Section 6.7.

6.2.12   Optional fields

This is a variable length list (usually absent) of optional bits and pieces, originally included in case the designers thought of something new they wanted to add to IP. Also it is for rarely used stuff, so we do not clutter the header with mostly unused fields. Every byte in the header is overhead that reduces the space left for our data, so it is good sense to make the header as small as possible in the common case.

Options include

- Security (encryption) and authentication (see Section 13.5.2). RFC 1108
- Record route: each router records its address in the datagram option header as it passes by.
- Timestamp: each router records its address and current time in the datagram option header as it passes by.
- Strict source routing: a list of addresses of routers that give the entire path from source to destination.
- Loose source routing: a list of addresses of routers that must be included in the path from source to destination.

All except the first are primarily for debugging the network, while the routing options are also used in Mobile IP (Section 6.11). The record route option is somewhat limited: as options are restricted to 40 bytes, this means that only nine routers can squeeze their addresses in (4 bytes per address, plus a couple of bytes for the option header itself). This is not enough these days when routes can easily be over 30 hops, so other techniques tend to be used today for debugging routes (see Section 6.12.2).

6.3   IP Addresses and Routing Tables

We now need to look at those 32 bit addresses. As mentioned previously, (roughly speaking) every machine on the Internet has its own unique address. This is so every machine can contact every other machine. These numbers are strictly controlled by the Internet Assigned Number Authority (IANA) – more about this later. They are not dished out at random, but are carefully allocated to make routing between networks that much easier.

Consider the complexity of the problem of finding a route between two arbitrary machines. If there were no structure on IP addresses, this would be impossible without gigantic tables that detail where each and every machine is located and the routes to get to them.

Instead, remember that the Internet is actually a collection of networks. The IP address is split into two parts: firstly the network number and secondly the host number. The host number defines the host uniquely on the network and the network number defines the network uniquely on the Internet.

To an end host, routing is trivial: if the destination is on the local network, simply put the packet out on the network. If the destination is not local, simply send the packet to the network gateway and let it deal with the problem.

> If we are running over Ethernet, the Ethernet hardware address on the packet will be that of the gateway, not the destination machine. Recall that the link layer can't know about IP addresses; all it knows is that this packet must go to the gateway. The gateway will send on the packet with a hardware address appropriate for the next hop and so on. In terms of ARPing for this packet, we make a request for the gateway's IP address.

Once a packet has arrived at the destination network its gateway simply sends the packet to the destination host. So, to a first approximation, the routing problem is that of directing packets between networks. This is much better, as there are significantly fewer networks than hosts.

A router contains a table of IP addresses, together with gateways and interfaces to be associated with those addresses. Each row of the table contains:

1. A destination address. This can be the address of a specific host machine, or the address of a network.
2. The address of the *next hop* router, i.e., the address of where to send this packet next. This is the address of an immediate next router that is directly connected to the current router.
3. The *interface* on which to send out the packet to get to the next router. A router has, of course, several interfaces, i.e., network connections, so we need to know which interface goes to the selected next router.

When a packet arrives at a router it checks its table:

1. If the packet destination address matches a host address in the table send the packet out to the indicated gateway on the indicated interface.
2. Else if the packet destination address matches a network address in the table send the packet out to the indicated gateway on the indicated interface.

3. Else find an entry in the table marked *default* and send the packet out to the indicated gateway on the indicated interface.

If none of the above works, drop the packet and send back an error message 'network unreachable'.

> The ICMP 'host unreachable' is returned when a destination is on the local network, but ARP fails to get a reply.

We return to the network routing problem later (Chapter 7), in particular how the information gets into the tables, but for now regard routers as machines with big tables that tell them where to send packets.

> Use `netstat -r` to see the routing table on a Unix machine.

Here is an example table:

Destination	Gateway	Genmask	Flags	MSS	Window	irtt	Iface
138.38.96.0	0.0.0.0	255.255.248.0	U	0	0	0	eth0
127.0.0.0	0.0.0.0	255.0.0.0	U	0	0	0	lo
default	138.38.103.254	0.0.0.0	UG	0	0	0	eth0

Every host has a routing table and for non-routers this generally this says to send packets destined for the local network out on the network interface and send all other packets to the default gateway. The above example table indicates that packets on the local network (138.38.96.0) should be sent out on interface eth0 and the default is to send to the gateway 138.38.103.254, which is also available on interface eth0.

The mask tells us how to split the IP address into network and host parts (see the next section and Section 6.5). The table is kept sorted with the longest (i.e., most 1 bits) masks first (recall that 255.255.248.0 is actually 11111111 11111111 11111000 00000000). Given an address, we work from the top of the table downwards, ANDing our address with each mask in turn. If the result equals the corresponding destination value, we route the packet out on the interface given by Iface. The `default` value actually stands for the destination 0.0.0.0, so this will entry always match.

There is also an entry for a *loopback network*, a virtual network internal to the machine, found on the (virtual) interface `lo`. This network connects a machine to itself and is useful for testing network programs amongst many other things.

Here is a table from a machine with more than one real interface:

Destination	Gateway	Genmask	Flags	Metric	Ref	Use	Iface
213.121.147.69	*	255.255.255.255	UH	0	0	0	ppp0
172.18.0.0	*	255.255.0.0	U	0	0	0	eth0
172.17.0.0	*	255.255.0.0	U	0	0	0	eth1
127.0.0.0	*	255.0.0.0	U	0	0	0	lo
default	213.121.147.69	0.0.0.0	UG	0	0	0	ppp0

There are three interfaces: eth0, eth1, and ppp0 (as well as lo). In this table:

- packets with address 213.121.147.69 go to interface ppp0, which, in this case, is a PPP (Section 4.4.2) connection;

- packets with address in the network 172.18 go to interface eth0;

- packets with address in the network 172.17 go to interface eth1;

- otherwise packets are sent to the gateway machine at address 213.121.147.69 on interface ppp0.

The first route is redundant in the presence of the last route, but shows that individual addresses can be routed.

More details on the meanings of the 'Flags' can be found in Chapter 7.

6.4   Networks and IP Addresses

RFC 950 So how are the addresses split into network plus host parts? If we give, say, 8 bits to represent the network and the rest to represent the hosts on the network, we will have $2^8 = 256$ networks each with $2^{24} = 16777216$ hosts. This isn't really enough networks and not many people require that many hosts. A few do, though. Splitting it up the other way, we could have 16777216 networks each with only 256 hosts. This is too small a network for many people, e.g., large corporations, but fine for small companies. Cutting it down the middle we can have $2^{16} = 65536$ networks with 65536 hosts. Still not really enough networks and too many or too few hosts per network according to taste.

As different people have different requirements, a compromise is used (Figure 6.5): we split the address in (essentially) three ways!

- *Class A* addresses, from 1.0.0.0 to 127.255.255.255, have 7 bits for the network and 24 bits for the host: this is 126 networks each containing 16777214 hosts. The address x.y.z.w has x as network, y.z.w as host.

- *Class B* addresses, from 128.0.0.0 to 191.255.255.255, have 14 bits for the network and 16 bits for the host: 16382 networks, 65534 hosts each. The address x.y.z.w has x.y as network, z.w as host.

- *Class C* addresses, from 192.0.0.0 to 223.255.255.255, have 21 bits for the network and 8 bits for the host: 2097152 networks, 254 hosts each. The address x.y.z.w has x.y.z as network, w as host.

There are also:

- *Class D* addresses, from 224.0.0.0 to 239.255.255.255, are *multicast* addresses. Multicast is sending a single packet to multiple hosts. This is in contrast to *broadcast*, which is sending to *all* hosts on a network. See Section 6.9.

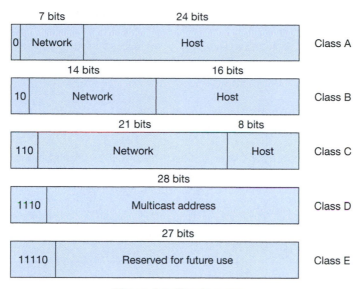

Figure 6.5 IP addresses.

- *Class E* addresses, from 240.0.0.0 to 247.255.255.255, are reserved for experimental and future use. This might include the transition to IPv6.

Various values are reserved for special purposes:

- Host part all zeros: 'this host'. Refers back to the originating host. Some implementations mistakenly used this as a broadcast address, so it is not commonly supported as a valid host address. For, say, a class B network 17.16, a packet sent to 172.16.0.0 *should* boomerang right back to the sender (but rarely does).

- Host part all ones: broadcast address to network. For example, 172.16.255.255 sends to all hosts on the 172.16 network.

- Network part all zeros: 'this network'. For example, 0.0.255.255 would broadcast to all hosts on the current network. Again, not often implemented.

- Network 127.0.0.0: the loopback network. Always implemented. The address 127.0.0.1 is commonly used as a way for a host to send a packet to itself over the internal loopback network. Note that this is different from the same host sending to itself via an external network (e.g., using the interface's own address) as the former packet probably won't go through the normal IP/Ethernet/whatever software and hardware.

The idea behind the class scheme is that the IANA can allocate big networks to those who want a lot of hosts and small networks to those who do not need so many. Thus we do not lose large chunks of the address space to small-time enterprises.

An example: the University of Bath has been allocated addresses in the network 138.38. This is a class B address and so there are 65534 possible hosts. General Electric Company has network 3, a class A address. The class C address 193.0.0 is allocated to Réseaux IP Européens (RIPE), the Internet Registry responsible for the allocation of IP addresses within Europe.

> This kind of information can be found using `nslookup` or `dig` and PTR queries and using `whois` to find who owns a name.

Although this way of dividing addresses has been historically very successful, the immense growth of the Internet has revealed several weaknesses with this kind of allocation. These days a *classless* allocation is employed: see Section 6.6.

6.5 Subnetting

RFC 950

Suppose you have your IP network address, a class B address, say, and you are building your network. You have 64000 host addresses to play with. Having a single network with 64k addresses on it is not a good idea: it is very hard to administer for a start, even before you get into technical or political reasons. The solution is to use *subnetting*. This allows you to split your network into smaller independent subnetworks. Each subnet can be administered independently, e.g., by different departments. The subnets will be joined by routers.

So you currently have 16 bits of (class B) address to play with. You can designate some of those bits to be (sub)network addresses and the rest to be host addresses on those subnets. Routers in your network will have to know which bits are which in order to be able to decide how to route a particular address.

A *subnet mask* is used (Figure 6.6). This tells you which part of the address is the subnet address and which is the host address. For example, the Department of Mathematical Sciences at the University of Bath has a subnet that contains addresses from 138.38.96.0 to 138.38.103.255, or 4096 values. In binary this is

network address	138.38.96.0	10001010 00100110 01100000 00000000
broadcast address	138.38.103.255	10001010 00100110 01100111 11111111
subnet mask	255.255.248.0	11111111 11111111 11111000 00000000

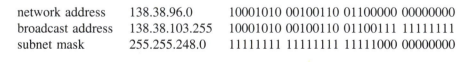

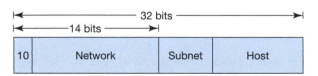

Figure 6.6 Subnetting a class B network.

A machine can tell if an address is on the local network if the host address ANDed with the mask gives the network address. Thus the address 138.38.100.20 is on the Maths subnet since

host address	138.38.100.20	10001010 00100110 01100100 00010100
mask	255.255.248.0	11111111 11111111 11111000 00000000
AND	138.38.96.0	10001010 00100110 01100000 00000000

but 138.38.104.20 is not, since

host address	138.38.104.20	10001010 00100110 01101000 00010100
mask	255.255.248.0	11111111 11111111 11111000 00000000
AND	138.38.104.0	10001010 00100110 01101000 00000000

Outside the network 138.38, subnetting is not visible, so no applications to IANA or changes to global routing tables are required if you move things about locally. A subnet can itself be subnetted for exactly the same reasons.

Use the Unix command
`ifconfig -a`
to see the way a network is configured. The format varies from machine to machine, but this will tell you

- `inet` the machine's IP address
- `netmask` the subnet mask

amongst other interesting stuff.

The Maths subnet can be described as '138.38.96.0, subnet mask 255.255.255.248.0', or more succinctly as '138.38.96.0/21', where 21 is the number of 1 bits in the mask. Subnetting does not actually require subnet masks to use the top n bits and we could have the Maths network as '138.38.0.96, subnet mask 255.255.0.248' if we really wanted. However, it is overwhelmingly the case that people follow the former format, particularly when *classless networks* are involved. (The short /n format only applies to the top-n-bits style of mask.)

RFC 1219

6.6   Classless Networks

Everybody wants a class B network, since a class C is too small and a class A is too large (you pay per address). This is called the *three bears problem*. Thus there are very few class B addresses left. One thing you might do is take several class C networks and link them together. This is not trivial, as you cannot have two network addresses on the same physical network. Thus you must have two networks, probably joined by a gateway. And every time the network grows, you have to apply for a new class C address and join it up to your existing system.

Additionally, having many small networks is a problem for routing: many networks mean large tables in routers. Again, this is not good.

Due to the massive growth of the Internet, some new way of managing the IP address space had to be invented. There are a few ways we can go:

1. Change the way classes of networks are defined: Section 6.6.1.

2. Use private networks with *network address translation*: Section 6.7.

3. Increase the number of addresses available by changing IP: Section 6.8.

The first two ways are backwardly compatible with the existing system. The third is a radical change.

6.6.1 CIDR

RFC 1519 This stands for *Classless InterDomain Routing*.

There are many class C network addresses left. CIDR is a way of packaging them up that (a) allows networks of larger than 254 hosts and (b) simplifies routing.

Firstly, blocks of class C networks are allocated:

- 194.0.0.0–195.255.255.255 Europe
- 198.0.0.0–199.255.255.255 North America
- 200.0.0.0–201.255.255.255 Central and South America
- 202.0.0.0–203.255.255.255 Asia and the Pacific

This gives each region about 32 million addresses. Another 320 million addresses from 204.0.0.0 to 223.255.255.255 are waiting for later allocation. Now routing to such addresses is easy: anything that starts 194 or 195 is routed to Europe. This is a single entry in a router table, rather than an entry for each network.

Within each region, the same idea is repeated. Contiguous blocks of class C addresses are allocated to ISPs or end users, say 192.24.0 to 192.24.7. This is described as network 192.24.0.0/255.255.255.248, or, more commonly, 192.24.0.0/21. As before, the 21 is the number of 1 bits required to mask off the network address part from the whole address.

192.24.0.0	11000000 00011000 00000000 00000000
192.24.7.0	11000000 00011000 00000111 00000000
255.255.255.248	11111111 11111111 11111000 00000000

And we now know that any packet with an address that has addr *AND* 255.255.248 = 192.24.0 should be routed to that ISP or user. For example, 193.0.0.0/22 is a collection of class C addresses allocated to RIPE.

This is a very clever update to the original class system, as the end machines do not need to know about CIDR. Once a packet has reached the destination network, it can be treated identically to a classed network. Only the routers need to know anything special and only those external routers that connect your network to the rest of the Internet. A classless network can be used just as a subnetted classed network and may even be subnetted further.

This has been a valuable addition to IP and has allowed the Internet to grow much further than once imagined. There are also extensions to CIDR to use class A addresses when this becomes necessary.

Compare CIDR with subnetting: CIDR merges small networks into a larger one, while subnetting divides a large network into smaller ones. In fact, CIDR is sometimes called *supernetting*.

6.7 Network Address Translation

Some IP addresses are reserved for private networks: RFC 1918

- Class A: 10.0.0.0–10.255.255.255

- Class B: 172.16.0.0–172.31.255.255

- Class C: 192.168.0.0–192.168.255.255

These are one class A network, 16 class B networks, and 256 class C networks. These addresses are guaranteed never to be allocated for use in the public Internet. Thus if you have a private IP network that is not connected to the Internet, these are safe addresses to use. How does this help if you *do* wish to be connected? There is a process known as *masquerading* or *Network Address Translation* (NAT) that converts a packet bound for the Internet with a private source address to one with a public source address and the returning packet with the public destination address back to the private address (Figure 6.7). RFC 3022

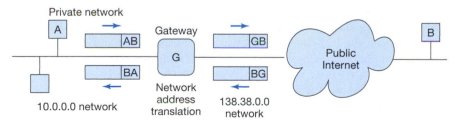

Figure 6.7 Network Address Translation.

A packet going from the private network to the Internet might have source address 10.0.1.1 and destination address 138.38.32.14. Let us suppose the gateway has address 138.38.32.252. The action of NAT is to make the Internet believe that this packet came from 138.38.32.252. We can do this by updating the source address in the IP header to be 138.38.32.252. This is done by the gateway. The gateway must remember that this has been done, so when a reply comes back (with source 138.38.32.14, destination 138.38.32.252), it can re-edit the header to replace the destination with 10.0.1.1 and pass the packet on to the private network.

Thus it appears to hosts on the private network that they are connected to the Internet, while it appears to the Internet that a lot of traffic is originating at the gateway. This has the added property that machines on the public Internet cannot refer to machines on the private network, as the addresses 10.0.0.0 can never be used on the Internet. This may seem a problem, but is actually an advantage to most people: it prevents external users hacking into the private network as they have no way of referring to the private machines. The gateway is careful only to let packets that are replies to travel inwards. See also Section 13.3 on firewalls for more on this issue.

There are problems with this technique: sometimes IP addresses are passed in the data part of the packet (e.g., FTP, Quake) as part of a higher layer protocol. This is often done to set up other connections to various places. In order for NAT to work in this case, the masquerading code has to be taught about such examples and where to look in the data for these addresses and how to update them. This is technically quite difficult, but can be done
RFC 2663
RFC 3027
RFC 3489
and is very effective. See RFC 2663, RFC 3027, and RFC 3489 for further considerations.

This technique is particularly good for home networks, where you can share one connection to the ISP between several hosts. Modems and routers that implement NAT are now commonly available.

A related concept is variously called *port address translation* (PAT) or *network address port translation* (NAPT) which acts on port numbers, rather than addresses. It can be used to redirect services: for example, translating traffic to port 80, a standard WWW port number, to port 3128, a standard Web proxy port number (see Section 12.8). Of course, NAT and NAPT are best used in tandem.

6.8   IPv6

The ultimate way of solving the address problem is to change IP itself.

RFC 2460
Here is a brief introduction to the next version of IP. Variously called IPv6 and IPng (*next generation*), it takes IPv4 in the light of modern experience and reworks things to be simpler and more efficient. It has has 128 bit addresses and uses a CIDR-style
RFC 3513
geographical allocation (amongst other types of allocation), which is what IPv4 really should have used in the first place. IPv6 is gradually being introduced, but it will be a long time before it replaces IPv4 everywhere.

IPv6 addresses various shortcomings of IPv4. Its aims are:

1. To give a larger address space.

2. To reduce the size of router tables.

3. To simplify the protocol so routers can process packets faster.

4. To provide security and authentication.

5. To pay attention to type of service.

6. To have better multicasting support.

7. To have mobile hosts with fixed IP addresses.

8. To allow room for evolution of the protocol.

9. To permit IPv4 and IPv6 to coexist during the transition.

IPv5 did exist: the experimental *Internet Stream Protocol* (ST). It was con- RFC 1819 nection oriented with QoS, designed to coexist with and complement the connectionless IPv4.

One thing the designers of IPv6 did was to make the names of the header fields clearer and more relevant to their actual use. The header (Figure 6.8) consists of:

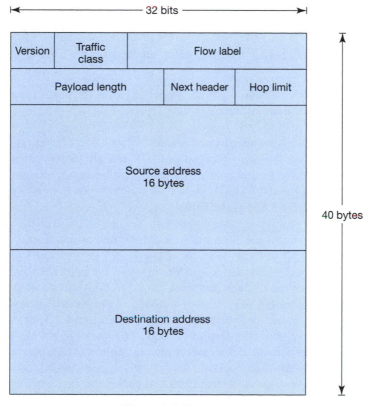

Figure 6.8 IPv6 header.

- Version, 4 bits. The number 6. This field is identical in position to the field in IPv4 and can be used to distinguish packets in mixed-version environments.

- Traffic class, 8 bits. Like TOS (or DSCP) in IPv4. This can be used to differentiate different kinds of traffic, e.g., video wants constant bit rate but can drop the occasional packet; file transfer allows variable bit rate but must be loss-free.

- Flow label, 20 bits. This allows routers to recognize packets as belonging to a single *flow*, i.e., a stream of packets from a certain host to a certain destination. Given this, the routers can endeavour to give special treatment to the flow, such as reserved bandwidth or minimal delay. This effectively sets up a virtual circuit for the flow that can guarantee, say, sufficient bandwidth for a video stream: thus IPv6 regains some of the advantages of a connection-based network. This field is set to 0 if flows are not being used.

- Payload length, 16 bits. The number of bytes that follow this fixed 40 byte header. Note that the IPv4 count included the header, while the IPv6 count does not need it since the header is a fixed length.

- Next header, 8 bits. This plays the role of the protocol field in IPv4, but also allows for IPv6 options. This field indicates which type of optional header (if any) follows the fixed header. If there are no optional headers (as is usually the case), this contains the code for a transport protocol, such as TCP or UDP.

- Hop limit, 8 bits. This is the TTL field, but renamed to make it clear what is actually happening.

- Source and destination addresses, 128 bits each. This is the biggest change in IPv6: addresses are four times as long.

The use of 128 bit addresses gives us a potential $2^{128} \approx 3 \times 10^{38}$ addresses. Initial allocations of addresses are following the lead of CIDR and are mostly geographical. But there is plenty of room for flexibility. This number of addresses is enough for 7×10^{23} addresses per square metre of the Earth's surface, or roughly enough to give an IP address to every molecule on the surface of the Earth.

RFC 3513 Some addresses are unicast, some are multicast (see Section 6.9). IPv6 adds *anycast* addresses: an anycast address identifies many machines, just as multicast, but instead of sending the packets to all of them, IPv6 picks one (often the 'closest') and sends the packet to this one. This can be used for load sharing. For example, the BBC might have an anycast Web server in the UK, and another in the USA. USA clients would contact the USA server, UK clients the UK one, but both would have the same IPv6 anycast address. This would save much traffic over the Atlantic link. See Section 6.9.3 for details.

IPv6 has no fragmentation field: instead of routers fragmenting an over-large packet, an IPv6 router just drops it and sends a 'packet too big' error message back to the source. The source can then resend smaller packets. An optional fragmentation header is available for the unlikely situation when the source cannot re-packet the data into smaller chunks: it proceeds very much like fragmentation in IPv4, but it is processed in the source and destination only. A router need never be concerned with fragmentation, which is a huge simplification over IPv4 and means that packets can be routed that much faster. IPv6 requires all links in the network to have MTUs of 1280 bytes or larger. If any link can't do this, a layer *below* IP must do fragmentation. Furthermore, a destination must be able to reassemble packets of size at least 1500 bytes.

IPv6 has no header length field. This is because the header length is fixed at 40 bytes.

IPv6 has no checksum field. Since most modern networks are fairly reliable, a checksum is not needed as much; and the transport layers (TCP and UDP) have checksums themselves anyway, so what's the point of duplicating work? Another problem with IPv4 checksums is that the IP header changes in every router as the TTL decreases, meaning the header checksum must be recomputed every hop. In IPv6 we avoid this work and so packets are again routed faster.

IPv4 has 13 fields in the fixed part of the header, while IPv6 has 8. IPv6 has addresses four times the size of IPv4, but the header is only twice the size, and is much simpler.

The *next header* field daisy-chains options, more properly called *extension headers*, together until it reaches the end. The last next header field contains the protocol of the data in the packet, e.g., TCP or UDP.

Extension headers are either of fixed length or have type, length and data fields (Figure 6.9). The top 2 bits of the type field indicate what to do if the header is not recognized:

- 00. Skip this option.

- 01. Discard this packet.

- 10. Discard this packet and send an error message back to the source.

- 11. Discard this packet and send an error message back to the source only if the destination was not a multicast address (so one bad packet will not produce millions of error messages).

Extension headers include, amongst others, routing options (cf. source routing in IPv4, p. 91); fragmentation management; authentication; security; jumbograms. A jumbogram is a very large packet, bigger than the $2^{16} = 64KB$ limit given by the payload field: a single jumbogram packet can be up to 4GB in length!

RFC 2675

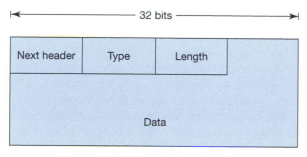

Figure 6.9 IPv6 extension headers.

UDP and TCP layer over IPv6 just as over IPv4, though small changes are needed in the way their checksums are computed. DNS (Chapter 8) adds a new RR type for an IPv6 address, namely AAAA.

The transition to IPv6 will be problematic: ideally the entire Internet would be taken down and brought back up with everybody using IPv6 addresses. As this is unlikely to happen, some transitioning strategies are in place.

RFC 2471

The plan was to grow groups of IPv6-connected machines, with the groups connected by IPv4: this network was called the *6bone* in analogy to the MBONE (see p. 107) which takes a similar approach for multicast traffic. As the groups grow, they eventually merge to make ever-increasing areas of IPv6, until the entirety of the public Internet is connected

RFC 3056

by IPv6. The *6to4* scheme describes how to manage IPv4 and IPv6 addresses to make this possible, translating between the two kinds of address where necessary and tunnelling IPv6 packets over IPv4.

In 2004 it was decided that the presence of IPv6 on the Internet at large was becoming sufficiently strong so that having a separate 6bone was no longer necessary, and it has

RFC 3701

now been phased out.

There has been a steady stream of opinion that IPv6 will never be necessary, or that it is too hard to change to IPv6, or that CIDR (Section 6.6.1) and NAT (Section 6.7) on IPv4 will always be enough. These opinions fail to take into account one of the most important aspects of the Internet: it is growing exponentially. One day the larger address space will be required: NAT may put off that day by a year or two, but nevertheless it will happen!

6.9   Broadcasting, Multicasting and Anycasting

There are three types of IP (version 4) addresses: *unicast*, *broadcast* and *multicast*. Unicast we are familiar with: an address specifies a single machine. Broadcast is similar to broadcast at the link layer: a single packet goes to every machine on the network, such as is used by ARP. The difference now is that we are talking about the IP layer, so the 'network' is everything on the IP network, which may be composed of more than one link layer network.

Multicast is something different: a single packet goes to several selected machines, more than one and probably less than all. The idea here is that it would be more efficient in certain circumstances, such as netcasting a TV programme, to send a single packet that multiple destinations can read rather than to send multiple copies of substantially identical packets to multiple destinations.

IPv6 adds a fourth kind of address, the *anycast* address. Roughly speaking, this may be regarded as the opposite to multicast. While multicast sends a single packet to multiple clients, anycast sends a single packet to potentially multiple servers. IPv6 chooses the best server, which might be the closest, least heavily loaded, or otherwise selected server. See p. 102 for an example of anycasting.

Notice that not all network layers support transmissions other than unicasting. For example, broadcast on a PPP link is not terribly enlightening. Use `ifconfig` to see what variants a network interface supports.

6.9.1 Broadcast

Broadcasting is conceptually simple: have a single packet that is read by all machines. This is better than sending unicast packets individually to all machines as we have a single packet on the network rather than ten or hundreds or whatever. But what do we mean by 'all'? Clearly some limitation on broadcast packets is needed, else the entire Internet would be permanently flooded.

We have, in increasing size:

- Limited broadcast. The address 255.255.255.255 sends to all hosts on the local network. A packet with such a destination is never forwarded by a router.

- Net-directed broadcast. When the host part of the network address is all ones, e.g., n.255.255.255 for a class A and $n.m$.255.255 for a class B. Routers forward such packets if they are connecting two subnets in the same network.

- Subnet-directed broadcast. Now we broadcast to all hosts on the local subnet. The address has a valid subnet part and the host part all ones. This is the most common form of broadcast. For example, 172.16.1.255 broadcasts on the subnet 172.16.1/24.

- All-subnets-directed broadcast. This is no longer used and has been replaced by multicast. It sends to a collection of subnets.

In fact, these broadcasts (apart from subnet-directed) are essentially obsolete due to CIDR (Section 6.6.1).

> If you want to annoy a lot of people, try `ping` to a broadcast address.
> To enable broadcasting on a socket, use `setsockopt`.

Only connectionless traffic (such as UDP) can be broadcast as one-to-many connections do not really make sense, particularly when you do not know how many recipient hosts there are in the broadcast domain.

6.9.2 Multicast

Multicast is used when we want to send the same packet to several hosts. For example, when streaming audio over the Internet we could unicast 100 packets to 100 people listening. Better, as there is less network traffic, we could broadcast one packet that is read by all hosts. Unfortunately, this must be read and processed by *every* host whether

RFC 1112

| 1 | 1 | 1 | 0 | Multicast group ID |

28 bits

Figure 6.10 Class D multicast addresses.

that host wants the audio stream or not. Furthermore, as broadcasts are generally not forwarded by routers, this doesn't work when the hosts are spread over many networks.

A better solution is to *multicast* a single packet that is read just by those 100 machines, leaving all other hosts alone. For example, multicast is used by OSPF (Section 7.3.4) to communicate routing data: a single packet informs all routers. Broadcast would inflict this data on *all* machines, not just the routers.

RFC 2908
Special multicast addresses are used and *multicast groups* (Figure 6.10) are formed of those machines that are interested in receiving packets from a given source, e.g., a group to listen to BBC Radio 4.

A *multicast group id* is a 28 bit number (nearly 270 million groups), with no further
RFC 3171
RFC 3307
structure. Multicast addresses fall in the range 224.0.0.0 to 239.255.255.255. The set of hosts listening to a particular IP multicast address is called a *host group*. A host group can span many networks and there is no limit on the number of members.

RFC 1700
Some group addresses are assigned as well-known addresses by IANA: these are the *permanent host groups*. For example, 224.0.0.5 for OSPF routers and 224.0.0.1 for 'all multicast-aware hosts on the subnet'. A host that claims to understand multicast should be part of the 224.0.0.1 group.

> `ping 224.0.0.1` will find all multicast-enabled hosts on your network and `ping 224.0.0.2` all multicast routers.

Not all hosts support multicast fully or at all. The extent of multicast support can be at different levels:

- level 0: no support;
- level 1: can send multicast, but can't receive (it is easier to send than receive as receiving involves understanding and joining groups);
- level 2: can receive and send.

RFC 1112
RFC 2236
RFC 3376
The process of joining and leaving host groups is governed by the *Internet Group Management Protocol* (IGMP). IGMP packets are transmitted within IP datagrams, but due to its use in the control of the network, IGMP is usually regarded as part of the network layer.

Multicast over LANs is reasonably simple, while the use of multicasting over a WAN is much harder: a multicast packet arriving at a router must be duplicated and sent to each subsequent network with a host that has joined the host group, so the router must be aware of which networks have hosts in which groups. When a host joins a multicast group it

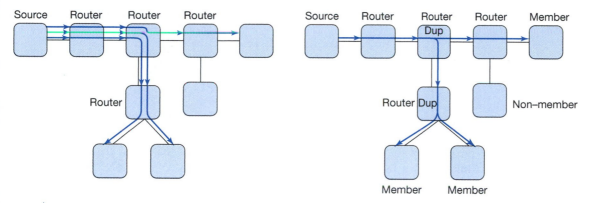

Figure 6.11 Unicast vs. multicast routing.

therefore uses IGMP to alert all routers on the path to the source. This relies on all routers between source and destination being multicast aware. All new routers support IGMP, but there are still many being used that don't. Tunnelling multicast in unicast packets can be used to get past unaware routers. To this end there is the *multicast backbone* (MBONE). This is a virtual network overlaying the Internet where 'islands' of multicast-aware hosts are joined by unicast tunnels. As more routers are updated, the islands grow and merge and eventually the tunnels will no longer needed. Very soon the MBONE will be much the same as the Internet proper.

As with broadcast, currently only connectionless traffic can be multicast.

RFC 1458

There have been some suggestions for reliable multicast and these consider the problem of how ACKs from the destinations can be scaled to large numbers of hosts. One suggestion is not to ACK every packet received, but to send a *negative acknowledgement* (NACK) for packets *not* received. This should scale much further.

The TTL (Section 6.2.8) field plays a special role in multicast IP. It defines the *scope* of a group, which is to say how wide an area a group may range over:

- 0 Host.
- 1 Subnet.
- < 32 Organization.
- < 64 Region.
- < 128 Continent.
- < 255 Global.

So to keep a multicast within your organization you set a TTL of not more than 32. Routers know the appropriate threshold values and only forward a packet if the TTL is

11111111	Flags	Scope	Multicast group ID

8 bits   4 bits   4 bits   112 bits

Figure 6.12 IPv6 multicast addresses.

bigger than it: this limits the packet to the site, region or whatever. The interpretations of terms like 'site' and 'region' are whatever you want them to be.

RFC 2365   A more flexible means of limiting scope is defined in RFC 2365 'Administratively Scoped IP Multicast' that uses addresses in the range 239.0.0.0 to 239.255.255.255.

> As with broadcast, multicasting is enabled with `setsockopt`. This can also be used to set TTLs.

Multicasting in IPv6 is similar to IPv4, but much simplified (Figure 6.12):

RFC 3513
- Multicast addresses are those that start with bit pattern 11111111 (hex FF).

- There are 4 bits of flags, of which only the last bit currently has a defined purpose. The T or *transient bit* is clear for a well-known address as defined by IANA; it is set for a non-permanent address.

- Next are 4 bits of scope. This separates scoping from the TTL/hop limit. Values include

1	interface-local	loopback only
2	link-local	local network
4	admin-local	an administration area, such as a department
5	site-local	for the site
8	organization-local	for the whole organization
14	global	everybody

Other values are available to the local administrator to set further boundaries.

RFC 2701   IGMP is replaced by the *Multicast Listener Discovery* (MLD) protocol, with MLDv1
RFC 3810   being an update of IGMPv2 and MLDv2 being an update of IGMPv3. IGMP and MLD are very similar, the most significant differences being the sizes of the addresses they carry.

Multicast and Ethernet Addresses

Many Ethernet interface cards support multicasting in hardware. What this means is that the card can be aware of which multicast groups the host requires and can filter out those multicast packets not in those groups. This hardware assist means less work for the IP layer software to do. To support this, special Ethernet hardware addresses are used for multicast packets.

Addresses in the range 01:00:5e:00:00:00 to 01:00:5e:7f:ff:ff are reserved for multicasting. This is 23 bits of address space. The lowest 23 bits of an IP multicast address are mapped directly into this space. There are 5 bits of the IP address left over, so this means that 32 different IP multicast addresses map to the same Ethernet multicast address. This means that the IP layer will have to do some filtering after all: it can't all be done by the hardware. On the other hand, it is unlikely that there will be a clash. Because of this, this combination of hardware plus software filtering of multicasting addresses is much better than unfiltered broadcasts.

Note that when we say 'multicast packets only go to a certain set of machines', what we really mean is 'only a certain set of machines process the packets'. The network interface in a host will (subject to the above) filter out multicast packets for groups it is not interested in, but the packets are still there occupying the network in a shared medium like Ethernet. Some switches are sufficiently clever and multicast aware to be able to forward a multicast packet only to those hosts that have joined the relevant multicast group. Otherwise, broadcasting and multicasting will result in the same number of packets on the local network, but fewer machines will be bothered by the multicast packets. And the other big difference is that broadcasts are restricted to the local network, while multicasts can roam wherever they are wanted.

6.9.3   Anycast

Anycasting in IPv6 tries to send a packet to one server chosen out of several that are suitable. It is sometimes likened to a *virtual server*. For example, DNS (Chapter 8) could be replaced by a single anycast address and then a DNS request would automatically be routed to the nearest DNS server. Thus DNS would be a service that requires no configuration. Other uses include distributed Web servers: a Web server could comprise multiple machines with a single global anycast address and each client would find that Web pages are being retrieved from the closest server, thus sharing the load.

RFC 1546
RFC 3513

There are two major Internet transport protocols, one connected (TCP) and the other connectionless (UDP). A connectionless protocol should not care if multiple requests to a server actually are served by different machines, it should get the same response whatever. A connected protocol, though, has state stored in the server and each packet in a connection *must* be serviced by the same host. This creates problems for anycast.

UDP is connectionless, so each packet can go to a different server with no ill effect.

TCP is connected: anycast would need to pick the same server for each packet in a TCP connection. Saving this information for every connection in every router along every path to every server is prohibitive, so an alternative solution is required. A couple of possibilities have been suggested.

The first says that anycast addresses should only be allowed in TCP in the first packet (the SYN handshake, see Section 9.4). The server replies with its *unicast* address in the reply (SYN-ACK), which TCP subsequently uses for the rest of this connection. A TCP option header *Source Identification* marks this as a return from an anycast address. Thus the anycast connection is transformed to a unicast connection and this ensures the whole connection is sent to a single server, though at some cost in blurring the layering.

The second solution is to use an *Anycast Address Mapper*. This determines a unicast address by sending an ICMP echo request (ping, section 6.12.1) to the anycast address. The server that gets the ping returns an echo reply using its unicast address. This address is extracted and used as the address to start a unicast TCP connection. This solution requires a time-consuming ping before any new TCP connection, which is potentially a problem when we use TCP heavily. Caching can be used to save the results, but if we use the same server for every fresh connection this defeats some of the purpose of having multiple servers to share the load.

RFC 3513
RFC 2526
RFC 3513 and RFC 2526 specify the form of IPv6 anycast addresses. In particular, RFC 3513 describes an anycast address as any unicast address that happens to be assigned to more than one server and that it is the responsibility of the routers to figure out what is going on. Thus anycast addresses are identical to unicast addresses. RFC 2526 narrows it down a little and recommends that the top 128 addresses of a subnet should be reserved for anycast addresses. A packet that wants to get to any of the anycast servers on a subnet will have the same routing up to that subnet's gateway, so externally this behaves identically to a unicast address.

Servers need to advertise to routers that they have joined an anycast group so the router knows it is a valid anycast destination. This can be done much as for multicast groups. Routing anycasts is simpler than multicasting, as routes to anycast addresses look just like multiple routes to unicast addresses, thus the 'nearest' anycast server is whatever the usual unicast routing algorithm decides. Tricks with TTLs are not needed.

RFC 3513
While the issues with anycasting are sorted out there are a couple of recommendations on the use of anycast addresses:

- An anycast address can only be given to an IPv6 router, never a host; this is to limit applications of anycasting until it is understood better.

- An anycast address must not be used as the source address field in an IPv6 header so ICMP errors can always know where to go.

Anycasting has lots of promise, particularly for configuration-free services, but still has some way to go!

6.10   Dynamic Host Configuration Protocol (DHCP)

Machines have IP addresses, so how does a machine go about getting one? It must lie within the local subnet, must be unique to the local network, and, if NAT is not being used, must be unique in the entire Internet. The simplest way is manual allocation by a systems administrator. This puts the onus of getting it right on a human. If someone does not wish to do this (or does not understand about IP addresses) we can use the protocol DHCP.

The *Dynamic Host Configuration Protocol* (DHCP) and its predecessor the *Boot Protocol* (BOOTP) expand on the functionality of RARP (Section 5.4.2) and are used to find the IP address of a diskless machine or to configure a transient machine. We start by looking at BOOTP, then move to DHCP as the two protocols share much in structure and intent.

RARP is at link layer level and has limitations on broadcast which BOOTP was designed to address. BOOTP runs on UDP (Section 9.3) on top of IP and so broadcast requests can be forwarded through gateways if desired. Further, BOOTP replies can supply the name of a host and a file on that host which should be downloaded and executed. This file will typically be the operating system for the client machine. RFC 903
RFC 951

In a BOOTP request the IP source address is 0.0.0.0, or can be the actual client address if already known. The IP destination is the broadcast 255.255.255.255 if the server address is unknown.

> The UDP destination port (Section 9.2) is 67, the BOOTP server port. Unusually, a fixed source port, 68, is used. This is because the server might want to broadcast a reply: if an ephemeral client port were used (as is more usual in a UDP transaction) the broadcast might confuse other machines on the network that happened to be listening on that same ephemeral port. By using a fixed client port, we know that only BOOTP clients will read BOOTP packets.

BOOTP uses a simple timeout and resend strategy in the case of lost packets. RFC 951 suggests starting at 4 seconds and doubling until 64 (including a bit of randomization), and keeping an average of about 60 seconds thereafter.

The BOOTP fields (Figure 6.13) are as follows.

- Opcode: 1 for a request and 2 for a reply.

- Hardware type: 1 for an Ethernet.

- Hardware address length: 6 for an Ethernet.

- Hop count: initialized to 0 and used by BOOTP servers that proxy to other servers.

- Transaction ID: a 32 bit random value generated by the client and returned in the response by the server. This is so the client can match the correct reply to its request amongst all the other BOOTP packets that are being broadcast on the network.

- Number of seconds: set by the client to the number of seconds that have elapsed since it started to boot. A primary BOOTP server can have backup servers that watch for this number getting too large. This indicates that the primary has crashed and the backup should take over.

- Client IP address: the client fills in its address, if known, else 0.

- Your IP address: in the reply this is the IP address that the server has allocated to the client or copied from the client IP address field if it was non-zero.

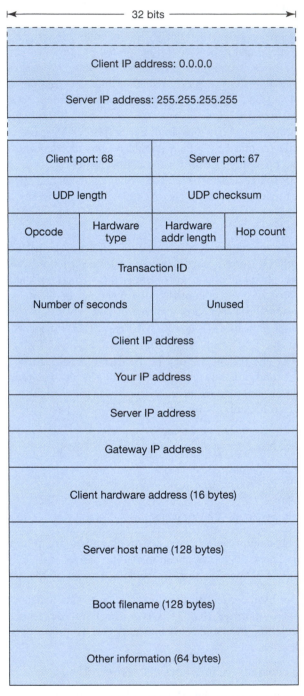

Figure 6.13 BOOTP packet format.

- Server IP address: the server also supplies its own IP address.

- Gateway IP address: and the address of a gateway for the local network.

- Client hardware address: the client puts its hardware address here. The hardware address can be used to guide the server in selecting an IP address for the client. Note that the hardware address is also in the link layer header, but repeating it here means the BOOTP server doesn't have to start digging into lower level headers itself.

- Server host name: the server can fill in its name, if it wishes.

- Boot filename: if the client is trying to boot, the server can supply the name of the boot file that the host should download.

- Other information: mostly used by DHCP, below.

If the client did not know its IP address then when the server sends out the reply there are two things it might do:

1. Broadcast the reply. The client will be able to recognize the reply aimed at it by the transaction ID. This works well, but broadcasts add to the general noise on the network and it would be better to unicast the reply to the client if possible.
2. But if the server does send a unicast packet the OS will need the client's hardware address to attach to the UDP packet and so will send out an ARP request. The client has no chance of replying to the ARP, of course, since it doesn't know its IP address yet. This is called the *chicken and egg problem*. This can be resolved by the server program directly informing its operating system kernel of the hardware/software address correspondence itself, often using a special system call. It can do this since all the relevant information is in the BOOTP packet.

One of the big advantages of BOOTP with UDP over RARP using the link layer is that the boot server can be a normal program rather than something that has to be dealt with at a lower level by the server operating system. This simplifies the implementation greatly.

DHCP (*Dynamic Host Configuration Protocol*) is a huge extension to BOOTP. It uses the same message format so that a DHCP server can respond to a BOOTP request if it wishes. While its main job is still to provide IP addresses, it does so in rather a different context.

RFC 2131

RFC 1534

Rather than dealing with diskless booting (which it still can do) it is more commonly used to configure machines that have non-permanent connections, e.g., laptops plugging into a network. DHCP enables the configuration of a host (IP address, subnet mask, DNS servers, and so on) in a simple, easily manageable manner. A DHCP server will respond to requests for configuration by supplying an IP address to a machine from a pool of numbers set aside for this purpose. When a client is done and wishes to disconnect, it signs off with the DHCP server and then the server can reuse that IP address for another client.

DHCP deals with machines leaving without signing off by giving *lease times* to IP addresses. This is a time limit on how long an IP address is allocated to a machine. If the client is still active at the end of the allocated time DHCP will renegotiate and probably renew the lease. If it is not active, the lease will expire and so release the IP address.

RFC 2132 DHCP provides all a machine needs to know to connect to a network, including:

- IP address
- subnet mask
- gateways
- DNS servers

amongst many other things such as lease times, MTU sizes, print servers, mail servers, time servers, boot servers and boot files (as for BOOTP), host name, Web servers, and so on as appropriate.

DHCP information is encoded in the BOOTP packet by a tag byte to indicate the type of data, a byte that contains the length of the data and then the data itself (Figure 6.14). Two special tags are 0 and 255 and they have no length or data. The 0 tag is a pad that can be used to align further fields and the 255 tag marks the end of the data. All data is in network byte order.

There are some more interesting points:

- When used as BOOTP the first 4 bytes of the extension area must be the *magic cookie* 99.130.83.99. This is what BOOTP expects and it signals that there is BOOTP data following.

- When a DHCP server is about to supply an IP address it should ping the network for that address. This is to see if any machine is already using that address without the server knowing. If the server gets no reply, it is assumed safe to supply that address.

- Once it has its new IP address, a client can send an ARP reply containing its own address. Again, this helps to flush out any hosts lurking with that address.

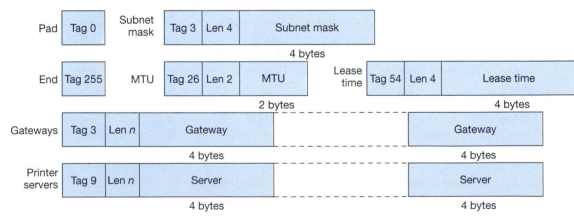

Figure 6.14 Examples of BOOTP/DHCP data.

Additionally, this *gratuitous ARP* tells the machines on the local network of the new address association so that they may update their ARP caches, if necessary, to reflect the new owner of the IP address.

6.11   Mobile IP

With the increase in mobile computing on laptops, PDAs and the like, there is a need for *Mobile IP*, so we are able to connect to the Internet wherever we are.

The naive solution of just using DHCP or something similar to get an IP address for the local network and using that is fine as far as it goes, but has one big problem: if someone else needs to initiate a connection to the mobile machine (say to send email to it), how do they know where that machine is and what IP address it currently has?

One approach, used by cellular phone companies (Section 5.2.5), is to give each device a fixed address, i.e., the telephone number, and hide the routing within the phone switching system. This requires the device always to connect to the same provider and clearly does not generalize to, say, a laptop connecting to an existing fixed Ethernet.

A general solution is to use the *Mobile IP* protocol. This was developed using IPv4 but sits better with IPv6 as the latter was designed with mobility as an objective. Mobile IP works, initially, by having a machine that keeps track of the current IP address of the mobile host and forwards traffic from other hosts to it.

RFC 3344

Forwarding traffic like this is relatively expensive and slow so Mobile IP has a protocol to tell remote hosts how to send their data directly to the mobile host.

We start with some terminology:

- MH is the mobile host.

- HN is the *home network* of the MH, the network of the organization the MH belongs to.

- HA is the *home agent*, a machine which will keep track of the location of the MH.

- FN is the *foreign network*, the network the MH is currently visiting and using for connectivity.

- C/O is a *care of* IP address, namely the address on the FN the MH is using.

- CH is the *correspondent host*, a machine that is trying to initiate a connection to the MH.

The MH has a fixed IP address on the HN, so any initial attempt of the CH to connect to the MH will route packets to the HN.

When an MH joins an FN it gets a C/O address from the FN somehow, say DHCP. In practice there will be questions of authentication, but Mobile IP does not address these. Then (see Figure 6.15):

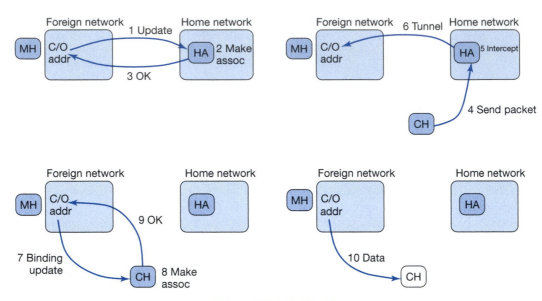

Figure 6.15 Mobile IP.

1. The MH sends a *binding update* request to the HA. This is a packet that contains the fixed address of the MH and the new C/O address.

2. The HA caches this association of fixed to C/O addresses. Mobile IP also looks after issues of timeouts and cache expiry.

3. If the binding update request had an acknowledgement flag set, the HA returns a confirmation packet back to the MH.

Suppose, now, that the CH wants to connect to the MH.

4. It sends to the fixed IP address of the MH. This packet will be routed to the HN.

5. The HA intercepts the packet (using proxy ARP, Section 5.4.1).

RFC 2003

6. It then tunnels it to the MH via the C/O address using IP in IP.

7. The MH sends a *binding update* request to the CH containing the current (mobile) IP address of the MH.

8. If the CH understands Mobile IP, it can cache the association of fixed to C/O addresses.

9. If the binding update request had an acknowledgement flag set, the CH returns a confirmation packet back to the MH.

10. Subsequent packets can then be sent to the fixed IP of the MH, but with an IP routing header (p. 91 or p. 103) that routes the packet via the C/O address.

If the CH does not understand Mobile IP, it can continue relaying via the HA.

This protocol has the advantages that:

- It does not require the CH to understand Mobile IP.

- But if it does, it can take advantage of direct routing to the MH.

- The layers above IP are unaffected, in particular TCP and UDP.

This is not a complete solution to roaming Internet connectivity. There are also problems of:

- Authentication of the MH to the FN and possibly vice versa.

- The FN will want to charge the MH for the connectivity and some protocol to negotiate this is required.

- Secrecy of data travelling through the FN. The MH could be using an FN of dubious integrity and so will want to secure its data from anyone in the FN (and elsewhere) who might be interested in reading their traffic.

This leads us naturally to questions of security and authentication: these will be dealt with in Chapter 13.

6.12   The Internet Control Message Protocol (ICMP)

In several places we have said things like 'drop a packet and return an error message to the source'. How is this error message sent? Well, the only mechanism we have for communication is to send packets, so the error message must itself be a packet. This is a normal IP packet, but has special contents. This kind of packet is called an *Internet Control Message Protocol* (ICMP) packet.

RFC 792

The ICMP is used for general control of the network as well as for indicating errors. It is layered on top of IP, but is usually considered for these reasons to be part of the Internet layer.

So an ICMP packet is enclosed in an IP packet, enclosed in (say) an Ethernet frame. The fields of an ICMP packet (Figure 6.16) are:

- Type. The kind of error message, e.g., 'TTL expired'; 'echo request'; 'destination unreachable'.

- Code. Extra information about the error, e.g., the 'destination unreachable' type has codes 'network unreachable'; 'host unreachable'; 'port unreachable'.

- Checksum.

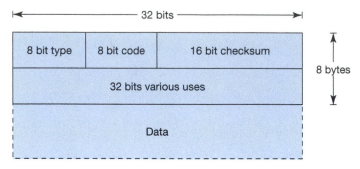

Figure 6.16 ICMP.

- The fourth field does different things for different ICMP types. Functions include a 32 bit gateway address, a 16 bit identifier, and a 16 bit sequence number for echo request and reply.

- Lastly, there is a general data field, the content of which depends on the message.

ICMP packets are IP packets and so are subject to the general foibles of IP, like being lost, delayed or duplicated. No provision is made in the protocol for loss of ICMP packets, though ICMP errors can be generated for ICMP packets just like any other IP packets, with certain reservations.

ICMP messages are classified as either *query* or *error*. For example, an ICMP 'echo request' (Figure 6.17) is a query, while a 'TTL expired' is an error. ICMP errors are never generated in response to:

1. an ICMP error message, e.g., if the TTL expires on a ICMP error packet;

2. a datagram whose destination is a broadcast (or multicast) address;

3. a datagram whose source is a broadcast (or multicast) address;

4. a datagram whose link layer address is a broadcast address;

5. any fragment other than the first.

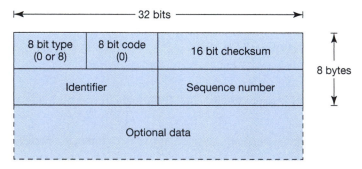

Figure 6.17 ICMP echo request and reply.

This is to prevent *broadcast storms* of ICMP packets, where a single error can be multiplied into many ICMP packets. Errors are not generated by non-first fragments as they won't contain enough identifying information for the receiving host to do anything useful with them (see Section 9.2).

Here are a few types of ICMP message:

RFC 1700

Type	Err	Code
ECHOREPLY		Reply from a ping
DEST_UNREACH	e	Network unreachable
	e	Host unreachable
	e	Port unreachable
	e	Fragmentation wanted but DF set
REDIRECT	e	Routing redirect for network
	e	Routing redirect for host
ECHO		Ping
TIME_EXCEEDED	e	TTL reached 0
	e	Fragment reassembly time exceeded

Messages marked 'e' are errors. There are many other types and codes, but the above are the most common in practice.

6.12.1   Ping

ICMP is used in the general running of the IP, but there are many clever ways we can exploit ICMP messages. For example, to discover whether a machine is up and running (ping), or to determine the route a packet took to get to a machine (traceroute).

Ping is a simple way to check whether a machine is alive or has crashed.

> ping www.yahoo.co.uk
> Hit ^C to terminate. Don't leave ping running. This uses bandwidth and annoys a lot of people.

This sends an ICMP *echo request* packet, waits a second, then repeats. This is ICMP type 0, code 0 with some random data. The required response from a host is to copy back the packet and its data in an ICMP *echo reply* packet (type 8, code 0).

The identifier field is some random number (often something like a process identifier) so that the operating system can distinguish replies when multiple pings are running on the same machine. The sequence number starts at zero and is incremented by one for each packet sent. This allows ping to determine if any packets were lost, reordered or duplicated.

When a ping echo response is received, the sequence number is printed, along with other useful information, such as the *round-trip time* (RTT) of the packet, the time between the sending of the ping request and the receipt of the reply.

```
% ping www.yahoo.co.uk
PING homerc.europe.yahoo.com: 56 data bytes
64 bytes from rc3.europe.yahoo.com (194.237.109.72): icmp_seq=0.
time=160. ms
64 bytes from rc3.europe.yahoo.com (194.237.109.72): icmp_seq=1.
time=154. ms
64 bytes from rc3.europe.yahoo.com (194.237.109.72): icmp_seq=2.
time=176. ms
64 bytes from rc3.europe.yahoo.com (194.237.109.72): icmp_seq=3.
time=159. ms
64 bytes from rc3.europe.yahoo.com (194.237.109.72): icmp_seq=4.
time=161. ms
^C
----homerc.europe.yahoo.com PING Statistics----
5 packets transmitted, 5 packets received, 0% packet loss
round-trip (ms)  min/avg/max = 154/162/176
```

There is variation in the RTT: the amount of variation increases with the distance the packet travels since WANs give us a lot of variance. It depends on how busy the remote host is, too, so ping RTTs are only a rough guide to network latency.

There is an IP option *record route* (Figure 6.18). This attempts to trace the path of a packet through the Internet by saving the IP addresses of machines as the packet passes by. If this is enabled on the echo reply, we will have a list of the hosts the packet travelled through to get to us. This is useful for debugging, or for simple curiosity.

Now, the options field in an IP packet can be up to 60 bytes so we can pack up to nine addresses (taking the option code and other fields into account). This is not very much. In the early ARPANET this was ample, but no longer. If the packet requires more than nine hops, only the first nine are recorded.

```
% ping -R www.yahoo.co.uk
PING homerc.europe.yahoo.com: 56 data bytes
64 bytes from rc3.europe.yahoo.com (194.237.109.72): icmp_seq=0.
time=168. ms
  IP options:  <record route> 138.38.29.254, bath-gw-1.bwe.net.uk
  (194.82.125.198), man-gw-2.bwe.net.uk (194.82.125.210), bristol.
bweman.site.ja.net (146.97.252.102), south-east-gw.bristol-core.j
a.net (146.97.252.62), south-east-gw.ja.net (193.63.94.50), 212.1
```

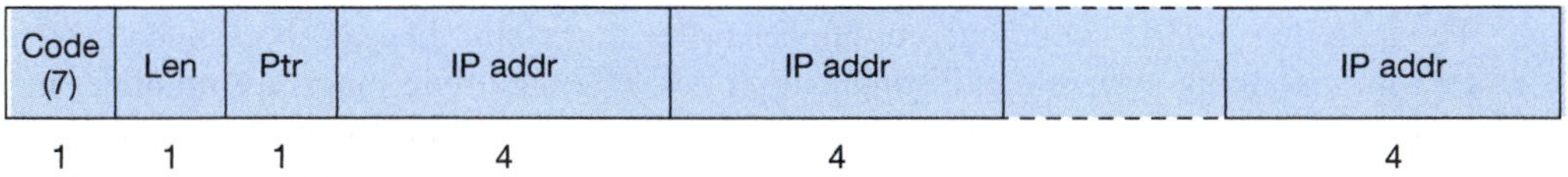

Code (7)	Len	Ptr	IP addr	IP addr		IP addr
1	1	1	4	4		4

Figure 6.18 IP record route.

```
.192.150, se-uk.uk.ten-155.net (212.1.192.110), se-aucs.se.ten-155
.net (212.1.194.25)
64 bytes from rc3.europe.yahoo.com (194.237.109.72): icmp_seq=1.
time=165. ms
   IP options:  <record route> 138.38.29.254, bath-gw-1.bwe.net.uk
   (194.82.125.198), man-gw-2.bwe.net.uk (194.82.125.210), bristol.
bweman.site.ja.net (146.97.252.102), south-east-gw.bristol-core.j
a.net (146.97.252.62), south-east-gw.ja.net (128.86.1.50), 212.1.
192.150, se-uk.uk.ten-155.net (212.1.192.110), se-aucs.se.ten-155
.net (212.1.194.25)
64 bytes from rc3.europe.yahoo.com (194.237.109.72): icmp_seq=2.
time = 167. ms
   IP options:  <record route> 138.38.29.254, bath-gw-1.bwe.net.uk
   (194.82.125.198), man-gw-2.bwe.net.uk (194.82.125.210), bristol.
bweman.site.ja.net (146.97.252.102), south-east-gw.bristol-core.j
a.net (146.97.252.62), south-east-gw.ja.net (128.86.1.50), 212.1.
192.150, se-uk.uk.ten-155.net (212.1.192.110), se-aucs.se.ten-15
5.net (212.1.194.25)
^C
----homerc.europe.yahoo.com PING Statistics----
3 packets transmitted, 3 packets received, 0% packet loss
round-trip (ms)  min/avg/max = 165/166/168
```

Record route can be used on any IP packet, but is mostly useful when pinging.

Some crackers search for machines to break into by pinging blocks of IP addresses until a response indicates they have found a live machine, so some people shut off the normal ICMP echo reply. Thus it could appear that a machine is not working (or not there) due to failed pings, but it is actually up and running. This is against the open spirit of the Internet, but is a small though useful element in modern security.

6.12.2   Traceroute

The IP option to record route has limited utility, since it can save only nine hosts and shows nothing if the destination machine is down. Traceroute is a clever means to discover the route a packet is taking that has neither of these problems. Traceroute works by deliberately generating errors and examining the ICMP packets returned.

Traceroute sends packets to the selected destinations that have an artificially small TTL. When the TTL drops en route to zero, an ICMP 'TTL exceeded' packet is generated and returned to the sender (Figure 6.19). The source address on the ICMP error packet tells us where the probe had got to.

So, to traceroute:

1. Send a packet with the destination address of the machine we wish to probe but with TTL set to 1.
2. This packet reaches the first gateway/router and the TTL is decremented to 0. The router drops the packet and returns an ICMP TTL exceeded.

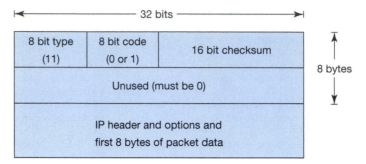

Figure 6.19 ICMP TTL exceeded.

3. This reaches the source, which records from where the packet originated, namely the router.
4. Send a packet with TTL set to 2. This gets to the next router before the TTL gets to 0 and the ICMP response identifies the second router.
5. Repeat with TTL 3, 4, and so on, until a packet manages to reach the destination. At each stage we get an ICMP error telling us of the router the packets reached.
6. When a packet gets to the destination it will be rejected with an ICMP 'port unreachable'. This is the sign that we can stop.

Just as in ping, traceroute computes the RTT for the probe and reply. In fact, traceroute sends *three* probes for each TTL, allowing us to see variance in RTTs.

```
% traceroute mary.bath.ac.uk
traceroute to mary.bath.ac.uk (138.38.32.14), 30 hops max, 46 byte
    packets
 1  136.159.7.1 (136.159.7.1)  0.779 ms  1.131 ms  0.642 ms
 2  136.159.28.1 (136.159.28.1)  1.369 ms  0.910 ms  1.489 ms
 3  136.159.30.1 (136.159.30.1)  2.339 ms  1.937 ms  0.988 ms
 4  136.159.251.2 (136.159.251.2)  1.458 ms  1.071 ms  1.831 ms
 5  192.168.47.1 (192.168.47.1)  1.434 ms  1.554 ms  1.008 ms
 6  192.168.3.25 (192.168.3.25)  29.192 ms  30.094 ms  25.374 ms
 7  REGIONAL2.tac.net (205.233.111.67)  25.413 ms  33.002 ms  32.677 ms
 8  * * *
 9  * 117.ATM3-0.XR2.CHI6.ALTER.NET (146.188.209.182)  82.403 ms
    58.747 ms
10  190.ATM11-0-0.GW4.CHI6.ALTER.NET (146.188.209.149)  56.376 ms
    67.898 ms  73.462 ms
11  if-4-0-1-1.bb1.Chicago2.Teleglobe.net (207.45.193.9)  66.853 ms
    46.089 ms  44.670 ms
12  if-0-0.core1.Chicago3.Teleglobe.net (207.45.222.213)  48.817 ms  *
    75.093 ms
13  if-8-1.core1.NewYork.Teleglobe.net (207.45.222.209)  106.198 ms
    94.249 ms  73.375 ms
14  ix-5-3.core1.NewYork.Teleglobe.net (207.45.202.30)  75.286 ms
    89.873 ms  98.789 ms
15  us-gw.ja.net (193.62.157.13)  143.686 ms  159.212 ms  166.020 ms
```

```
16   external-gw.ja.net (193.63.94.40)  172.803 ms  189.216 ms
     191.260 ms
17   external-gw.bristol-core.ja.net (146.97.252.58)  206.403 ms
     185.438 ms  192.989 ms
18   bristol.bweman.site.ja.net (146.97.252.102)  196.685 ms 206.221 ms
     183.763 ms
19   man-gw-2.bwe.net.uk (194.82.125.210)  197.968 ms * 174.809 ms
20   bath-gw-1.bwe.net.uk (194.82.125.198)  209.307 ms  221.512 ms
     199.168 ms
21   * * *
22   mary.bath.ac.uk (138.38.32.14)  250.670 ms *  186.400 ms
```

Some versions of `ping` support setting the TTL, e.g., the `-t n` option is common. This can be used to mimic `traceroute` by hand, but using ICMPs rather than UDP packets.

There are many things that can happen in a traceroute:

- Three asterisks in line 8: an error packet was not received. This can be for many reasons. For example, some routers return an ICMP error with a TTL equal to whatever was left in the original datagram. This is guaranteed not to reach us.

- If the last half of the routers are asterisks, this means that the destination has this bug: the TTL is ramped up until it is double the hop length of the route and then the ICMP reply can reach us. The destination is really only half the advertised number of hops away.

- Another possibility (on longer routes) is that the router is setting a TTL too small to reach us.

- A third possibility is simply that the router refuses to send ICMP errors for TTL exceeded in a misguided attempt at security.

- An asterisk before the machine name in line 9: the DNS name lookup (see Chapter 8) took so long that traceroute decided to stop waiting for the name and carry on. The name subsequently turned up.

- Sometimes the same line is repeated twice: this is because some routers forward datagrams with TTL of 0. This is a bug.

There are many bugs out there in real routers!

ICMP errors must contain the IP header and at least 8 bytes of data of the datagram that caused the problem. This is so the source machine can match up the ICMP datagram with the program that sent the original packet. Eight bytes are just enough to contain the interesting parts of the header of the next layer (TCP or UDP).

In fact, it is now recommended that the ICMP error contains 'as many bytes of the original datagram as possible without the length of the ICMP datagram exceeding 576 bytes'. (Recall that 576 is the minimum segment maximum.) This is so that as much information as possible is returned without the chance of fragmentation.

RFC 1812

6.13   Exercises

Exercise 6.1 Write detailed notes on each field of the IPv4 header. What limitations do the sizes of each field imply?

Exercise 6.2 Investigate the effect that packet size and therefore fragmentation has on performance: find a machine where you can alter the MTU and discover the effect it has on the speed of sending large files.

Exercise 6.3 Find the most distant host (in terms of hops) that you can (using `traceroute`, Section 6.12.2). Does geographic distance have any bearing on the TTL distance? Explain with examples.

Exercise 6.4 IP optional headers are not often used. Look in detail at the record route and timestamp options and formulate reasons why this is so.

Exercise 6.5 Write down the differences between

   (a)   uni-
   (b)   broad-
   (c)   multi- and
   (d)   anycasts.

Give examples of applications that each is best suited to.

Exercise 6.6 Describe the issues related to broadcast on

   (a)   an Ethernet,
   (b)   a token ring,
   (c)   a point-to-point connection, such as PPP (Section 4.4.2),
   (d)   a tunnel over a connection-based protocol, such as ATM (Section 4.6).

Exercise 6.7 Some broadcasters are starting to support multicasting to distribute their TV and radio programmes. Find out the level of support for multicasting for various machines that are available to you.

Exercise 6.8 Discuss the problems and solutions of connection-oriented multicasting. How far have proposed solutions progressed?

Exercise 6.9 Discuss the problems and solutions of connection-oriented anycasting. How far have proposed solutions progressed?

Exercise 6.10 Look at the IP addresses on several machines that are available to you. Determine which classes of network they are in, or whether they are CIDR. Next, look at their router tables and determine the kind of subnetting your machines employ.

Exercise 6.11 Repeat Question 6.1 but for IPv6.

Exercise 6.12 If your machine has DHCP, find out what the lease time is. Also find out what other information the DHCP server has provided to your machine.

Exercise 6.13 Investigate the way your mobile phone copes with mobile networking. This may involve digging into the way GSM (Section 5.2.5) works.

Exercise 6.14 Write detailed notes of the purpose of each type and code of an ICMP message.

Exercise 6.15 Use `ping` to find out whether various machines across the Internet are alive. Sometimes ping reports a machine down, but nevertheless the machine is active in some other way, e.g., serving Web pages. Explain what is happening and discuss other ways of determining is a machine is live.

Exercise 6.16 Use `traceroute` to find the route that packets take to various machines across the Internet. Try remote countries. Do the routes taken correspond to your intuition?

Exercise 6.17 Find a destination such that packets regularly take more than one route to get there. Investigate why.

Exercise 6.18 Some systems administrators block ICMPs as they think they are a security risk. Go through the list of ICMP messages and determine those for which this is true and those for which this view is counterproductive.

7

ROUTING IP

7.1   Introduction

In this chapter we look at one of the fundamentals of IP: its routing. As already mentioned, an IP packet does not know how to get from source to destination, but relies on the intermediate machines, the routers, to send it in the right direction. So now we must address the problem of how the *routers* know which way to send each packet.

A packet may pass though many routers on its travels. Each router is typically connected to a handful of other routers, so how, for example, can a router in England know that to send a packet to Australia it needs to forward it to America first?

Routing falls generally into two classes: local routing where a packet travels within an organization (requiring an *interior gateway protocol*) and non-local routing where a packet travels between organizations (requiring an *exterior gateway protocol*). The requirements for the two classes of protocol are quite different, with the most important being that exterior protocols are more driven by politics and economics than engineering.

We shall start with interior gateway protocols. We have already alluded to routing tables (Section 6.3). Small tables can be set up by hand and the tables in most hosts contain only two routes of interest: to the local network for local traffic and to the gateway for non-local traffic. We now look a little more closely at these tables.

The routing table on a machine can often be inspected, for example, by the `netstat -r` command:

```
Destination      Gateway         Genmask          Flags Metric Ref Use Iface
213.121.147.69   *               255.255.255.255  UH    0      0   0   ppp0
172.18.0.0       *               255.255.0.0      U     0      0   0   eth0
172.17.0.0       *               255.255.0.0      U     0      0   0   eth1
127.0.0.0        *               255.0.0.0        U     0      0   0   lo
default          213.121.147.69  0.0.0.0          UG    0      0   0   ppp0
```

To recap from Section 6.3, the address on a packet is ANDed with the mask. If the result is equal to the destination, the packet is sent out on the corresponding interface. We proceed from top to bottom in the table; the default is always matched if it is reached.

The flags vary between operating systems, but generally we have:

- U. The route is up (i.e., working).

- G. The route is to a gateway/router. Without a G the route is directly connected to the network on the interface.

- H. The route is to a host. The destination is a host address, not a network address.

- D. The route was created by ICMP *redirect*.

- M. The route was modified by ICMP *redirect*.

The `Ref` indicates the number of (TCP) connections currently using this route. The `Use` is the number of packets that have passed via this route. The `Metric` is the number of hops (i.e., intermediate routers) to the destination. Not all of these fields get used.

A *static route* is one added by hand, typically by means of the `route` command. For example,

```
route add default gw 213.121.147.69
```

would add a default route to the indicated gateway. Different operating systems have different arguments to `route`, but the principles are similar. Routing tables on most non-router hosts are set up manually by the operating system at boot-time.

7.2 ICMP Redirect

Sometimes the routing tables are not perfectly set up.

Suppose host H1 in Figure 7.1 wants to send to host H2, but H1's routing table directs all packets to router R2. When the packet reaches R2, R2 looks at its table and realizes the packet should be forwarded back through the interface it came in on. This is an indication to R2 that H1's table needs improving. R2 forwards the packet to R1, but also sends an ICMP *redirect* message to H1. H1 uses the information in the message to update its table

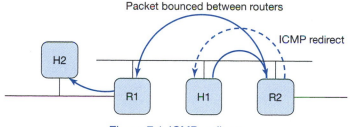

Figure 7.1 ICMP redirect.

(which is marked by the D or M flag). The next time H1 wants to send to H2 it will send the packet directly to R1 thanks to the modified route.

This allows small improvements in routing to accumulate over time.

RFC 1256

Another mechanism for generating router tables involves *router advertisement* using ICMP *Router Discovery* messages. A host can broadcast a *router solicitation* message and one or more routers can respond with messages containing routes via themselves.

7.3 Dynamic Routing Protocols

ICMP redirects fix small things, but in general routers need something more substantial. Their tables can be set up by an administrator, but it is better is to let them do it for themselves.

Dynamic routing is the passing of routing information between routers. ICMP redirects are a limited form of dynamic routing, but they are generally classed as static routes.

Routers can transmit routing tables between themselves using some protocol. There are several protocols commonly used, including the *Routing Information Protocol* (RIP), the *Open Shortest Path First* (OSPF) protocol and the *Border Gateway Protocol* (BGP).

RFC 1930

The Internet uses many routing protocols. It is organized as a collection of *autonomous systems* (ASs), each of which is administered by a single entity, e.g., a university or a company. Each AS chooses its own routing protocol to direct packets within the AS. These are *interior gateway protocols* (IGPS) (or *intradomain routing protocols*), e.g., RIP or OSPF. Between ASs run *exterior gateway protocols* (EGPS) (also called *interdomain routing protocols*), e.g., BGP.

Typically a router will run a *router daemon*, a program whose sole purpose is to exchange routing information and update the routing table. For example, the `routed` program talks RIP and `gated` talks RIP, OSPF and BGP.

7.3.1 Distance-Vector and Link-State Protocols

When collecting routing information a router gets all kinds of information on who is connected to whom and in what manner. There must be some means of collating this information to produce something that can be put into a routing table. There are two major classes of ways to do this: *distance-vector* protocols and *link-state* protocols.

A router using a distance-vector protocol gathers collections (the vectors) of hop counts (the distances) from its neighbouring routers to selected destinations. From these it computes its own vector of distances. See RIP, below, for an example of this type of protocol.

On the other hand, a router using a link-state protocol gathers complete maps of connectivity from all the routers in the AS (or some subset thereof) and then uses these to compute its own map. OSPF, below, is an example.

Distance-vector protocols, while being much simpler, have several problems. Link-state protocols are more sophisticated and harder to implement, but have several advantages.

We investigate these problems and advantages by considering two concrete proponents of the two classes of protocol, RIP and OSPF.

7.3.2 RIP

The *Routing Information Protocol* (RIP) is a widely used protocol on small to middle-sized networks. It is a distance-vector protocol.

RFC 1058

In Figure 7.2 a *command* of 1 is a request, while 2 is a reply. Other values are not often used. The *version* is generally 1, though a newer version of RIP has 2.

The next 20 bytes specify a route: the *address family* is 2 for IP addresses; an IP address; and a metric. The *metric* is the number of hops to the destination. This should be interpreted as 'I know a route to this destination that takes this number of hops'. RIP regards routes of fewer hops to be preferred over routes of more hops.

The limit of 25 routes is to keep the total packet size less than 512 bytes, a size that should never need to be fragmented.

When the router starts, it broadcasts a request (command value 1) on all its interfaces with address family 0 and metric 16. This is a 'send me all your routes' message. When another router receives such an RIP request, it replies with all its table's entries in one or more RIP replies (the vector of distances).

RIP packets are layered over UDP. Also, because broadcasts are used, only immediate neighbours can communicate with each other.

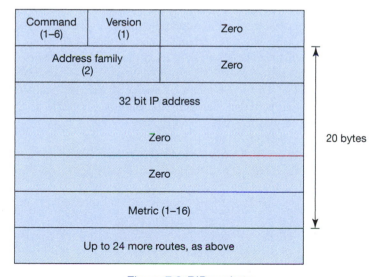

Figure 7.2 RIP packets.

Otherwise a RIP request is a request for a route to a specific address (or several addresses). A response to this is our metric for the route, or 16 to signify infinity or 'no route'.

When a response is received, we can update our routing table appropriately. Our metric is the received metric plus one for the hop to the router that replied. If a new route arrives with a smaller metric than an existing route we can replace the old route with the new one: this happens if a new path arises that is shorter than the old one. A shorter path is always deemed better in RIP.

RIP also sends a chunk of the current routing table every 30 seconds to all its neighbour routers. Routes are timed out if they haven't been reconfirmed for 3 minutes (six updates). The metric is set to 16, but the route is not deleted for 60 seconds. This ensures that the invalidation is propagated.

Suppose R3 (Figure 7.3) has a route to H with metric 1. An RIP message between R2 and R3 allows R2 to learn that there is a route to H via R3 with metric 2. Then an RIP message between R1 and R2 allows R1 to learn there is a route to H via R2 with metric 3. Notice that R2 will then get a message from R1 saying that it knows a route of metric 3 to H3, but it ignores this as it already knows a better route.

There are a few problems with RIP. Firstly, the time RIP takes to settle down after a change, e.g. when a new router is added, or a router crashes: this can be several minutes. This is called *slow convergence* or the *count to infinity problem*. Suppose that the link from R3 to H in Figure 7.4 breaks. R3 starts sending RIP messages with metric 16 (infinity) for the route to H. R2 picks this up. But now R2 gets a message from R1 with a metric of 3. So R2 replaces its route to H to go via R1 with metric 4. R1 now sees that R2 has a route to H metric 4 and so updates its metric to 5 in its table. This bounces back and forth between R1 and R2 until eventually they both reach infinity at 16. Only now can the route to H be deleted. This takes about 4 minutes. Meanwhile, real data packets are also being bounced between R1 and R2 adding to the confusion. The problem is that R2 does not know that R1's advertised route is actually via R2 itself.

Another problem is that RIP is not suitable for use between ASs as it exposes too much (possibly confidential) internal network information and it is ignorant of subnetting. As broadcast is used, routers only ever talk to their immediate neighbours, thus a global view of the network can be difficult to obtain as only local pieces of the network configuration are available.

Furthermore, the limit of 15 on the metric is too small for the Internet where paths can easily be 30 hops long. Note that increasing the limit is not viable as it would make the slow convergence even worse.

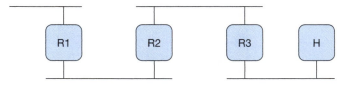

Figure 7.3 RIP routing.

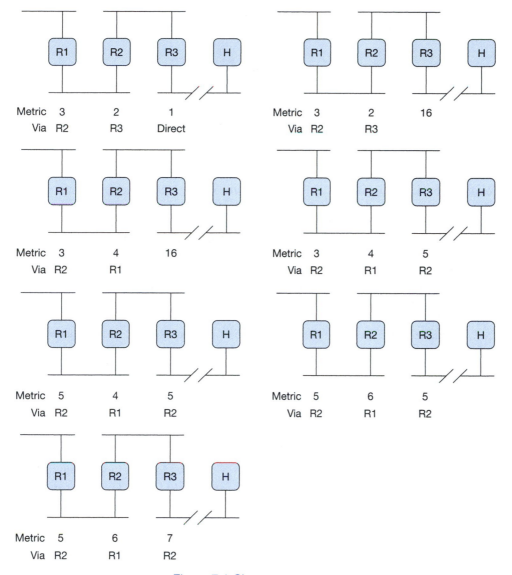

Figure 7.4 Slow convergence.

The use of a hop count as a metric is somewhat simplistic: it is not always the case that the fewest hops is the best route to take. Other considerations like network speed, network bandwidth, and cost should be taken into account when computing a route.

Nevertheless, RIP is quite suitable for small to medium-sized networks. RIP version 2 addresses the questions of subnets and EGPs, but OSPF is more popular. RFC 2453

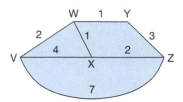

Figure 7.5 Example for Dijkstra's algorithm.

7.3.3 Dijkstra's Algorithm

We need to take a brief detour to describe *Dijkstra's algorithm*. This algorithm is used in several routing protocols to find the best route to a destination, in particular it is used in OSPF, below. Dijkstra's algorithm is a simple way of computing shortest paths though a network where 'shortest' means 'least cost', for whatever cost measure you have chosen.

Suppose we want to find the shortest/cheapest path between V and Z in Figure 7.5, where the cost of each hop is as indicated. With each node we shall associate a *predecessor* node and the cost *c* of getting to that node. Also we shall mark each node as 'determined' or 'undetermined':

1. Initialize all costs to ∞, predecessor names to blank, and all to be undetermined.

2. Initialize cost of the starting node V to zero.

3. While there are any undetermined nodes:
   (a) pick an undetermined node with lowest current cost and call it node C;

   (b) mark C determined;

   (c) for each undetermined neighbour N of C

       if cost to C + cost N to C < cost to N we have found a shorter path to N via C; make the cost of N be cost to C + cost N to C and the predecessor of N be C

Determined nodes are those for which we definitely know the cheapest route; undetermined nodes are those where we might yet find a better route.

For example:

- Start with

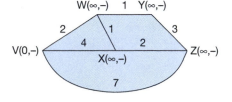

V	W	X	Y	Z
0	∞	∞	∞	∞
–	–	–	–	–
Undet	Undet	Undet	Undet	Undet

- Pick the cheapest undetermined node: this is V.

- Make it determined, and consider its undetermined neighbours W, X, and Z.

- All have infinite current cost, so all three get revalued and their predecessor set to V

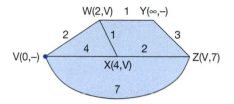

V	W	X	Y	Z
0	2	4	∞	7
–	V	V	–	V
Det	Undet	Undet	Undet	Undet

- Pick the cheapest undetermined node: this is W.

- Make it determined, and consider its undetermined neighbours X and Y.

- Cost to X via W is $2 + 1 < 4$ so revalue X; cost to Y via W is $2 + 1 < \infty$ so revalue Y

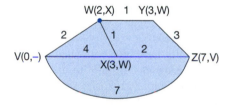

V	W	X	Y	Z
0	2	3	3	7
–	V	W	W	V
Det	Det	Undet	Undet	Undet

- Pick the cheapest undetermined node: this is X (Y could be chosen here, too).

- Make it determined, and consider its sole undetermined neighbour Z.

- Cost to Z via X is $3 + 2 < 7$ so revalue Z

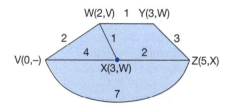

V	W	X	Y	Z
0	2	3	3	5
–	V	W	W	X
Det	Det	Det	Undet	Undet

- Pick the cheapest undetermined node: this is Y.

- Make it determined, and consider its undetermined neighbour Z.

- Cost to Z via Y is $3 + 3 \geq 5$ so do not revalue Z

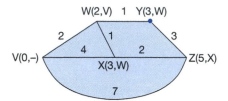

V	W	X	Y	Z
0	2	3	3	5
–	V	W	W	X
Det	Det	Det	Det	Undet

- Pick the cheapest undetermined node: this is Z.

- Make it determined, so it has no undetermined neighbours, and we are done.

The final costs are

V	W	X	Y	Z
0	2	3	3	5
–	V	W	W	X

The cheapest path from V to Z is of cost 5. We actually have also computed the cheapest costs from V to every other node *and* all the cheapest *paths* from V to each node. The paths are read from the table in reverse: for example, start with Z and successively take the predecessor, Z X W V, so V W X Z is the cheapest path from V to Z.

We are now equipped to consider OSPF.

7.3.4 OSPF

RFC 2328 *Open Shortest Path First* (OSPF) is an interior gateway routing protocol that addresses the problems of RIP. It is a link-state protocol. In essence, RIP measures simple hop counts while OSPF considers the states of neighbouring routers and passes this information throughout the AS. Each router takes this state information and builds its own view of the network and from this its own router table. This allows OSPF to *converge* faster than RIP in the case of a change in the network.

OSPF is layered directly on top of IP (RIP is on UDP on IP), and has many advantages over RIP:

- OSPF can have different routes for different IP types of service.

- An interface is assigned a *cost*. This is a number that is computed from anything relevant, e.g., reliability, throughput, round-trip time.

- If more than one equal cost route exists, OSPF shares traffic equally between them (*load balancing*).

- OSPF understands subnets.

- A simple authentication scheme can be used to help prevent spoofing of routes.

- OSPF uses multicast (Section 6.9) rather than broadcast, so only hosts that are interested have to listen to OSPF traffic.

- The use of multicast also allows routing information to flow beyond the local network and, indeed, anywhere within the AS.

On the other hand:

- RIP requires virtually no setup or administration while setting up the various costs in OSPF can be complex.

- OSPF requires more computational power than RIP as it needs to run Dijkstra's algorithm rather than a simple comparison of hop counts.

- OSPF is a complex protocol that is hard to implement, containing several message types and having to carry out its own reliability mechanisms.

- Serious problems (like routing loops) may arise if the routers' views of the network get out of sync.

In OSPF a router:

- tests for its neighbors by multicasting to the address 240.0.0.5, called the *AllSPFRouters* address (the TTL on these packets is set to 1 as they should not be forwarded);

- periodically multicasts its link-state tables to the routers in the AS;

- multicasts the updates when there are changes to the network;

- receives the link-state information from other routers in the AS;

- updates its link-state table in light of this information;

- computes its routing table from the link-state using, say, Dijkstra's algorithm.

An AS can be subdivided into smaller chunks called *areas* if a whole AS is too large to compute comfortably.

The cost of a link in OSPF can be set according to any desirable criteria and they can be technical (e.g., bandwidth of link, round-trip time of link), or economic (e.g., one route may go via a carrier that is more expensive than another), or political (e.g., traffic from Research to Development may not pass through Accounting), or anything else that is codifiable by a value. This is called *policy-based routing*.

OSPF has many desirable properties. It:

- reacts quickly to network changes;

- requires minimal network traffic overhead (we do not want to take bandwidth away from actual data traffic!);

- enables multiple routes between hosts;

- enables policy-based routing;

- allows multiple networks to be grouped together, thus simplifying routing;

- is ideal for a large, complex network as might be used in a large, complex organization.

7.3.5 BGP

RFC 1771 The *Border Gateway Protocol* (BGP) is an *exterior gateway protocol* (EGP) and so is used for routing between ASs.

An EGP has a different problem to an IGP: now the problem is to route between ASs rather than networks or hosts, and politics (and policy-based routing) becomes a dominant factor.

> For example, suppose there is a Canadian law to the effect that all traffic beginning and ending in Canada must not leave Canada at any point. So no intermediate AS can route traffic out of the country under such circumstances.

In BGP ASs are classified into three types:

1. A *stub* AS. This has only one connection to any other AS and only carries local traffic.

2. A *multi-homed* AS. This has more than one connection, but refuses to carry anyone else's traffic.

3. A *transit* AS. This has more than one connection and will carry traffic from one AS to another (usually with certain policy restrictions).

Just like OSPF, BGP allows policy-based routing. BGP is layered on top of TCP and is a distance-vector protocol like RIP, but rather than giving simple hop counts BGP passes on the actual AS-to-AS routes. This fixes some of the problems associated with distance-vector protocols. On the other hand, ASs do not change very much, so there is not a big problem with slow convergence.

7.4 Exercises

Exercise 7.1 Identify the main differences between interior and exterior gateway protocols. Is there any protocol that could be used as both? Explain.

Exercise 7.2 Discover what routing protocols are being used in your local networks and find the policy decisions that lie behind them.

Exercise 7.3 Implement Dijkstra's algorithm and use it to determine some shortest paths within example networks.

Exercise 7.4 Look at the *Bellman–Ford* algorithm for finding shortest paths. Compare it to Dijkstra's algorithm.

Exercise 7.5 Identify the AS your network lives within. Find the ASs of several other networks and determine the routes between them.

Exercise 7.6 Identify the security problems that can arise from using an unauthenticated routing protocol.

Exercise 7.7 Multicast routing (i.e., routing of multicast traffic) is very different from unicast routing. Explain why this is so and investigate the various routing solutions.

THE DOMAIN NAME SYSTEM

8

8.1 Introduction

RFC 1034
RFC 1035
RFC 1591

The Domain Name System (DNS) is the means by which we can convert names like `news.bbc.co.uk` to IP addresses like 212.58.226.30. The benefit of having human comprehensible names rather than a jumble of numbers is clear. We *could* learn numbers to refer to machines (we do manage to learn telephone numbers), but names tend to stick much better in the mind.

In the early days of the Internet, all machines could keep a table of every host name and corresponding IP address that existed. This lives on in files like `/etc/hosts`. Soon, though, this became untenable as the Internet grew. The DNS was developed as a hierarchical system to *resolve* names and is *distributed*: that is, no single machine on the Internet knows all the names of all the machines, but the mapping is spread about over very many machines.

`www.llanfairpwllgwyngyllgogerychwyrndrobwllllantysiliogogogoch.com` is a valid name.

8.2 The Hierarchy

The DNS hierarchy (Figure 8.1) is a tree with root at the top. The root has name `"."` (dot). Other nodes in the tree have *labels* of up to 63 characters. A *fully qualified domain name* (FQDN) is a sequence of labels terminated by a dot, e.g., `www.bbc.co.uk.`.

A name without a terminating dot is incomplete and must be completed before we can look up the IP address. When given a name that is incomplete, any software that wants to look up a name will need to complete it by appending strings such as given in `/etc/resolv.conf`. A machine on the University of Bath network would have the string `"bath.ac.uk"` in its `/etc/resolv.conf`, so the name `mary` would be completed to `mary.bath.ac.uk.`. The `bath.ac.uk` is the network *domain*.

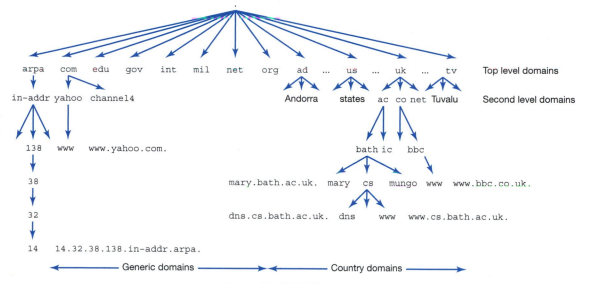

Figure 8.1 DNS hierarchy.

For a long while there were just seven *generic domains*, each three characters long. These included labels like `com`, `org` and `edu`. They mostly refer to machines in the USA (where the DNS was invented), but some, e.g., `com`, are used worldwide. More recently, new labels like `biz` and `info` have been added. The `arpa` domain is used for the reverse problem of getting names from numbers, Section 8.4.

The two character names are *country domains*, and refer to the appropriate country. These names come from ISO 3166, the list of official country name abbreviations, except that the UK uses `uk` instead of the ISO `gb`.

ISO 3166

Each level of the tree represents different management and responsibility for the names. The *top level domains* (TLDs) are managed by IANA, which has delegated responsibility to The Internet Corporation for Assigned Names and Numbers (ICANN). To get a new name at this level, you would have to apply to ICANN – but it wouldn't give you one, as this level is essentially determined politically.

Every other layer is managed by some other entity. For example, labels under `uk` are managed by the UK Network Information Centre (NIC), run by a company called Nominet. Again, this level is fixed and it is hard to get a name at this level.

The beauty of the DNS is the shared responsibility. The labels under `ac.uk` are managed by the United Kingdom Education and Research Networking Association (UK-ERNA). You have some chance of getting a name from these people as long as you are connected with the UK academic community. Labels under `co.uk` happen also to be managed by Nominet: you can readily get a label here for the right price. Labels under `bbc.co.uk` are administered by the BBC. And so on.

Another thing to note is that names administered by one authority can refer to machines anywhere in the world: `bill.acme.com` might be in Rangoon, while `ben.acme.com` might be in Tunbridge Wells. Furthermore, some countries happen to have ISO names that have other interpretations. For example, Tuvalu has `tv` and it makes a bit of money selling labels under this domain to television companies. Thus `bbc.tv` is again owned by the BBC and has nothing to do with Tuvalu!

Apparently the South Pacific Polynesian nation of Tuvalu has done very well out of this serendipity and the proceeds form a significant part of its income. Never say the Internet never did anyone any good!

Delegation of names allows us to put some structure on them. For example, the `uk` domain is divided into subdomains as follows:

`.ac.uk`	for academic establishments
`.bl.uk`	for the British Library
`.co.uk`	for commercial enterprises
`.gov.uk`	for government bodies
`.ltd.uk`	for limited companies
`.me.uk`	for personal domains
`.mod.uk`	for Ministry of Defence establishments
`.net.uk`	for Internet service providers
`.nhs.uk`	for National Health Service organizations
`.org.uk`	for not-for-profit organizations
`.plc.uk`	for public limited companies
`.police.uk`	for police forces
`.sch.uk`	for schools

Labels under `bath.ac.uk` are managed by The University of Bath Computing Service, while labels under `cs.bath.ac.uk` are managed by the Department of Computer Science in the university. Other organizations manage their parts of the tree differently. For example, Germany does not have an `ac.uk` equivalent, but rather has names like `uni-paderborn.de`. This is a shame because it loses the ability to distribute responsibility for names. The shape of the DNS was initially determined by technological requirements: as is so often the case, those requirements have been overtaken by political considerations. These days it is a question of who controls names that is important.

A *zone* is a subtree that is administered separately, `bath.ac.uk`, for example. A zone can have sub-zones (e.g., `cs.bath.ac.uk`).

The authority for a zone must set up some *name servers*. A name server is (a program on) a machine that has a database of the labels for that zone. Names are added or deleted at this level by changing this database. To provide resilience, there must be a *primary name server* and one or more *secondary name servers* in case the primary goes down. The primary gets its information from the database, while the secondaries get theirs from the primary using *zone transfers*, which is just the copying of the zone database. A secondary queries the primary every 3 hours typically. Good practice has at least one secondary off-site to increase resilience even further.

If a machine requests a lookup from the name server for a name that is in its own zone, it can reply with an *authoritative* response. Otherwise lookup is harder and this brings us to the main purpose of the DNS.

8.3 Recursive Lookup

If the request is for a name outside the zone, the name server must ask around for the name. Firstly, it contacts a *root name server* (Figure 8.2). A root name server is one of (currently) about 80 machines dotted about the world that are responsible for the TLDs (the root zone). Using load sharing these machines share just 13 IP addresses. Current name servers are named `a.root-servers.net` to `m.root-servers.net`, but our name servers will have their IP addresses in a file stored locally (otherwise we will never get started!).

All the root servers contain the same data: the replication is to spread load and add resilience (and to defend against attack).

Suppose we want to find the IP address of `news.bbc.co.uk`. Our name server `ns` in Figure 8.3 doesn't have responsibility for the `bbc` zone. So `ns` asks a random root server the question 'who is responsible for the `uk` domain?' This is a *start of authority* (SOA) request. The root server answers with `ns1.nic.uk` or some such. Or course, it also supplies the IP address of `ns1.nic.uk`!

Now `ns` asks `ns1.nic.uk` 'who is responsible for the `co.uk` domain?' and gets `ns1.nic.uk` again. It just happens that `ns1.nic.uk` is responsible for both `uk` and `co.uk`. Next, `ns` asks `ns1.nic.net` for the SOA for `bbc.co.uk` and gets `ns.bbc.co.uk`. Finally, it asks `ns.bbc.co.uk` for `news.bbc.co.uk` and gets the IP address 194.130.56.40. At last `ns` can hand the IP address back to us. This is `ns` doing a *recursive lookup*.

Of course, these responses are cached by `ns` so it doesn't have to go through a complete lookup every time. Each response has a *time to live* attached that indicates how long the server should keep the information before asking again. The next request for a `bbc.co.uk` address can go directly to `ns.bbc.co.uk` without bothering a root server or `ns1.nic.uk`.

Our host could go through this lookup process itself rather than rely on the name server (a *non-recursive lookup*), but an additional benefit of caching in the name server is that an organization-wide name server may well have done and cached several or all of the steps already for some other host's request. This means a reduction in network traffic and a faster response for the user.

The distributed nature of the DNS is also a great strength. In October 2002 there was a denial of service attack (Section 13.2) on the root servers: many subverted machines across the world were instructed to flood the root servers with DNS requests and managed to produce 30–40 times the normal amount of traffic. The intent was to give the servers so much fake work that real requests would not be serviced and the Internet would grind to a halt. The effectiveness of the attack can be gauged by the fact that barely anyone noticed. The operators of the root servers *did* notice, of course, as it effectively disabled 7 of the 13 servers, but they estimated that the efficiency of DNS lookup dropped to about 94% of its normal value.

```
;           This file holds the information on root name servers needed to
;           initialize cache of Internet domain name servers
;           (e.g. reference this file in the "cache  .  <file>"
;           configuration file of BIND domain name servers).
;
;           This file is made available by InterNIC
;           under anonymous FTP as
;               file                    /domain/named.root
;               on server               FTP.INTERNIC.NET
;           -OR-                        RS.INTERNIC.NET
;
;           last update:    Jan 29, 2004
;           related version of root zone:   2004012900
;
;
; formerly NS.INTERNIC.NET
;
.                           3600000  IN  NS      A.ROOT-SERVERS.NET.
A.ROOT-SERVERS.NET.         3600000      A       198.41.0.4
;
; formerly NS1.ISI.EDU
;
.                           3600000      NS      B.ROOT-SERVERS.NET.
B.ROOT-SERVERS.NET.         3600000      A       192.228.79.201
;
; formerly C.PSI.NET
;
.                           3600000      NS      C.ROOT-SERVERS.NET.
C.ROOT-SERVERS.NET.         3600000      A       192.33.4.12
;
; formerly TERP.UMD.EDU
;
.                           3600000      NS      D.ROOT-SERVERS.NET.
D.ROOT-SERVERS.NET.         3600000      A       128.8.10.90
;
; formerly NS.NASA.GOV
;
.                           3600000      NS      E.ROOT-SERVERS.NET.
E.ROOT-SERVERS.NET.         3600000      A       192.203.230.10
;
; formerly NS.ISC.ORG
;
.                           3600000      NS      F.ROOT-SERVERS.NET.
F.ROOT-SERVERS.NET.         3600000      A       192.5.5.241


...


;
; operated by WIDE
;
.                           3600000      NS      M.ROOT-SERVERS.NET.
M.ROOT-SERVERS.NET.         3600000      A       202.12.27.33
; End of File
```

Figure 8.2 Excerpt from the root DNS servers file.

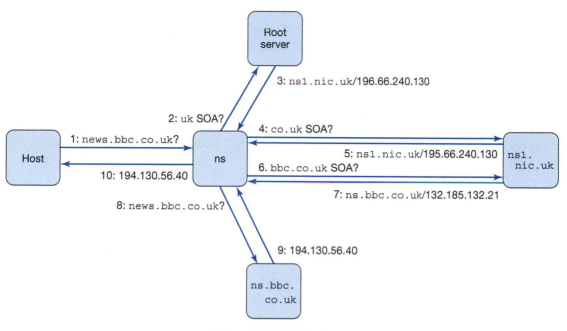

Figure 8.3 DNS lookup.

We can use the command `dig` to look up names via DNS:

```
% dig news.bbc.co.uk

...

;; QUESTION SECTION:
;news.bbc.co.uk.                        IN      A

;; ANSWER SECTION:
news.bbc.co.uk.          360     IN     CNAME    newswww.bbc.net.uk.
newswww.bbc.net.uk.      62      IN     A        212.58.226.19

;; AUTHORITY SECTION:
bbc.net.uk.              162395  IN     NS       ns0.thdo.bbc.co.uk.
bbc.net.uk.              162395  IN     NS       ns0.thny.bbc.co.uk.

;; ADDITIONAL SECTION:
ns0.thdo.bbc.co.uk.      211     IN     A        212.58.224.20
ns0.thny.bbc.co.uk.      211     IN     A        212.58.240.20

...
```

(Some output elided.)

This reply contains a lot of information. More than one name can map to the same IP address: `newswww.bbc.net.uk` is an alternate name for `news.bbc.co.uk`. In fact, `newswww.bbc.net.uk` is the *canonical name* or CNAME for this machine, while `news.bbc.co.uk` is an *alias*. Aliases are useful to give mnemonic names to machines, e.g., `www.bath.ac.uk` was at one time an alias for `jess.bath.ac.uk`. If we decide to run the Web server on a different machine, we can transfer the alias to the new machine and nobody else needs to be aware anything has changed.

The reply from `dig` also tells us about the name servers (`NS`) and their addresses (`A`).

A useful property of `dig` is that it will display the recursive lookup for you: use `dig +trace`:

```
% dig +trace news.bbc.co.uk

...

.                             137487   IN      NS      e.root-servers.net.
.                             137487   IN      NS      f.root-servers.net.
.                             137487   IN      NS      g.root-servers.net.
...
.                             137487   IN      NS      b.root-servers.net.
.                             137487   IN      NS      c.root-servers.net.
.                             137487   IN      NS      d.root-servers.net.

...

uk.                           172800   IN      NS      NSC.NIC.uk.
uk.                           172800   IN      NS      NSD.NIC.uk.
uk.                           172800   IN      NS      NS1.NIC.uk.
...
uk.                           172800   IN      NS      NS7.NIC.uk.
uk.                           172800   IN      NS      NSA.NIC.uk.
uk.                           172800   IN      NS      NSB.NIC.uk.

...

bbc.co.uk.                    172800   IN      NS      ns1.thny.bbc.co.uk.
bbc.co.uk.                    172800   IN      NS      ns1.thls.bbc.co.uk.
bbc.co.uk.                    172800   IN      NS      ns1.thdo.bbc.co.uk.
bbc.co.uk.                    172800   IN      NS      ns1.bbc.co.uk.

...

news.bbc.co.uk.               900      IN      CNAME   newswww.bbc.net.uk.
newswww.bbc.net.uk.           294      IN      A       212.58.226.19
```

```
bbc.net.uk.                    170057  IN    NS     ns0.thny.bbc.co.uk.
bbc.net.uk.                    170057  IN    NS     ns0.thdo.bbc.co.uk.
```

A name can map to more than one IP address: `www.yahoo.com` has

```
www.yahoo.com.                 221   IN    CNAME  www.yahoo.akadns.net.
www.yahoo.akadns.net.          26    IN    A      68.142.226.39
www.yahoo.akadns.net.          26    IN    A      68.142.226.41
www.yahoo.akadns.net.          26    IN    A      68.142.226.43
www.yahoo.akadns.net.          26    IN    A      68.142.226.46
www.yahoo.akadns.net.          26    IN    A      68.142.226.49
www.yahoo.akadns.net.          26    IN    A      68.142.226.54
www.yahoo.akadns.net.          26    IN    A      68.142.226.56
www.yahoo.akadns.net.          26    IN    A      68.142.226.32
```

which is eight different machines.

When this happens, the IP address to use is taken in a round-robin fashion. This is usually done to balance load so different people will be trying to get the same Web page from different machines. Usually, all the machines are configured identically so it doesn't matter which machine we actually contact. Note that these machines can be entirely independent and distributed throughout the world!

> Even better, some clever DNS servers look at your IP address and return the address of the server closest to you. For example, a request from North America for `news.bbc.co.uk` will elicit a response 212.58.240.35, a machine in New York. The same request from a machine in Great Britain gets 212.58.226.40, a machine in the UK. This kind of load balancing requires a rough idea of how blocks of IP addresses are allocated to countries: of course, it doesn't matter too much if you get it wrong if all your servers are identical. If you are using this technique to restrict services to specified regions (e.g., a video licensed only to Europe) you need to be a little more careful.
>
> To find the authority for a domain, use `dig` *domain* `soa` (start of authority) and to find an authoritative name server, use `dig` *domain* `ns`.

8.4   Reverse Lookup

There is another branch of the DNS tree with TLD `arpa`. This branch allows us to do the reverse lookup of IP address to DNS name. This is very useful for determining the source of a packet when you only know its IP address.

A DNS name has the most significant part last, e.g., the uk in mary.bath.ac.uk, and we delegate downwards from that end. An IP address has its most significant part first, e.g., the 138 in 138.38.32.14, and the values are delegated from that end.

> In the early days the UK community used the order uk.ac.bath.mary to be consistent. But the rest of the world disagreed, and eventually the UK changed.

The subdomain in-addr is the start of the part of the tree that contains IP values as labels. Looking up the *pointer* (PTR) record for the address 14.32.38.138.in-addr.arpa. will reveal that the IP address 138.38.32.14 belongs to mary.bath.ac.uk. The authority for the numeric domain is generally the same as the authority for the name domain, though it need not be.

RFC 2050
> CIDR causes complications here as networks are no longer necessarily divided on byte boundaries.

Setting up a name server authority properly requires the management of two databases: one from names to numbers and the other, the reverse. Some people forget to set up the number-to-name map, or change the name-to-number map and forget to update the reverse, and so on. This causes all sort of problems as, for example, sometimes reverse lookup is used in authentication of connections.

Use dig to find PTR records:

```
% dig 14.32.38.138.in-addr.arpa ptr
...
14.32.38.138.in-addr.arpa. 104879 IN    PTR    mary.bath.ac.uk.
```

It is easier to use -x with the forward IP address:

```
% dig -x 138.38.32.14
...
14.32.38.138.in-addr.arpa. 104786 IN    PTR    mary.bath.ac.uk.
```

which reverses the address and queries for a PTR.

The domain for IPv6 reverse lookup is ip6.arpa.

8.5   Other Data

The DNS can give you more than just IP addresses. We have seen that 'A' records give us IP addresses, while 'PTR' records give us names. There are many others, about 50 in total.

Name	Type	RFC	
A	1	1035	IP address
AAAA	28	2874	IPv6 address (128 bit)
NS	2	1035	Authoritative name server
CNAME	5	1035	Canonical name
SOA	6	1035	Start of authority
PTR	12	1035	Pointer (IP address to name lookup)
HINFO	13	1035	Host info
MX	15	1035	Email exchange
SRV	33	2782	Server selection
AXFR	252	1035	Zone transfer
ANY	255	1035	All records

HINFO is some snippet of information about the machine, e.g., operating system. Not many people like to publish this kind of information as it could possibly be used to aid an attack on the machine.

Mail exchange, MX, gives the IP address of one or more machines that will accept email for a given domain:

```
% dig bath.ac.uk mx
...
bath.ac.uk.          102931   IN      MX      20 kelly.bath.ac.uk.
bath.ac.uk.          102931   IN      MX      20 roche.bath.ac.uk.
bath.ac.uk.          102931   IN      MX      10 bucs.bath.ac.uk.
bath.ac.uk.          102931   IN      MX      20 binda.bath.ac.uk.
bath.ac.uk.          102931   IN      MX      20 coppi.bath.ac.uk.
```

The integers before the FQDNs are *preferences*. One of the hosts with the smallest preference is contacted first. If that host is down, we try a host with the next smallest. Note that no machine with the name bath.ac.uk need actually exist, but we can still send email to somebody@bath.ac.uk. This allows us to dedicate a single mail address to serve a large number of people using a variety of different machines.

NS gives an authoritative name server for the domain.

AXFR is for a zone transfer, namely a transfer of a zone's records, usually from a primary name server to a secondary.

ANY fetches all available records associated with a name.

SRV is slightly different. Its purpose is for *service discovery*, such as finding a printer on the local network. Sending a DNS request for _lpr._tcp.example.com would return the address of a machine or machines that are willing to supply a printer service on the example.com network. Similarly, _www._tcp.example.com would find a Web server. The service name and protocol have underscores to prevent accidental clashes with normal DNS labels.

RFC 2606

The reply contains other information including:

- A priority, like the preference for MX.

- A weight, which allows selection between machines of the same priority. A server might choose to vary the weight returned according to its current load.

- The port number the service is on.

The SRV record is not widely used currently, but the Zeroconf Working Group of the IETF is set to use it to provide *zero configuration IP networking*. The aim is to have a user simply plug a computer (or general appliance) into a network and have it configure itself (IP address, gateway, and so forth) and discover its service requirements (printer, Web server, and so on) all automatically. This overlaps some of the functionality provided by DHCP (Section 6.10), but is intended to be even easier to use and not to require a DHCP server when only local addresses are needed.

It has been predicted that Zeroconf will be most useful in the wireless world: a machine can roam into the range of a wireless network and be automatically configured.

> An alternative to Zeroconf is Microsoft's *Universal Plug'n'Play* (UPnP) which is a much more heavyweight XML-based protocol.

8.6   Packet Format

The message format for DNS has a fixed 12 byte header, followed by four variable length fields (Figure 8.4).

The *identification* is a number selected by the client in the query message and is returned by the server in the reply. This allows the client to match up responses with queries if there are several in flight simultaneously.

The flags (Figure 8.5) are:

- QR. This bit is 1 for a query, 0 for a response.

- Opcode. Usually 0 for a standard request, but can be other values.

- AA. This bit is set on an authoritative answer.

- TC. *Truncated*: couldn't fit the reply within 512 bytes (see later).

- RD. *Recursion desired*: the name server should do the recursive lookup. Otherwise, the name server returns a list of other name servers for the client to contact (an *iterative lookup*). This bit is normally set.

- RA. *Recursion available*: this name server can do a recursive lookup. Normally set.

- Rcode. A 4 bit return code: 0 is no error, while 3 is *name error*, a response from an authority saying the requested name does not exist.

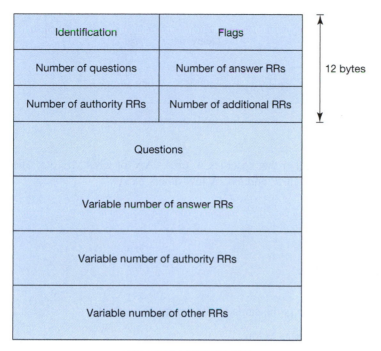

Figure 8.4 DNS format.

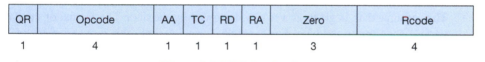

QR	Opcode	AA	TC	RD	RA	Zero	Rcode
1	4	1	1	1	1	3	4

Figure 8.5 DNS header flags.

The next four fields give the numbers of each type of *resource records* (RRs) that follow. Usually these are 1, 0, 0, 0 for a request and 1, 1, 0, 0 for a reply (the question is returned with the answer).

8.6.1 Query

The question format (Figure 8.6) starts with the name we want to resolve. It is a sequence of one or more labels, where a label is stored as a single byte containing the number of characters in the label followed by those characters. The name is terminated by a 0 byte. Recall that the length of a label is not more than 63 characters:

```
4mary4bath2ac2uk0
```

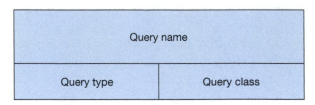

Figure 8.6 DNS question format.

The *query type* is a number that specifies A, or AAAA, or CNAME, etc. The *query class* is normally 1, denoting an IP address. A few others exist.

8.6.2 Response

As shown in Figure 8.7:

- The domain name is the same as for the question field.

- Type and class are as before.

- The *time to live* is a time, in seconds, when the name server should cache this data. A popular value is 2 days. When the TTL expires, the name server should re-query the authority for this data.

- The resource data is given as a length, followed by the data. The format of the data varies according to the type. For example, for an A reply this is just 4 bytes of IP address.

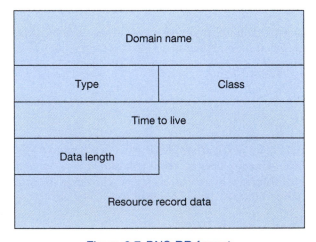

Figure 8.7 DNS RR format.

8.7 Other Stuff

The DNS hierarchy allows machine names at any level: for example, `channel4.com` is both a zone name and a machine name. As a machine name it (currently) happens to resolve to the same IP address as `www.channel4.com`.

> The DNS runs over both UDP and TCP. Typically UDP is used for speed, but there is a twist. To avoid possible fragmentation, a DNS server will never return an answer in a UDP datagram larger than 512 bytes. Instead, the response has the *truncated* (TC) bit set. Then the two machines start up a TCP connection and try again.
>
> Zone transfers are done using TCP as large amounts of data can be transferred and the TCP connection overhead is small in comparison.

A simple form of compression can be used if the RRs contain repetitive data, e.g., the same root repeated many times.

The DNS does have problems: in particular, there is no authentication. If I get a message telling me that `www.bath.ac.uk` has IP address 138.38.32.14 can I be certain this is not the IP address of somebody else? It is possible that one of the DNS servers in the hierarchy from the root to `bath.ac.uk` has been subverted and made to hand out an incorrect address or SOA.

For example, the Web server of the security company RSA was subverted by spoofing DNS (Figure 8.8). An authority for `.com` was convinced somehow that the authority for `rsa.com` was a machine other than the real one (`dnsauth1.sys.gtei.net` is a real one). Let's say `dns.spoofed.com` was made the authority. This was an innocent machine somewhere that had been cracked. Now `dns.spoofed.com` resolved `www.rsa.com` to some IP address of its own choosing, let's say the address for `www.spoofed.com`. A replacement Web page for RSA was set up on `www.spoofed.com`. So when users tried to get the Web page for `www.rsa.com` they were actually directed to the Web page from `www.spoofed.com`, which said uncomplimentary things about RSA, the company. Note

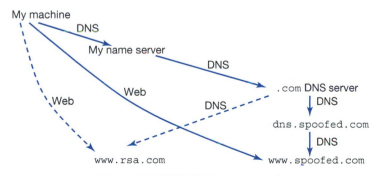

Figure 8.8 RSA Web page spoof.

that there was absolutely no compromise of any of RSA's machines: none of them were ever touched.

> A more subtle attack is *DNS cache poisoning*. In this an attacker sends a DNS request to a server which then recursively sends off a request to the appropriate authority. The attacker then sends a spoof packet to the server which appears to come from the authority: this just involves getting the right

- IP address of the authority,
- port number the server used, and
- DNS identification field.

> The IP address of the authority will be easy to find: just look it up. To get the other information the attacker should send a valid query to the server just before the spoofed one. Ephemeral ports are often assigned consecutively, giving a good hint. Old versions of the BIND DNS server also assigned identifications consecutively, too.
>
> This meant that the attacker could spoof a DNS record to the server, which would then cache it for a while – usually a long while if the time to live in the RR was cranked up high. Note that this attack can happen remotely.
>
> Modern versions of BIND (and other DNS servers) choose random identifications to avoid this attack. The response of the attacker is to send a large number of spoof requests which can either determine how good the random number generator is and perhaps crack it, or use the Birthday Paradox and send a large number of potential spoofed replies. The Birthday Paradox greatly increases the probability that one of the spoof replies matches a spoof request.

RFC 4033
RFC 4034
RFC 4035
There is a solution to this in *Secure DNS* (DNSSec), which uses public key authentication, involving cryptographically secure authentication certificates. It hasn't really taken off, possibly due to unfamiliarity with the concepts. And it doesn't really make sense until many people use it and nobody is going first.

RFC 2136
RFC 3007
Dynamic DNS (DDNS) is a protocol that enables hosts to update their DNS entries. It is mostly aimed at hosts that occasionally change IP address but want to keep their DNS name. This would include hosts that get their IP address through dynamic means like PPP (Section 4.4.2) or DHCP (Section 6.10). Rather than get an administrator to update the DNS tables, this protocol does it automatically. When a host gets a new address, it sends an (authenticated in RFC 2137) request to update to its DNS server which can then change the A and PTR records. The change will then percolate throughout the Internet. Note that such records should have TTL values comparable to the rate the IP address changes, else hosts will keep using the old associations in their caches.

The DNS has been coopted in the fight against spam email. A *Realtime Blackhole List* (RBL) is a list of IP addresses that are associated with spammers. That is, a list of addresses that have been repeatedly reported by users as being an origin of spam. It is *realtime* since the list can be interrogated as each email arrives. The *Mail Abuse Prevention System* (MAPS) technique uses the DNS to look up the database: if an email arrives from, say, 10.0.0.1, the receiving host does a DNS lookup for `1.0.0.10.bl.spamcop.net`. Here `spamcop.net` is a provider of RBL services; several others exist. If the source is in the RBL, then an IP address such as 127.0.0.2 is returned. If it is not, then a 'name not found' is returned. Thus the host can quickly determine whether the email is likely to be spam and can take appropriate action, such as marking it as likely spam or even simply dropping it.

The `whois` command can be used to find the current owner of a domain name:

```
% whois google.com
```

8.8   Exercises

Exercise 8.1 Look up ISO 3166 and determine the latest country code additions to the DNS. Similarly investigate the latest generic TLDs.

Exercise 8.2 The precise locations of the root servers are kept secret for security reasons. Use `traceroute` (or other) to get a rough idea of where in the world some of them might be situated.

Exercise 8.3 The DNS is a simple distributed database, designed for a specific purpose. Find out about other kinds of distributed database and discuss whether they could be a suitable replacement for the DNS.

Exercise 8.4 Make notes on the various kinds of record that the DNS supports. How many are in common use?

Exercise 8.5 Determine how to host a DNS name, both on your own machine and using a commercial hosting service.

9
THE TRANSPORT LAYER

9.1 Introduction

The Internet Protocol has three main protocols that layer over IP. Two are for data transmission, the third for control. The data protocols are complementary, one (UDP) being fast, unreliable and connectionless, and the other (TCP) being more sophisticated, reliable and connection oriented. Arguably, the third, ICMP, is a transport layer since it runs on top of the IP layer, but it is usually regarded as a network layer due to its function.

We have already looked at ICMP in Section 6.12, so we now turn to UDP and TCP.

9.2 Ports

Both UDP and TCP use the concept of *ports*. At any time there may be many services available on a server machine that a client may want to use, e.g., Web page serving, email delivery, telnet login, FTP, and so on. How does a client indicate which service it requires? In IP it is done by the use of *ports*.

A port is simply a 16 bit integer (1–65535). Every transport layer connection (using UDP or TCP) has a source port and destination port. When a service starts (i.e., a program that will deal with that service) it *listens* on a port. That is to say, the program informs the operating system that it wishes to receive data directed to that port. The OS checks that the port is not already being used and subsequently arranges for UDP/TCP packets that arrive with that port number to be passed to our service program. If the port is already being used by some other service, our program receives an error from the OS.

One analogy is to think of a host as a block of flats or apartments. Inside the block there are many occupants, doing many different things. The block has a single street address so if you want to deliver a letter you need a flat number as well as the main address.

TCP ports and UDP ports are completely separate: one service can be listening for TCP packets on the same port number while another service is listening for UDP packets.

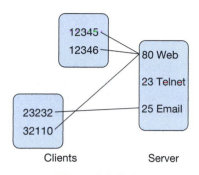

Figure 9.1 Ports.

The OS can distinguish the two as they are using different protocols. It is important to note that TCP and UDP are completely separate protocols and do not interact at all at the transport level.

Certain *well-known ports* are reserved for certain services (Figure 9.1), e.g., a Web server on TCP port 80, a mail server on TCP port 25; a selection of other ports are only available to privileged programs; most ports are available to any program that wants to use them. See RFC 1700 *et seq* (now kept on a Website) for allocations of well-known port numbers, or look at the file /etc/services which keeps a partial local copy.

RFC 1700

It is important to realize that this is pure convention and is for convenience only. There is nothing special about any port number and you can run any service on any number. You can run a Web server on port 25 if you are so inclined, but you will just confuse anyone who wants to send you mail.

Also the use of ports solves another problem: that of several connections between two machines. There can be several users on the client machine all connecting to the same port on the server, e.g., several people retrieving Web pages. The source port allows us to distinguish connections and hand the replies back to the correct client program. Source port numbers are generally chosen afresh for each connection from the pool of currently unused numbers: these are called *ephemeral* ports, as they only live for the lifetime of the connection. There is no difference technically between an ephemeral port and a well-known port, it's just that the latter has a conventional meaning assigned to it and the former doesn't.

The quad (source address, source port, destination address, destination port) identifies a connection uniquely. A pair (address, port) is sometimes called a *socket*, while a full quad is sometimes called a *socket pair*.

> More accurately, the protocol (TCP or UDP) plus socket pair combination defines a connection.
> Use a Unix command like
> `netstat -f inet` or
> `netstat --inet`
> according to the flavour of OS to see the current Internet connections on a machine. The reply uses the format `machine.port` or `machine:port` for

source, then destination. `Port` is either a port number, or a name like www or
domain (DNS) from `/etc/services`.

RFC 1812

Both UDP and TCP have ports fields in their headers. In fact both have these fields at
the very start of their headers, as this allows the port numbers to be included in the 'IP
header and 8 bytes of data' that an ICMP error message contains (p. 123). This is so
that the OS can identify which of the currently running programs sent the original packet
(from the source port) and can direct the ICMP message back to it.

9.3   The Transport Layer: UDP

The *User Datagram Protocol* (UDP) is the transport layer for an unreliable, connectionless
protocol. As usual, we use 'unreliable' in its technical sense of 'not guaranteed reliable'.
UDP is not much more than IP with ports.

9.3.1   UDP Header

The UDP header (Figure 9.2) is very short:

- Ports. First there are two 16 bit port numbers for the source and destination.

- Length. This 16 bit field contains the length of the UDP packet, including the
  header, which is always 8 bytes long. This field is not strictly necessary as this can
  be computed as the length of the IP packet (as given in the IP header) minus the
  length of the IP header, but repeating the information helps layer independence.

- Checksum. Next is a checksum of the UDP header, the data, and some of the fields
  from the IP header. Filling in this field is optional, but recommended, in IPv4. If
  you do not want to compute the checksum (presumably for extra speed), put 0 here.
  The checksum is mandatory in IPv6. Incorporating some IP header fields into the
  checksum breaks the principle of layering and unnecessarily intertwines UDP and
  IPv4. This means that, e.g., in the transition to IPv6 (Section 6.8), this checksum
  RFC 2460 computation has to be changed.

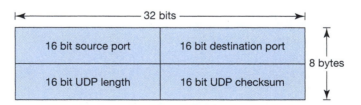

Figure 9.2 UDP header.

9.3.2 Comments

UDP is a thin layer on top of IP as we only add the minimum needed for a transport layer. It is as reliable or unreliable as the IP implementation it is based upon and just about as fast and efficient as IP, with only a small overhead.

UDP is widely used as it is good in two areas:

1. One shot applications, where we have a single request and reply. One example is the DNS.

2. When speed is more important than accuracy, such as audio or video streaming, where the occasional lost packet is not a problem, but a slow packet is.

No provision is made for lost or duplicated packets in this protocol. If an application uses UDP then it must deal with these issues itself, if necessary. For example, it can set a timer when it sends a request datagram. If the reply takes too long in coming, it assumes the datagram (either the request or the reply) was lost and resends a copy. This is how DNS over UDP works. Duplicated datagrams are not a problem to the DNS as the answer should be the same every time, but they might be a problem to other applications.

> In January 2003 a worm, variously called 'Slammer' and 'Sapphire', exploited a bug in Microsoft SQL Server. This was a tiny piece of code (376 bytes long) that simply tried sending a copy of itself to randomly selected IP addresses to infect any SQL server it happened to find. The sheer volume of traffic of the worm sending packets was enough to severely weigh down the Internet, causing widespread denial of service as real data couldn't squeeze through. As it used UDP it could simply 'send and forget', not having to wait to see if the packet was received successfully. It managed to reach 90% of vulnerable computers within 10 minutes, cumulatively doing more than 55 million scans per second after about 3 minutes. This earned it the title of a 'Warhol worm' as it could infect the entire Internet in 15 minutes.
>
> If TCP had been used the propagation would have been much slower due to the timeouts required in the initial handshake.

9.4 The Transport Layer: TCP

The *Transmission Control Protocol* (TCP) is the transport layer for a reliable, connection-oriented protocol. Often called *TCP/IP* to emphasize its layering on top of IP, it is hugely more complicated than UDP as it must create a reliable layer from an unreliable IP. Most of this complication is in the handling of error cases, though some is in the details to improve performance and flow control.

The basis of the reliability in TCP is the use of acknowledgements (ACKs) for every packet sent. So if A sends a packet to B, B must send a packet back to A to acknowledge the arrival of the packet. If A doesn't get an acknowledgement, then it resends the packet.

The use of acknowledgements raises the question of the *two army problem*. Two armies A and B wish to coordinate an attack on a third army C. So A sends a message to B, saying 'Attack at dawn'. How does A know that B got the message? A cannot safely attack until it is sure B got the message. So B sends an acknowledgement back to A. This may seem enough, but the acknowledgement may be intercepted, so A may not discover that its message got through and A cannot yet attack. B realizes this and cannot attack. To fix this, A must send a second acknowledgement to B, to say it received B's acknowledgement. But this might not get through, so B must send a third acknowledgement back to A. And so on to infinity.

To overcome the two army problem TCP uses packet retransmissions. A starts a *retransmission timer* when it sends the packet: if the timer runs out before the ACK is received, A resends. This repeats until A gets an ACK. We shall go into this protocol in detail later, but consider some of the problems to be solved:

- How long A should wait before a resend: this may be a slow but otherwise reliable link and resending too soon will just clog the system with extra packets.

- How many times to resend before giving up: it may be that the destination has gone away completely.

- How long B should wait before sending an ACK to A: you can piggyback an ACK on a normal data packet (see next section), so it may be better to wait until some data is ready to return rather than sending an empty ACK as this will reduce the total number of packets sent.

- IP packets can arrive out of order, so we need some way to recognize which ACK goes with which packet.

- How to maintain order in the data stream: again, IP packets can arrive out of order so we need some way of reassembling the data stream.

- How to manage duplicates: IP packets can be duplicated through resends, so we need some way to recognize and discard extra copies.

- Flow control: how to increase the rate of sending packets when things are going well and how to decrease the rate when things are getting overloaded.

Packets in a TCP connection are often called *segments*. As TCP needs to solve many complex problems a TCP segment header contains many fields (Figure 9.3).

9.4.1   Ports

The header starts with two 16 bit port numbers for the source and destination. This is identical to UDP (on purpose).

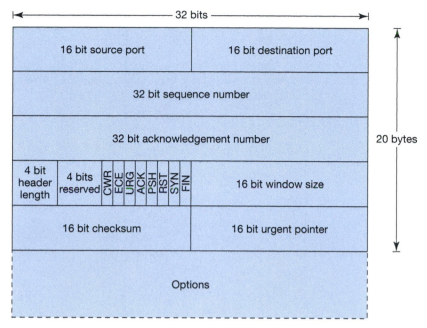

Figure 9.3 TCP header.

9.4.2 Sequence and Acknowledgement Numbers

These are at the heart of the reliability of TCP. Each byte in the data stream from source to destination is numbered. This 32 bit unsigned *sequence number* starts off at some random(ish) value at connection initialization, and increases by one for each byte sent, so if a segment contains 10 bytes of data, the next segment will have a sequence number 10 greater. The sequence number in the header is the number of the first byte in the segment's data.

The destination acknowledges those bytes it receives by setting the corresponding value in the ACK field. The acknowledgement field is only active if the ACK flag (see below) is set. The reverse connection from destination to source has its own sequence number, as TCP is full duplex. Also note that a host may not immediately get the whole segment that was sent due to IP fragmentation in which case it will have to reconstruct the TCP segment before it can ACK.

> TCP is full duplex at the IP layer: it may or may not be full duplex at the link layer.

If the sequence number is 10000 and 10 bytes are received, the ACK is the sequence number of the next byte the destination expects to receive, namely 10011. Note that you can use ACK in a normal data segment: this is called *piggybacking* the ACK, as the ACK

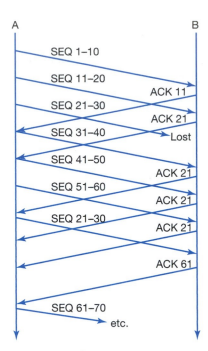

Figure 9.4 TCP acknowledgements.

gets a 'free' ride on top of the returning data segment. More importantly, this reduces the amount of network traffic as we do not always require a separate packet purely for the ACK.

In Figure 9.4 A is sending 10 byte segments to B at regular intervals and B is ACKing them. But the segment containing bytes 21–30 gets lost (perhaps a router could not cope with the load, or someone kicked a transmission cable). When B gets a segment with bytes 31–40 it ACKs again with value 21: it expected byte 21 next. While the ACK is traveling back to A, A is still sending. Each time, B ACKs with 21.

So eventually A receives *duplicate ACKs* for 21. If this happens, A can tell something is wrong. So A resends bytes 21–30. If B gets this segment then it is able to ACK all the way up to byte 60.

There is much more to be said on ACKs later.

The sequence number wraps round at $2^{32} - 1$: this can cause problems with very-high-bandwidth connections. For example, this would wrap in less than 10 seconds for a 10 gigabit Ethernet. It is easy to imagine a segment being delayed on the network for this order of time. Thus, when the straggler does turn up, it might be confused with other segments with similar sequence numbers. For such cases, it might be wise to use RFC 1323 protection against wrapped sequence numbers, or PAWS. This coopts the timestamp TCP option (Section 10.2) and uses it to distinguish segments with the same sequence number that were sent at different times.

9.4.3 Header Length

The header has a variable length as we can have options. This 4 bit field gives the header length in 32 bit words. Thus the header can be up to 60 bytes long. It is always at least 20 bytes.

9.4.4 Flags

This part of the header contains several 1 bit flags that perform a variety of functions. The four reserved bits should be set to 0. Note that the ECE and CWR flags were introduced relatively recently.

- URG. Urgent data. Section 9.4.7.
- ACK. The acknowledgement field is active. Section 9.4.2.
- PSH. Push this data to the application as quickly as possible.
- RST. Reset (break) the connection. Section 9.4.12.
- SYN. Synchronize a new connection. Section 9.4.10.
- FIN. Finish a connection. Section 9.4.11.
- ECE. ECN-Echo.
- CWR. Congestion window reduced.

The last two flags are part of the *Explicit Congestion Notification* (ECN) mechanism and are discussed in Section 10.6.3.

9.4.5 Window Size

Also called *advertised window size*, this is used for flow control. The destination has only a limited amount of buffer memory that it can store newly arrived segments in. If the application is not reading the segments as fast as they are arriving, eventually the buffer will be filled up. The *window size* is the number of bytes that the server is willing to accept, i.e., the amount of buffer it has left. It puts this number in the next segment that it sends to the client. If the window size is very small, the client can slow down sending until the window increases again. The 16 bit field gives us a window of up to 65535 bytes, but there is a header option to scale this to something larger.

Note that the advertised window size is the amount of space free when a returning segment is *sent*. More space may have been freed up when the client gets around to sending more data. Thus the value of window size that the client has is not a wholly accurate measurement and it gets more inaccurate as time passes. Nevertheless, it is safest to assume that the advertised window size is the largest amount of data that can be sent until we get a segment with a different window size. See Section 10.2 for more on windows.

9.4.6 Checksum

This is a checksum of the TCP header, the data, and some of the fields from the IP header. Just as for UDP, incorporating some IP fields into the checksum breaks the principle of layering and causes problems when changing the network layer. Moving to IPv6 is a case in point.

RFC 2460

9.4.7 Urgent Pointer

This is active if the URG flag is set. It is an offset into the TCP data stream indicating the end of the current urgent data block. Urgent data includes things like interrupts that need to be processed before any other data that is buffered (e.g., hitting Ctrl-C to interrupt a big file transfer). While the original intent was for URG to mean 'somewhere in the data up to this point there is something important', it has ended up meaning something more like 'read and act quickly on the data up to this point'.

> There is a feature/bug in TCP that, when the advertised window closes and no more data can be sent, there is no way for an URG to be transmitted. And when the remote machine stops responding like this is precisely the kind of situation when you would want to send an signal to interrupt the connection. For this reason, RFC 793 specifies that the receiver must process the URG field of a segment even when the window is 0 and the segment data is rejected.

RFC 793

9.4.8 Options

There are several of these, including the window scale option and *maximum segment size* (MSS). Some of these are discussed below.

9.4.9 Data

Finally, the data. This can be empty and is often so while setting up or tearing down a connection, or for an ACK when there are no data to be returned.

9.4.10 Connection Establishment Protocol

Setting up a connection is a complicated business. The connection state is to be initialized (e.g., sequence numbers) which will be used throughout the connection. TCP is a

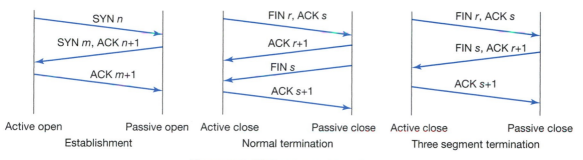

Figure 9.5 TCP setup and teardown.

connection-oriented protocol. UDP, on the other hand, is connectionless and *stateless*, as each segment is independent of all others.

At the other end, tearing down a connection is not trivial either, as we need to make sure that all segments in flight have been received and ACKed safely: you can't just drop a connection as the other end may still be awaiting ACKs and segments may need to be resent. Thus a connection will hang around for a little time after closing to ensure everything is tidied up nicely.

Three segments are used to create a new connection (see Figure 9.5):

1. The initiator (normally called the *client*) sends a SYN segment, i.e., a segment with the SYN flag set, containing the *initial sequence number* (ISN), n, say. This is some randomly generated integer.

2. The receiving host (the *server*) replies with another SYN segment containing its own ISN, m say. It also ACKs the client's segment, i.e., sends a segment with the SYN and ACK flags set and the ACK field set to $n + 1$. The SYN flag consumes one sequence number. Consider why this is: so we can ACK the SYN independently of the first data byte. These initial segments can be lost just as much as any other!

3. The client ACKs the server's SYN with $m + 1$.

In all three segments the data field is empty: these segments are overhead in setting up the connection. Once the connection is established we can start sending data.

This is called the *three way handshake*. The initiator is said to do an *active open*, while the server does a *passive open*. The ISN is a number that should change over time. RFC 793 suggests that it should be incremented every 4 microseconds. The reason to change the ISN is so that late-arriving segments from an earlier connection to the same machine and port cannot be confused with the current connection.

RFC 793

These days, it is better to choose random ISNs to avoid IP attacks which start with a malicious person guessing the ISN for someone else's connection and inserting their own segments into the connection.

RFC 1948

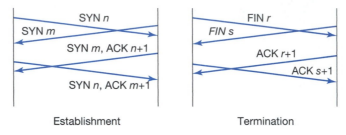

Establishment   Termination

Figure 9.6 TCP simultaneous open and close.

It is possible, but hard, to do a *simultaneous open* (Figure 9.6). This is when both ends send a SYN and the segments cross in flight. This is defined to result in one new connection, not two.

9.4.11 Connection Termination Protocol

Four segments are normally needed to take down a connection (see Figure 9.5). This is because a connection can be *half closed*. Since TCP is full duplex, we can close one direction of traffic independently of the other (Figure 9.7).

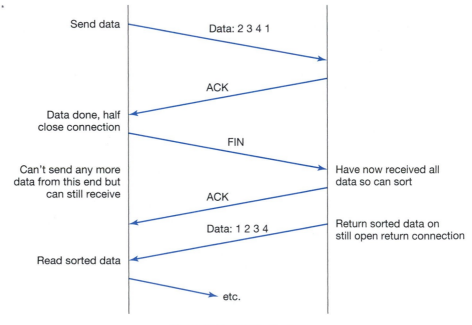

Figure 9.7 TCP half close.

The classic example of a reason for doing this is sending a sequence of integers to a server to be sorted: closing the client end of the connection is used to indicate the end of the sequence, while the reverse connection is kept open to receive the reply.

The FIN flag is set to indicate close. More precisely, a FIN indicates a half close and that no more data will be sent from this end of the connection. Data still can be received at this end. The FIN will be ACKed by the other end and a FIN consumes one sequence number. Later, when the other end is done, it will send a FIN and get an ACK back.

There are many variations on this. Either end can send the first FIN in an *active close* and then the other end will do a *passive close*. The FIN of the passive end can be piggybacked on the ACK of the active FIN, so that only three segments are used. The ends can do a *simultaneous close*, i.e., both send a FIN before receiving one: the protocol still works (Figure 9.6).

9.4.12 Resets

There is another way for connections to end: by a *reset* (RST) segment. This is normally for cases in error, e.g., a segment arrives that doesn't appear to be for a current connection. This can happen when a server crashes and reboots, but the client is still trying to send data. Recall that a connection is characterized by the quad (source IP address, source port, destination IP address, destination port). If a segment arrives from a client to a server that is not expecting it, the server returns an RST (i.e., an empty segment that has the RST flag set). When the client gets the RST it terminates the connection immediately. This is usually seen by the user as a 'connection reset by peer' error message.

Another example of RST is when a client attempts to make a TCP connection to a server port that has no process listening on it. An RST is returned to the client to indicate that a connection cannot be made. UDP, in contrast, would send an ICMP error packet in such an event.

A connection that terminates using FINs is said to have an *orderly release*, while one terminated by an RST is called an *abortive release*. An RST will discard all buffered segments for that connection and pass an error message up to the application layer.

RST segments are not ACKed: the connection stops right here.

And RSTs must always be processed, even if the advertised window is 0. RFC 793

9.4.13 TCP state machine

The transitions between states in TCP are complicated. There is a standard TCP state transition diagram (Figure 9.8) that indicates how a TCP connection must act, though note that this only covers the non-error conditions, and does not say what to do when, for example, getting an RST while ESTABLISHED, or receiving a SYNFIN segment. A typical timeline of a connection is shown in Figure 9.9. RFC 793

RFC 1337

You should spend some time working through examples of TCP connections on this diagram, following how you progress from state to state. You may wish to try: open,

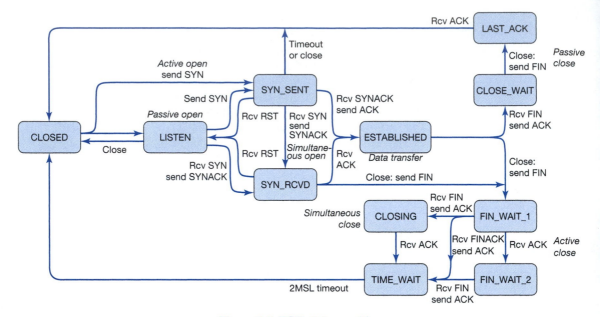

Figure 9.8 TCP state machine.

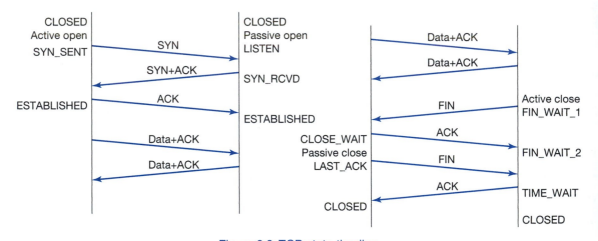

Figure 9.9 TCP state timeline.

orderly close, simultaneous open, simultaneous close, abortive close. You start (and end) in the CLOSED state. Note that this state diagram is applied for *each* TCP connection, i.e., for *each* socket pair.

There is one state in the active close that is worth spending some time on. This is the TIME_WAIT state, also called the 2MSL state. Each implementation must choose a value for the *maximum segment lifetime* (MSL). This is the longest time a segment can live in the network before being discarded. This time is bounded, as the TTL field in the IP header ensures segments will die at some point.

RFC 793 specifies an MSL of 2 minutes. You will find values of 30 seconds, 1 minute and 2 minutes being used in implementations. RFC 793

When TCP does an active close, it must stay in the TIME_WAIT state for twice the MSL. This is in case the final ACK was lost and gives the other end chance to time out and retransmit its final FIN. Any other segments that are received in this state are simply dropped. This means that the connection (i.e., the quad above) cannot be reused until 2MSL has elapsed. This is not a problem if the client does an active close, as it is likely using an ephemeral port, and any other port will do if we need to make a new connection within the 2MSL. On the other hand, if the server does the active close there is likely a problem. Since servers often listen on specific well-known ports, a server cannot restart until the 2MSL has passed.

There is a slight problem if a machine in the 2MSL state crashes, reboots, and starts a new connection with the same quad all within 2MSL. There is a chance that delayed segments from the old connection will be interpreted as part of the new connection. To remedy this, RFC 793 states that TCP should not create any new connections until MSL after rebooting: this is called the *quiet time*. Not many people implement this, as it usually takes more time than this to reboot, though many get close and high-availability machines can be back up very quickly. RFC 793

Another state of interest is FIN_WAIT_2, where we have sent a FIN and the other end has ACKed it, but not yet sent its FIN. If the remote machine crashes we can be stuck here waiting for ever. Many implementations set a timer on this state and if nothing is forthcoming for a decent period they violate the protocol and move to TIME_WAIT. Timeouts from 60 seconds to 10 minutes are common, with smaller values being preferred on heavily loaded servers.

9.4.14   TCP options

An option starts with a 1 byte *kind* that specifies what this option is to do (see Figure 9.10). Options of kinds 0 and 1 occupy 1 byte. All other options next have a length field that gives the total length of this option. This is so that an implementation can skip an option if it does not know the kind. RFC 793
RFC 1323

The No Operation (NOP) option is to pad fields out to a multiple of 4 bytes so that they are nicely aligned.

Maximum segment size (MSS) specifies how large a segment we can have without fragmentation. The bigger, the better, of course, as this reduces the overheads of headers. MSS occupies 2 bytes and so has a maximum value of 65535. This value is strongly affected by the interface MTU. For an Ethernet, whose physical layer allows 1500 bytes, the MSS can be as large as 1460 bytes when we take the 20 byte IP header and 20 byte

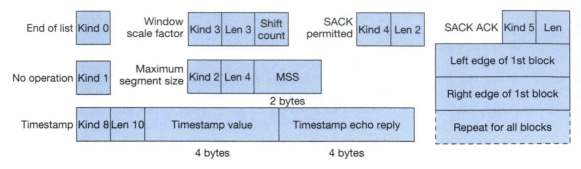

Figure 9.10 Some TCP options.

TCP header into account. For non-local networks, the MSS often defaults to the minimum of $576 - 40 = 536$ bytes.

Modern fast networks like an advertised window size larger than the 65535 that the standard header allows, so the *window scale* option gives the number of bits to scale the TCP window size, from 0 to 14. A value of n multiplies the size by 2^n. This gives up to $65535 \times 2^{14} = 1073725440$ bytes in a window. A gigabyte is a big buffer! Though for a 10Gb/s connection, that's about a second's worth of data.

Timestamp puts a time-of-day value in a segment, allowing us accurately to measure how long segments are taking to travel through the network. This is useful for computing retransmission times. See Sections 10.7 and 10.12.

Selective acknowledgement (SACK) *permitted* is a modern option that allows us to be more specific about which bytes we are ACKing in a segment. See Section 10.13.

Many options are only available in SYN segments, e.g., window scale, MSS and SACK permitted. This is because some things (like buffers) need to be prepared in advance of a new connection and varying them mid-connection makes little sense. For example, the turmoil that would be caused by deciding to start using SACK half way through would be more trouble than it is worth.

9.5   Exercises

Exercise 9.1 What are the differences between UDP and IP? Why?

Exercise 9.2 Investigate some common services that use UDP. How do they cope with the problems of lost or duplicate packets?

Exercise 9.3 Compare the effect of a lost packet in

   (a)   an audio stream
   (b)   a DNS request
   (c)   copying a payroll file.

Exercise 9.4 Find the port numbers for various services you commonly use (Web, ssh and the like). Some services (such as NFS, Section 12.6) do not have fixed port numbers. Discuss the pros and cons of this.

Exercise 9.5 TCP was actually developed before UDP. Read up on the history of the development of transport layer protocols in IP.

Exercise 9.6 Variants on UDP exist: read up on UDP-Lite from RFC 3828. What are its advantages and disadvantages?

Exercise 9.7 Use tcpdump to watch the packets sent in a connection that, for example, fetches a Web page. Make sure you understand connection setup and teardown and the use of sequence numbers and ACKs in the ESTABLISHED state.

Exercise 9.8 Work through the TCP state machine with several variants of connection open and close. Take the data from the previous exercise and follow through the state machine.

Exercise 9.9 Try to find a Web server for which the connection is unreliable (e.g., one a long way away or heavily loaded). Use tcpdump to see how packet loss is treated. (If all else fails, you can unplug the network cable for a couple of seconds.)

Exercise 9.10 Use tcpdump to inspect the optional headers used in a typical TCP connection. Distinguish between headers in SYN and non-SYN packets.

Exercise 9.11 Discuss how a *packet insertion attack* might be done in (a) UDP, (b) TCP. Which of the two is more secure against such attacks?

TCP STRATEGIES

10

10.1 Introduction

TCP gets its reliability by acknowledging every segment sent. Does this mean that there are two segments for every packet? It is possible to implement TCP like this, but you would get poor performance. Instead, TCP implementations use a variety of strategies to improve performance, but still sticking to the letter of the law of the TCP protocol.

10.2 Sliding Window

As data arrives at its destination it is put into a buffer, waiting for the relevant application to read it at its leisure. The TCP header in a returning segment contains the advertised window field that informs the sender of how much buffer space is free at the destination. This amount of free space depends on two things:

1. how fast the sender is sending data, and

2. how fast the destination application is consuming the data.

If the sender is producing data faster than the application reads it, the buffer space will soon be used up. The *advertised window* is the mechanism used to tell the producer to slow down. This is a form of *sliding window* protocol that operates as a *flow control*.

The idea of the sliding window is that it describes the range of bytes that the sender can transmit: the sender should never send more bytes than the window size. If the receiver is having problems keeping up, the window gets smaller and the sender will send fewer bytes. When space is freed up in the receiver, the window gets bigger and the sender can transmit more. The sliding window is a dynamic value that the sender recomputes every time it receives an ACK.

The sliding window has its left hand edge defined by the last ACK value and the right hand edge by the TCP window size field. The window size is filled in by the receiver

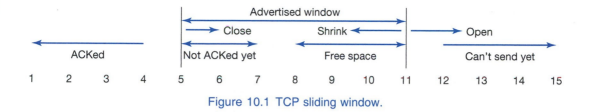

Figure 10.1 TCP sliding window.

on every ACK returned and it represents an upper bound on the range of bytes that the destination is willing to receive at that time. As more ACKs are returned, the window *closes* by the left edge advancing. As data is removed from the buffer by the application, the window *opens* by the right edge advancing. There is the fairly unusual possibility of the window *shrinking* (the right edge receding), perhaps when the amount of buffer space available to a TCP connection is reduced due to it being needed elsewhere.

In Figure 10.1 bytes to the left of the window (bytes 1–4) are ACKed and safe. Bytes to the right (12 and onward) cannot yet be sent. Bytes within the window range fall into two classes: not ACKed yet and free space. The unACKed bytes (5–7), usually a fairly small range, are those that have been read, but the ACK has not yet been sent. The free space (8–11) is the actual range of bytes that the receiver can buffer. The sender can compute this as the advertised window minus the number of unACKed bytes.

It is not uncommon for the window size to reduce to zero. If this happens the sender will have to wait before sending any more data. When the receiver is ready for more data it will send a duplicate ACK with the same ACK value but with a new different window size: this is a *window update* segment.

Complications arise here if window updates get lost: see the *persist timer* (Section 10.8).

All this computation of windows and flow control is done by the operating system. In fact, all the hideous details of TCP (and UDP) are dealt with by the kernel so the applications programmer need know nothing about what is going on.

10.3   Delayed Acknowledgements

Instead of immediately ACKing every segment, maybe we should wait a little until we return a data segment and piggyback the ACK on it. If no return data is forthcoming, we send a normal ACK.

For example, when using telnet to log in to a remote machine, each keystroke is echoed back to your screen by the remote machine (Figure 10.2). An immediate ACK would use four segments: data plus ACK for the keystroke, then data plus ACK for the echo. Delaying the first ACK just a little allows it to piggyback on the echo segment, reducing the traffic by one segment.

The total time taken for the exchange is the same, but fewer segments are used. Fewer segments means less traffic and this is good, particularly in the case of a heavily loaded network.

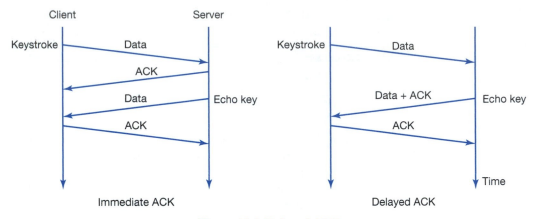

Figure 10.2 Delayed ACK.

An additional benefit is that we may be able to ACK more than one segment at a time. If we receive, say, three segments in the period when we are delaying our ACK, we may simply ACK the last segment: the ACK for the first two is implicit, since an ACK indicates which byte we are expecting *next*. This, again, reduces traffic.

The big question is: how long do we delay an ACK? If we delay too long, the sender might think the segment was lost and resend; if we delay too short, we do not get as many free piggybacks. In practice, a typical implementation will delay an ACK for up to 200 ms.

RFC 2581 The TCP standard says you must not delay an ACK for more than 500 ms.

This is one of many *timers* associated with TCP. Each time you receive a segment you (i.e., the TCP software) must set the timer for that segment that runs out after 200 ms. If the segment has not yet been ACKed, do so then. In fact, many implementations cheat and have just one global timer (rather than a timer for each segment received) that goes off every 200 ms and any outstanding segments are ACKed then. This means there is a maximum of 200 ms delay, but it could be much shorter. A single timer is much easier to implement, of course.

If you receive an out-of-sequence segment (the sequence number is not the one you are expecting next), e.g., when a segment gets lost, then you must not delay, but send an ACK immediately. This may mean resending an ACK you have sent already: a *duplicate ACK*. This is to inform the sender as quickly as possible that something has gone wrong.

10.4   Nagle's Algorithm

RFC 896 When sending individual keystrokes using TCP over a network there is a big waste of bandwidth going on. One keystroke is typically 1 byte. This is sent in a TCP segment with 20 bytes of header, which is sent in an IP datagram with 20 more bytes of header. Thus we are sending a 41 byte packet for each byte of data: such a small segment is sometimes called a *tinygram*. On a LAN this is not too bad as LANs generally have plenty of bandwidth, but on a WAN this proliferation of tinygrams causes additional congestion.

John Nagle invented an acknowledgement strategy that reduces this effect. This applies to the sending side (the client) rather than the receiving side (the server). This is *Nagle's algorithm*:

> A TCP connection can have only *one* unacknowledged small segment outstanding. No additional small segments should be sent until that acknowledgement has been received.

Any small waiting segments are collected together into a single larger segment that is sent when the ACK is received. This segment can also be sent if you buffer enough tinygrams to fill a segment, or have exceeded half the destination's window size.

This leaves open the definition of 'small' and there are variants that choose anything from '1 byte' to 'any segment shorter than the maximum segment size'. The latter is more appropriate when combined with other strategies (see 'silly window syndrome', Section 10.5).

This is a very simple strategy to apply and reduces the number of tinygrams without introducing extra perceived delay (over the delay that results from a slow WAN). The faster the ACKs come back, the more tinygrams can be sent. When there is congestion, so ACKs come back more slowly, fewer tinygrams are sent. When a network is heavily loaded, Nagle's algorithm can reduce the number of segments considerably.

> Note that it is to the client's advantage to hold back and not flood the system with tinygrams, as this reduces overall congestion and improves the client's own throughput.
> Use `setsockopt` with `TCP_NODELAY` to disable Nagle on a socket.

Sometimes it is better to turn off Nagle's algorithm. The usual example of this is using a graphical interface over a network. Each mouse movement translates to a tinygram. It would not be good to buffer these up, as that would cause the cursor to jump erratically about the screen. Such applications can call a function to disable Nagle for this connection.

10.5   Silly Window Syndrome

Another problem that can cause bad TCP performance is *silly window syndrome*. Recall that segments advertise a window: that is, they say how much space there is available to buffer incoming segments. This is intended to slow down a sender if the recipient can't keep up with the data flow.

Consider what can happen if the sender (A) is sending large segments (Figure 10.3), but the receiver (B) is reading the data slowly 1 byte at a time:

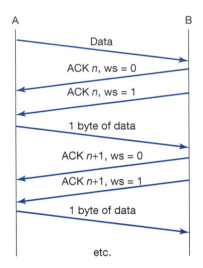

Figure 10.3 Silly window syndrome.

- B's buffer fills up and B sends a segment (probably the ACK of A's last segment) saying 'window size 0'.

- B reads a byte.

- B send a window update segment: 'window size 1'.

- A gets this and sends a segment containing 1 byte.

- B ACKs, with 'window size 0'.

- B reads a byte.

- Repeat.

We are back to the two segment, high overhead per byte scenario. This is the silly window syndrome, where the advertised window is not helping throughput. It would be better for B to wait until a decent sized window is available before it sends a window update. Clark's algorithm to avoid SWS is never to send window updates for 1 byte. Instead, only advertise a new window when either enough buffer space is available to accommodate a maximum segment size, or the buffer is half empty, whichever is smaller.

RFC 813

This also answers the question of 'small' in Nagle's algorithm. If 'small' means 'less than the maximum segment size', Nagle and Clark fit together naturally.

10.6   Congestion Control

Congestion happens when more traffic is sent to the network than it can handle. There are several strategies that deal with congestion in TCP connections.

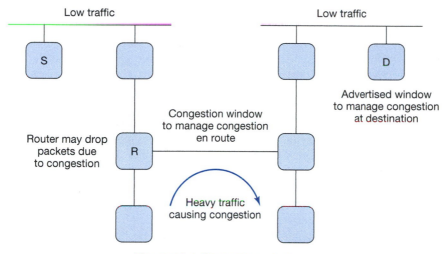

Figure 10.4 Congestion windows.

One point arises: how can we spot that congestion is happening, given that it may be in a part of the network many hops away from us? The trick is to watch for segment loss. Segments can be lost through poor transmission, or through being dropped at a congested router or destination. In these days of high-quality fibre optic transmission the former almost never happens, so it is safe to assume that all segment loss is due to congestion. So TCP implementations watch for segment loss (missing ACKs) and treat this as an indication of congestion.

Congestion can happen in two places, see Figure 10.4: firstly in a router somewhere on the path to the destination due to lack of capacity in the onward link; secondly in the destination itself if the destination is just too slow to receive data at the full rate the network can deliver.

The TCP advertised window size is there to deal with congestion at the destination. The path congestion needs to be addressed in a different way.

10.6.1   Slow Start and Congestion Avoidance

If we have a lot of data to send we do not want to wait for an ACK before we send each segment. Instead, we can use the network's bandwidth much better if we send off several segments before stopping to wait for ACKs to see if the segments were successfully received. We want to avoid too much waiting as this is wasted time when we could potentially be sending more segments. However, sending *too* many segments at a time is just as bad if the network is congested and cannot cope with that many segments. We need a way to estimate the capacity of the network in order to send as many segments as we can, but not too many. If we get it right, we can have a continual stream of data segments being sent out while a continual stream of ACKs are coming back.

RFC 2581 The *slow start* algorithm tries to estimate the path congestion by measuring the number of ACKs that come back.

Slow start adds a new window, the *congestion window*, which is an estimate of the capacity of the path. This will be an additional constraint on the amount of data to transmit: the sender can send data up to the minimum of the advertised window size and the congestion window size.

The congestion window size is initialized to the maximum segment size of the destination. Also, a variable, the *threshold*, is initialized to 64KB. Every time a timely ACK is received, the congestion window is increased by one segment. So at first the sender can send only one segment; then two at a time; then four at a time; and so on.

The technique is called 'slow start' (Figure 10.5), but actually this is an exponential increase in the congestion window over time. It is 'slow' in comparison to earlier versions of TCP that started off by blasting off as many packets as they could even before the performance of the connection was known.

This doubling only repeats until we reach the current threshold. When the congestion window reaches the threshold, the slow start algorithm stops and the *congestion avoidance* algorithm takes over. Rather than an exponential increase, congestion avoidance uses a linear increase of 1/(congestion window size) each time (Figure 10.6).

Eventually the network's limit will be reached and a congested router somewhere will start discarding segments that it cannot forward. The sender will realize this when ACKs stop coming. At this point, the threshold is halved and the current window is dropped back to one segment size again.

Slow start takes over until the new threshold is reached, then congestion avoidance starts, and so on. The sender eventually converges on a rate that is neither too fast, nor

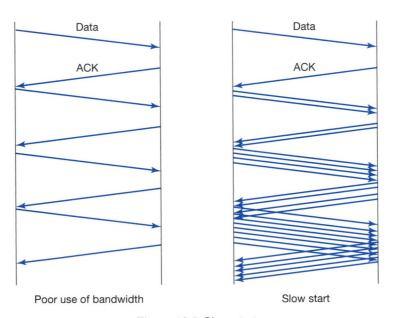

Figure 10.5 Slow start.

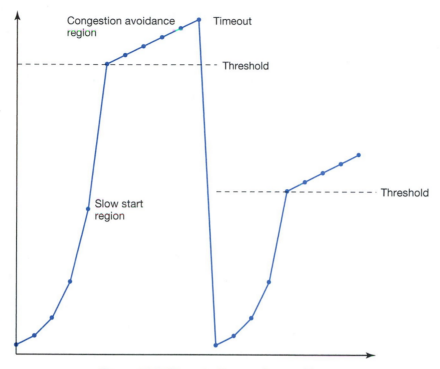

Figure 10.6 Slow start/congestion avoidance.

too slow. If conditions on the network change, it soon adapts to the new best rate, be it faster or slower.

If no congestion occurs, the congestion window grows until it reaches the advertised window size: in this case the receiver is the limiting factor, not the network.

> Other congestion strategies have been proposed. For example, proponents of 'Fast TCP' note that halving the threshold on a packet loss seems far too severe and instead reduce the window by an amount based on the RTT.
>
> One thing to consider is the effect on other users of using another strategy. You may be able to boost your own throughput, but this might well be at the expense of other users.

10.6.2   Fast Retransmit and Fast Recovery

When an out-of-order TCP segment is received, the TCP calls for an immediate ACK: it must not be delayed. This is to inform the sender as soon as possible which segment sequence number was expected. We saw above how duplicate ACKs arise from a lost segment.

Jacobson's *fast retransmit* takes the idea that several duplicate ACKs are indeed symptomatic of a lost segment. The argument is that one or two duplicated ACKs might just

RFC 2581

be due to out-of-order delivery of segments. But three or more and something is badly wrong. If this happens, retransmit the indicated segment immediately, without waiting for the usual timeout.

Next, perform congestion avoidance and do not go into slow start. This is the *fast recovery* algorithm. We do not want slow start, as a duplicate ACK indicates that later data has actually reached the destination and is buffered by the destination. So data is still flowing and we do not want to abruptly reduce the flow by going into slow start.

10.6.3   Explicit Congestion Notification

RFC 3168 Another mechanism for congestion avoidance is *Explicit Congestion Notification* (ECN). This gives routers the ability to put a mark on packets as they go past that indicates that that route is becoming congested. This can be used to give prior notification to the hosts to slow down before packets start getting dropped.

ECN uses bits 6 and 7 in the type of service (TOS) field in the IPv4 header (Section 6.2.3). These are bits that previously were unused and were set to 0. Bit 6, the *ECN-capable transport* (ECT) bit, indicates that the hosts are aware of the ECN mechanism. This is to provide backward compatibility with hosts that do not understand ECN, as those hosts should already be setting bit 6 to 0. Bit 7, the *congestion experienced* (CE) bit, is set when a router is congested and the endpoints are ECN aware.

IPv6 has corresponding bits in its traffic class field (Section 6.8).

On receipt of a CE packet, a host is recommended to act as if a single packet had been dropped. For example, with TCP, this would trigger congestion avoidance and halve the congestion window. Two bits of the TCP header are used to support ECN (Section 9.4.4): bit 8 in the flags field is *ECN-Echo* (ECE) and bit 9 is *congestion window reduced* (CWR). Further, TCP option headers are used in the SYN handshake to negotiate whether both ends are ECN aware.

RFC 3168 The details of ECN over TCP are fairly complicated and are covered in RFC3168, but in essence:

1. A client sends a packet (with ECT set in the IP header).

2. A router that has congestion imminent sets the CE bit in the IP header.

3. The server receives the packet, notes the CE bit, and sets the ECE bit in the TCP header of the ACK packet.

4. The client reads this and acts as if a single packet has been dropped.

5. The client sets the CWR bit in the TCP header of the next packet it sends to the server to acknowledge it has received the congestion notification.

Unfortunately, in the early deployment of ECN some ECN-unaware routers treated packets with TOS bit 6 set as corrupted and dropped them. This meant that ECN-capable hosts sometimes could not reach hosts beyond ECN-unaware routers. Until all routers en route are at least *aware* of ECN (even if they do nothing about it) the only practical recourse is to turn off ECN for that destination.

A technique called *Random Early Detection* (RED, aka *Random Early Drop*) can be used in routers to gauge when congestion is about to happen. This monitors the queues of packets that are waiting to be relayed onwards and notifies congestion when the average queue length exceeds a threshold. Previously, the only way to notify congestion was to drop the packet, but now ECN is available.

RFC 2309

Performance measurements show ECN to be good, as early notification of congestion allows IP to slow down before segments are dropped and has the added benefit of fewer retransmits consuming the already limited network bandwidth. Theoretically, a fully ECN-enabled Internet would have no packet loss due to congestion.

RFC 2884

10.7   Retransmission Timer

We now look at the timer that determines when to resend a segment in the absence of an ACK. Too short a time is bad since we might just be on a slow connection. But we do want as short a time as is reasonable so that our data gets though as fast as possible.

What would be better than a fixed timeout would be to have a dynamic timeout interval that adjusts itself to the current network conditions: if the network slows down (e.g., extra traffic somewhere en route), the timeout should increase. If the network speeds up (e.g., a quiet period), the timeout should decrease.

Jacobson gave an easy to implement algorithm that does this for us. For each connection TCP keeps a variable, RTT, that is the best current estimate for the expected *round-trip time* of a segment going out and its ACK getting back.

RFC 1122

When a segment is sent, the timer is started. If the ACK returns before the timeout, TCP looks at the actual round-trip time M and updates RTT:

$$RTT = \alpha RTT + (1 - \alpha)M$$

where α is a smoothing factor, typically set to $7/8$. Thus RTT is an estimate that smoothly increases and decreases as conditions change and doesn't get unduly upset by the occasional straggler that is excessively slow (or fast).

Next, we need to determine a timeout interval given RTT. Jacobson suggested taking the standard deviation into account: if the measured RTTs have a large deviation it makes sense to have a larger timeout. The standard deviation is hard to compute quickly (square roots), so instead Jacobson used the *mean deviation*

$$D = \beta D + (1 - \beta)|RTT - M|$$

D is close to the standard deviation and is much easier to calculate. A typical value for β is $3/4$.

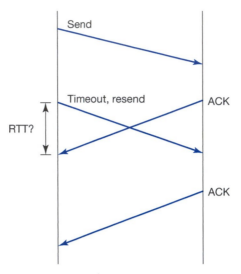

Figure 10.7 Retransmission ambiguity.

The timeout interval is set to

$$T = RTT + 4D$$

The 4 was found to be good in practice. When sending a segment we set the retransmission timer to expire after a time T.

So what should we do if the segment is sent and the timeout is triggered? Firstly, of course, we resend the segment. But we also need to increase RTT somehow. Simply using the RTT of the resent segment is not a good idea, as we might get the ACK of the original segment (the *retransmission ambiguity problem*, Figure 10.7). In this case the value would be severely undersized and we wouldn't want to update the RTT using it.

Karn's algorithm is to double the timeout T on each failure, but not to adjust RTT. When segments start getting though, the normal RTT updates resume and the RTT value quickly reaches the appropriate value. The doubling is called *exponential backoff*.

10.8   Persist Timer

RFC 793
RFC 1122

TCP needs several timers. The most obvious is the retransmit timer. Another is the 2MSL timer. There is also the *persist timer* (aka *persistence timer*). Its role is to prevent a deadlock through lost window update packets (Figure 10.8):

1. A sends to B.

2. B replies with an ACK and a window size of 0.

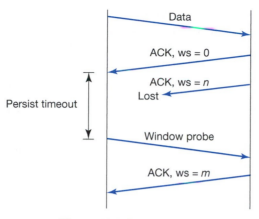

Figure 10.8 Persist timer.

3. A gets the ACK and holds off sending to B.

4. B frees up some buffer space and sends a window update to A.

5. This gets lost.

At this point A is waiting for the window update from B and B is waiting for more data from A. This is deadlock.

To fix this, A starts a persist timer when it gets a window size 0 message. If the timer goes off, A prods B by sending a 1 byte segment. The ACK of this *zero window probe* will contain B's current window size. If this is still 0, the persist timer is reset and the process repeats. If B's buffer was still full, the ACK will indicate that the data byte will have to be resent.

The persist timeout starts at something like 1.5 seconds, doubling with each probe, and is rounded up or down to lie within 5 to 60 seconds. So the actual timeouts are 5, 5, 6, 12, 24, 48, 60, 60, 60, ... The persist timer never gives up, sending window probes until either the window opens, or the connection is terminated.

The persist timer is unset when a non-zero window size is received.

10.9   Keepalive Timer

Yet another timer in TCP is the *keepalive timer*. This one is not required and some RFC 1122 implementations do not have it since some people regard its use as controversial.

When a TCP connection is idle no data flows between source and destination. This means that some part of the path could break and be restored without the connection being any the wiser. This is often a good thing. On the other hand, sometimes the server wants to know whether the client is still alive: maybe the connection uses some resources in the server that could be better used elsewhere. If the client has crashed, the server can reallocate the resources.

To do this the server sets the keepalive timer when the connection goes idle. This typically is set to time out after 2 hours. When the timer goes off, a *keepalive probe* is sent. This is simply an empty segment. If an ACK is received, all is well. If not, then the server may well assume that the client is no longer listening.

We can be in one of four states:

1. The client is up and running: the keepalive probe is ACKed and everybody is happy. The keepalive timer is reset to 2 hours.

2. The client machine has crashed or is otherwise not responding to TCP: the server gets no ACK and resends after 75 seconds. After 10 probes, 75 seconds apart, if there is no response the server terminates the connection with 'connection timed out'.

3. The client machine has crashed and rebooted: the client will get the probe and respond with an RST. The server gets the RST and terminates the connection with 'connection reset by peer'.

4. The client is up and running, but not reachable (e.g., a router is broken): this is indistinguishable from scenario 2 as far as the server is concerned, so the same sequence of events ensues. It may be that an ICMP 'no route to host' is returned by an intermediate router in which case this information can be passed up to the application rather than 'connection timed out'.

If a machine is shut down normally (rather than crashing), normal closedown of processes will cause TCP to send FINs for any open connections. These allow the server to close the connections.

There are a few reasons not to use keepalive:

1. It can cause a good connection to be dropped because of an intermittent failure on a router.

2. It uses bandwidth.

3. Some network operators charge per packet.

Reasons 2 and 3 are not particularly good arguments as keepalive is just a couple of segments every 2 hours. It is usually possible to disable the keepalive feature in applications: indeed some people think keepalive should not be in the TCP layer, but should be handled by the application layer.

10.10   Path MTU Discovery

RFC 1191
RFC 1981   The *path MTU* (Maximum Transmission Unit) is the size of the largest packet that can be sent from source to destination without being fragmented somewhere along the way.

Strictly defined, it is the smallest MTU of *any* path that connects the source to destination, as a packet could conceivably use one of several paths.

Sending packets with sizes not larger than the path MTU means that they will not be fragmented: this is generally good as the costs of fragmentation are quite high. It is possible to think of a scenario where using the path MTU is slower than using a larger MTU (say, a packet traversing several networks with large MTUs followed by one with a small MTU, where the advantage of using a large MTU on the initial networks outweighs the cost of fragmentation at the final network), but this is rare.

Path MTU discovery tries to find the path MTU by adjusting the sizes of the packets it sends. When a connection starts, it uses an MSS which is the smaller of the MTU of the interface and the MSS announced by the other end. If the other end does not specify an MSS, it uses the value 536. With this value IP can be sure that segments will not be fragmented because of the inability of the source or destination to cope.

Next, all subsequent IP datagrams are sent with the DF (Don't Fragment) flag set. If fragmentation is needed en route, the segment is dropped and an ICMP 'fragmentation needed but DF set' is returned. The source can then reduce the MSS and try again. This emulates the IPv6 approach to fragmentation.

Modern versions of ICMP return the *next hop MTU* in the ICMP error message and the source can use this. Older implementations do not and the source just picks a suitable smaller value from a table of MTUs:

65535	Hyperchannel, maximum MTU	RFC 1044, RFC 791
32000	Just in case	
17914	16Mb/s Token Ring	
8166	Token Passing Bus 802.4	RFC 1042
4464	4Mb/s Token Ring (maximum MTU)	
4352	FDDI	RFC 1188
2048	Wideband network	RFC 907
2002	4Mb/s Token Ring (recommended MTU)	
1500	Ethernet	RFC 894
1492	IEEE 802.3	RFC 1042
1006	SLIP	RFC 1055
576	X.25	RFC 877
512	NETBIOS	RFC 1088
296	Point-to-point (low delay)	RFC 1144
68	Minimum MTU	RFC 791

If such an ICMP error occurs with a TCP connection, its congestion window should remain unchanged, but a slow start should begin.

You should try larger MTUs once in a while since routes can change dynamically. The recommended time is 10 minutes, but you will see intervals of 30 seconds being used. RFC 1191

Some poorly configured routers are set never to return ICMP messages, allegedly for 'security'. Such routers do not respond to pings. Also, these routers fail to operate with path MTU discovery if they have a small MTU: your packets are dropped and you never RFC 1435 RFC 2923 get an ICMP error. Turning off the DF will allow the packet to be fragmented and get through the router. Thus, sometimes you can get a working TCP connection only if you turn off path MTU discovery! Clearly, this is a poor state of affairs, even worse than the ECN problem (Section 10.6.3), since systems administrators should know better.

10.11   Long Fat Pipes

WANs have quite different problems to LANs. Instead of bandwidth being the major limiting factor, the difficulty lies with the speed of light: the actual time the bits take to travel to the destination now dominates.

The *bandwidth–delay product* is a measure of the capacity of a network:

$$\text{capacity in bits} = \text{bandwidth in bits/s} \times \text{round-trip time in seconds}$$

The 'Fat Pipe' which at one point connected JANET in the UK to the USA contained ATM links running at 155Mb/s. The RTT was approximately 140 ms (as measured by `ping` at the time). This gives a bandwidth–delay product of roughly 22Mb (2.8MB). This is the total number of bytes that can be in flight within the Fat Pipe. An Ethernet, running at a fairly good 5Mb/s and with a reasonable 500 μs RTT, has a capacity of 312 bytes. A gigabit network running over a satellite link (delay 0.5 s each way) has a capacity of 125MB.

A network with a large bandwidth–delay product is called a *long fat network* (LFN, or 'elephant') and a TCP connection over an LFN is a *long fat pipe*.

Long fat pipes have some problems:

1. To be used efficiently, there must be a huge advertised window, much bigger than the 65535 limit that standard TCP gives us. The *window scale* option exists to fix this. This is because we can't afford to wait for ACKs with such a large RTT.

2. Packet loss in an LFN is disastrous. If a packet is lost the subsequent reduction in congestion window size in the slow start/congestion avoidance algorithms hits us badly.

3. The TCP sequence number counts bytes using a 32 bit value. This wraps around after 4 GB and in a 10 gigabit network we can easily transmit this in less than 10 seconds. It is possible that a segment could be lost for this amount of time and reappear to clash with a later segment with the same sequence number. The *protection against wrapped sequence numbers*, or PAWS option, coopts the time-stamp TCP option (Section 10.12) and uses it to distinguish segments with the same sequence number that were sent at different times.

RFC 1323

The biggest problem is *latency*, or the time a packet takes to get to the destination. If we want to send a megabyte across the Atlantic this will take about 76 ms on a 155Mb/s link. The first bit arrives after about 70 ms and the last 6 ms later. If we could increase the bandwidth of the Fat Pipe ten-fold to 1550Mb/s, the first bit would *still* arrive after 70 ms (it's the speed of light!) and the last just 0.6 ms later, for a total of 70.6 ms. The ten-fold increase has reduced the latency by just 7%.

Clearly, with such a fast wide network we are latency limited, not bandwidth limited. The problem is much worse with a satellite link with a delay of 0.5 s.

10.12   Timestamps

The TCP header can contain an optional *timestamp*. This is a 32 bit value, not necessarily a time, that should be echoed unchanged back to the sender in the ACK. The timestamp option is negotiated during the SYN handshake: if both ends include a timestamp option in their SYN segments then timestamps can be used for this connection (Figure 10.9).

RFC 1323

This is a mechanism for the sender to make accurate RTT measurements and therefore better estimates for the retransmission timeout. The timestamp value is simply a value that gets incremented once in a while and the period should usually be between 1 ms and 1 s. A typical value is 500 ms. The sender notes its system time when a timestamped segment is sent and thus can compute the RTT when the timestamp returns.

RFC 1323

However, the destination may choose to ACK more than one segment in a single reply: which segment's timestamp should it put in the reply? The timestamp used is the one for the next expected segment. So if the destination receives two segments and sends one ACK, it uses the timestamp of the first segment. This is so the source can compute RTTs including the ACK delay. If a segment arrives out of sequence, the destination will still use the timestamp for the expected segment when it finally arrives.

PAWS also uses the timestamp option, as noted above.

RFC 1323

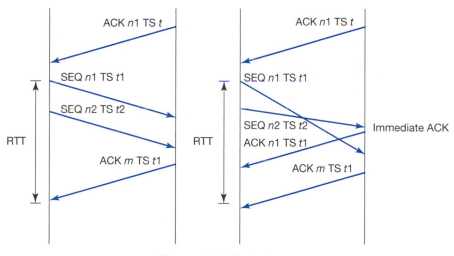

Figure 10.9 Timestamps.

10.13 SACK

Selective Acknowledgement (SACK) is an optional mechanism for finer control of acknowledgements than simple ACKs provide. It extends the single value in the ACK by a list of blocks of bytes that have been safely received. Suppose, for example, that a client is sending segments to a server, Figure 10.10, but a couple of segments are lost.

At point A, the server gets an unexpected sequence number, so it sends an immediate duplicate ACK. The client eventually gets the duplicate ACK (after sending more data) at B, resends the segment and slows down. (The client should also go into Jacobson's fast retransmit and recovery at C, the third duplicate ACK.)

The data arrives safely at D and gets ACKed. Note that the server can ACK up to byte 41 as it has the data that the client continued sending after the initial lost segment. However, the single ACK value cannot notify the client that the server also has bytes 51–60 and that the client didn't need to resend that segment at E.

This is where SACK comes in. The ACK field plays its normal role, but the server is able to use SACK to tell the client the additional information of which extra segments it has received at F. So, at G, the client knows that segment 51–60 is safe and so can immediately continue sending with segment 61–70.

The result is fewer segments resent unnecessarily and faster recovery.

As with timestamps, whether to use SACK is agreed during the SYN handshake using the SACK Permitted option in the TCP header.

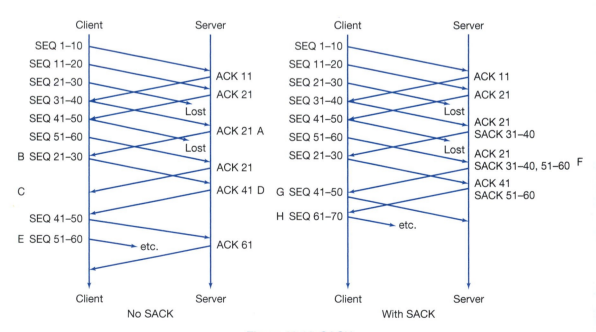

Figure 10.10 SACK.

10.14   Theoretical Throughput

Standard Ethernet is rated at 10Mb/s. When the physical, IP and TCP headers are taken into account and the minimum interpacket gap and ACK packets, and so on, the theoretical maximum throughput of a TCP connection on 10Mb Ethernet can be calculated as 1183667 bytes/s. Implementations have measured 1075000 bytes/s, which is pretty close. Faster networks are correspondingly better, but the final limitations are:

1. the speed of light;

2. the TCP window size.

The latter can be tweaked, but not the former! If you have a network running significantly slower than this, the problem is in the hardware or the software implementation, not TCP!

TCP has been a major success. From 1200 bits/s telephone lines to gigabit and beyond, it has turned out to be massively flexible and scalable – not without a lot of work from a lot of people, though!

RFC 2525

10.15   Alternatives to TCP

There have been several experimental approaches to improving on TCP. While there is still scope for tuning TCP itself (such as alternatives to slow start), some people have looked at changing the basic protocol.

10.15.1   TCP for Transactions

One approach is *TCP for Transactions* (T/TCP). This tries to combine the efficiency of UDP (fewer packets sent) with the reliability of TCP. It is designed for use in *transactions*, specifically:

RFC 1379
RFC 1644

1. Asymmetric. The two endpoints take different roles; this is a typical client–server role where the client requests the data and the server responds.

2. Short duration. Normally, a transaction runs for a short time span.

3. Few data packets. Each transaction is a request for a small piece of information, rather than a large transfer of information both ways.

T/TCP is an extension of TCP, using the standard TCP header, but with some new options to indicate T/TCP (Figure 10.11). The trick is to put the request data in the SYN segment sent to the server and get back the response in the SYN plus ACK of SYN in the reply to the client. Then one last ACK of the reply. This transaction takes three segments in the

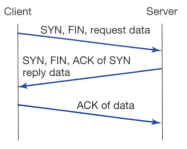

Client   Server

SYN, FIN, request data

SYN, FIN, ACK of SYN
reply data

ACK of data

Figure 10.11 T/TCP.

no-error case, only one more than UDP. A normal TCP connection takes three segments to establish; three for request, reply plus ACK of request, and ACK of reply; then up to four for closedown.

In case of lost segments, the normal TCP timeouts and resends apply.

If the server does not understand T/TCP, the client drops back to the normal TCP handshake and resends the request in a normal TCP connection. T/TCP would be of great benefit to HTTP (the protocol used to fetch Web pages, Section 12.8) but has not been widely adopted because of worries about problems with the protocol. For example, the client is sending data into an unknown, possibly zero, sized window.

10.15.2   Stream Control Transmission Protocol

RFC 2960
RFC 3257
RFC 3286

Another alternative to TCP is the *Stream Control Transmission Protocol* (SCTP).   This protocol has several features that make it well adapted for streamed data, in particular telephony. It is a protocol designed using the experience of TCP and it aims to keep the good parts of TCP whilst fixing the not-so-good parts.

SCTP, like TCP, is connection oriented and reliable. Unlike TCP:

- SCTP can deliver multiple message streams within a single connection. This allows for better utilization of the bandwidth between a pair of hosts.

- SCTP allows for transparent *multi-homing*, where either or both ends of a connection are multi-homed, i.e., has more than one network interface. If one endpoint fails, SCTP can automatically switch from one endpoint to another, so providing fault tolerance.

- SCTP preserves message boundaries. A TCP connection is just a stream of bytes and there is no way (within TCP) to tell the end of one message from the start of the next. Sometimes this is convenient, but not always. SCTP messages are always distinguishable within a stream. SCTP is *message oriented*, rather than *byte oriented*.

- SCTP can provide unordered reliable delivery. If ordered delivery is not required, SCTP doesn't force it on you. This may be reflected in improved data rates. For example, when loading a Web page with several images, it doesn't matter in what order the pictures arrive.

On the other hand, SCTP is unicast only and operates between exactly two endpoints (which may be multi-homed, of course).

When serving, say, Web pages over an SCTP connection, the multiple objects on a page (text, pictures and so on) can all be streamed over the same connection. Thus they share the same flow and congestion control mechanisms, which reduces the work required at the transport level.

SCTP separates the ideas of data transmission and data delivery. Each data packet in SCTP has *two* sequence numbers:

1. The *Transmission Sequence Number* (TSN) governs the transmission of messages and detects message loss.

2. The *Stream Sequence Number* (SSN) is used to determine the sequence of delivery of received data.

If a packet is lost there will be a gap in the TSN. One of the streams in the connection will also have a corresponding gap in its SSN. Only one stream has to wait for the retransmission of the packet; the other streams can carry on unaffected. This again improves throughput.

The structure of SCTP is centred around the idea of a *chunk*. A packet contains one or more chunks. User data is one kind of chunk and control is effected by means of other types of chunks. A simple header (Figure 10.12) common to all packets contains just:

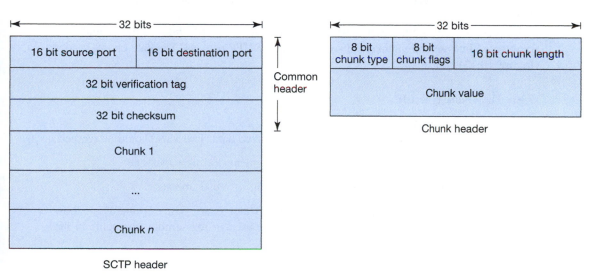

Figure 10.12 SCTP headers.

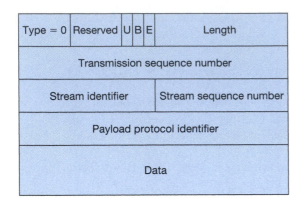
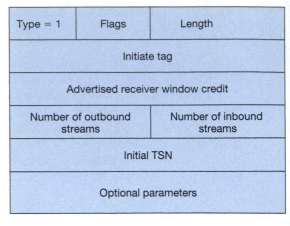

Data chunk   INIT chunk

Figure 10.13 SCTP chunks.

- source and destination port numbers;

- a verification tag which marks a current connection and guards against stale packets from old connections (and against blind packet insertion attacks); and

- a checksum.

The common header is followed by a sequence of chunks. Some chunks deal with connection setup, others with connection teardown; still more deal with flow control, SACK, and so on. Chunk headers all include a type field, a flag field and a chunk length field (Figure 10.12).

Data chunks contain the user message. If a message cannot fit into a single chunk it is fragmented into several chunks and sent in several SCTP packets. The data chunk header (Figure 10.13) contains:

- The chunk type (0).

- Three 1 bit flags:
    - U: unordered. Set to indicate this is unordered data. The SSN should be ignored.

    - B: beginning. Set to indicate the first fragment of a user message.

    - E: ending. Set to indicate the last fragment of a user message.

    An unfragmented message will have both B and E set. Thus B and E are how we can tell message boundaries. The TSN is used to reassemble fragments in the correct order.

- The chunk length.

- The TSN.

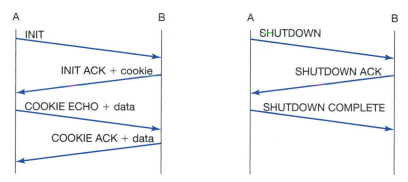

Figure 10.14 SCTP setup and teardown.

- The *Stream ID* (SID) identifies the stream to which the data belongs.

- The SSN. All fragments of a single message have the same SSN.

- A *Payload Protocol Identifier* (PPI), not used by SCTP but passed on to a higher layer for its benefit.

- The data itself.

Connection setup between hosts A and B is a four way handshake using INIT chunks (Figure 10.14):

1. A sends an INIT chunk (type 1). This contains a verification tag value in the initiate tag field and an initial TSN. The window credit field plays the role of TCP's window size. A packet containing an INIT chunk cannot contain any other chunks.

2. B replies with a INIT ACK (type 2) chunk. This has structure identical to an INIT chunk. B replies with its own verification tag value, window credit and initial TSN. Also, B must provide a cookie value as an extra parameter, described below. A packet containing an INIT ACK chunk cannot contain any other chunks.

3. A returns a COOKIE ECHO (type 10) chunk to B containing a copy of the cookie. A may also include data chunks in this packet, too.

4. B returns a COOKIE ACK (type 11) chunk to A, ending the handshake. Furthermore, B may also include data chunks (and SACK chunks) in this packet.

Now the connection is established, A and B may exchange (further) data chunks.

The cookie is an arbitrarily sized value that encodes enough information for B to recognize the returning COOKIE ECHO chunk as a reply to a valid INIT ACK that it had sent previously. Up to this point B need not (in fact, *must not*) allocate any resources

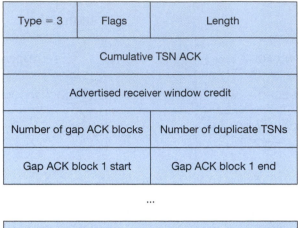

Type = 3	Flags	Length
Cumulative TSN ACK		
Advertised receiver window credit		
Number of gap ACK blocks		Number of duplicate TSNs
Gap ACK block 1 start		Gap ACK block 1 end

...

Duplicate TSN 1

...

Figure 10.15 SCTP SACK chunk.

for this putative new connection. The reasoning behind this is to prevent SYN flood attacks. See Section 13.2.1.

Data is acknowledged by SACK chunks (Figure 10.15). At the very least, such a chunk contains:

- A *cumulative TSN ACK*, which acknowledges all TSNs up to that value. This corresponds to the acknowledgement field in the TCP header.
- A window credit, giving the current window size.

This chunk can also contain TCP-SACK-like blocks of individual acknowledgements and also a list of TSNs that have been duplicated.

SACK chunks are sent after the first data chunk is received and then periodically for subsequent data chunks. Guidelines are to:

- send a SACK at least every second packet (note, this is not necessarily every second data chunk); and
- at most within 200 ms of receipt of the data.

SCTP shutdown is shorter than TCP shutdown (Figure 10.14). Either host may initiate:

1. A (say) sends a SHUTDOWN (type 7) chunk to B. It will only do this after all data chunks sent to B have been acknowledged.

2. When received by B, B carries on as normal until all its data chunks have been acknowledged. B then sends a SHUTDOWN ACK (type 8).

3. A replies with a SHUTDOWN COMPLETE (type 14) chunk. A packet containing a SHUTDOWN COMPLETE chunk cannot contain any other chunks.

There is also an ABORT chunk which corresponds to TCP's RST.

Packet retransmission and congestion avoidance algorithms are based on TCP but with a few changes for multi-homing and unordered streams. In particular, SCTP uses delayed ACKs, slow start, congestion avoidance, and fast retransmit and recovery. This means, additionally, that SCTP traffic will coexist comfortably alongside TCP traffic on the same network.

RFC 2581

SCTP has several advantages over TCP:

- Startup is faster: data flows from the third segment onwards.

- Multiple streams share a single connection, thus sharing flow control.

- Multiple streams mean better throughput in the case of packet loss.

- SCTP allows for unordered but reliable streams.

- SCTP maintains message boundaries.

- Protection against various types of connection attack are built into the protocol.

- There is a uniform way of extending the protocol by introducing new kinds of data or control via new types of chunk.

On the other hand:

- The minimum protocol overhead for TCP is a header of 20 bytes per packet. SCTP has 12 bytes for the common header plus 12 bytes for the data chunk header, making 24 bytes total. We then need to add in SACK chunks, which contribute at least 16 bytes every other packet. (This extra overhead is possibly offset by the lack of a need to add message delimiters at the application layer.)

- SCTP does not support half-closed connections (though message boundaries might be used to counter this).

- TCP is well understood, has many highly tuned robust implementations and is available everywhere, while SCTP support is as yet minimal.

SCTP is a well-designed protocol that shows much promise. It takes the good features of TCP, makes several of the optional improvements to TCP mandatory and generally fixes up weaknesses that have been discovered over the years of using TCP.

It is too early to tell if it will be a success or not.

10.16   Exercises

Exercise 10.1 Read about the history of the development of TCP, with particular regard to the strategies that have been proposed to increase throughput. How much faster is a modern TCP implementation than an early implementation?

Exercise 10.2 `tcpdump` shows the current advertised window of a connection. Investigate how the window opens and closes for various kinds of traffic, e.g., keystrokes, a video stream, data file transmission.

Exercise 10.3 While copying a large file using FTP (or other), watch (using `tcpdump`) how slow start and congestion avoidance work. Try to find a congested connection to see the effect of packet loss on throughput.

Exercise 10.4 The slow start mechanism is a one MTU increment per received ACK. This is called *TCP Tahoe*, later modified to become *TCP Reno*. An alternative congestion scheme is *TCP Vegas* which tries to anticipate congestion. Read up on these variants and describe how they work.

Exercise 10.5 Suppose we wanted to extend the Internet to the rest of the Solar System. What would we have to do to TCP? (For example, the Moon is about 1 second away; Mars varies between 3 and 22 minutes away.)

Exercise 10.6 ECN can be turned off or on in some operating systems. For example, `/proc/sys/net/ipv4/tcp_ecn` in Linux. By connecting to various hosts (e.g., Web servers) discover how many routers are still treating ECN-enabled packets as corrupt.

Exercise 10.7 By using `pchar` or `pathchar`, or the equivalent, determine some path RTTs. You might also be able to gain some information about the kinds of network you are testing by using `traceroute`.

Exercise 10.8 `ping` and `traceroute` can both be used to measure the time a packet takes to make a hop. Find the longest hop time you can that is accessible to you. What kind of network link does it correspond to?

Exercise 10.9 Read up and explain why TCP for Transactions has not been successful.

Exercise 10.10 Read up and explain why SCTP might well be successful.

THE PRESENTATION LAYER

11

11.1 Introduction

The job of the presentation layer is to ensure data at one end of a connection is interpreted in the same way when it reaches the other end. For example, how do we encode the letter 'A'? One popular method is to use a 7 bit number, namely 65. The *American Standard Code for Information Interchange* (ASCII) is one standard for encoding letters, digits and sundry punctuation marks. However, it is not the only standard and this is precisely the problem.

11.2 Character Encodings

At the time of the birth of the Internet IBM's *Extended Binary-Coded Decimal Interchange Code* (EBCDIC) was still strong. The purpose of EBCDIC is exactly the same as ASCII: it is an encoding of characters as numbers. The difficulty is that a file containing the bytes 108, 97, 110 would read as 'lan' on an ASCII system but as '%/>' when it is copied to an EBCDIC system. This is because ASCII says 108 is the letter l, while the EBCDIC standard says 108 is a percent sign, and so on. The *presentation problem* is how to ensure that the file always reads as 'lan' when copied to *any* other system.

Note that there is a question of philosophy here. The bits are the same, but it is our *interpretation* that changes. To maintain a consistent result of interpretation, we must therefore change the bits. Not only do we have to know *how* to translate the data to the alternate representation, but also we must know *when* to do so. If the 'lan' file above is a text file, we should translate it to keep its meaning constant. If the file is, say, the IQs of three people, we should *not* translate. Everything depends on the final *interpretation*, not the bits themselves. This is a subtle and hard-to-grasp concept, but it is at the heart of the presentation problem.

These days everybody has more or less settled on ASCII as the encoding to use for simple Roman letters and digits so presentation issues are minimal for this kind of data. On the other hand, the issue of encoding other character sets (Chinese, Russian, Klingon, etc.) is still somewhat in flux, with the *Universal Character Set* (UCS) plus *Unicode*   ISO 10646 looking to be the winning solution. UCS is a character encoding that uses 31 bits rather than just 7, which gives ample room for all the characters from all written languages in the world. Unicode takes UCS and adds extra information like direction of writing (left to right, or right to left, or bidirectional), defining alphabetic orders, and so on.

However, simply using 4 bytes per character would not be acceptable to many programmers since it would

- break the 'one character equals 1 byte' assumption that many programs make;

- make data files four times as large when the original data is encoded in ASCII; and

- the zero byte is conventionally used to indicate 'end of string' so a value such as (hex) 12340078 is open to misinterpretation.

Therefore there are some intermediate systems that are defined. Some of these have the useful property that they are backwardly compatible with ASCII in that characters with (hex) values 00 to 7f are the same as their ASCII encodings. The simplest and most obvious encoding method, UCS-4, translates ASCII to UCS by inserting three 00 bytes before every ASCII byte (using the big endian convention). This has the expansion problem, of course. Less inflationary is UCS-2 which inserts a single 00 byte, so only doubling the size of an ASCII file. These zeros are problematic to both schemes, since 00s mean end of string in C and this would break just about every C program ever written. Furthermore, UCS-2 can't represent all the characters in UCS.

RFC 3629
ISO 10646

Thus UTF-8 was devised. This *UCS Transformation Format* has the property that ASCII characters are transformed into themselves (i.e., still 7 bit, single byte values) while still being able to encode the full UCS.

The way it works is this:

- UCS values 00000000 to 0000007f are transformed into bytes 00 to 7f. Thus an ASCII file is a valid UTF-8 file.

- UCS values 00000080 to 000007ff become 2 bytes 110xxxxx 10xxxxxx. The bits from the UCS values are simply copied across to the x's. Thus the £ sign, UCS 000000A3, binary 00000000 00000000 00000000 10100011, transforms to 11000010 10100011 (00010/100011 → 110/00010 10/100011).

- More generally:

UCS range (hex)	UTF-8 (binary)
00000000–0000007F	0xxxxxxx
00000080–000007FF	110xxxxx 10xxxxxx
00000800–0000FFFF	1110xxxx 10xxxxxx 10xxxxxx
00010000–001FFFFF	11110xxx 10xxxxxx 10xxxxxx 10xxxxxx
00200000–03FFFFFF	111110xx 10xxxxxx 10xxxxxx 10xxxxxx 10xxxxxx
04000000–7FFFFFFF	1111110x 10xxxxxx 10xxxxxx 10xxxxxx 10xxxxxx 10xxxxxx

Thus some characters may require up to six bytes, but the commonly used ones require only three or fewer. The ASCII range requires just 1 byte.

UTF-8 has several good features:

- An ASCII file is already UTF-8 encoded and so there is no expansion when regarding it as UCS.

- The convention of using 0 as end of string still works.

- Most common UCS characters are expanded into three bytes or fewer.

- When dipping at random into a UTF-8 encoded file it is easy to find the start of the next character: just search until you find the next byte starting with 0 or 11.

- The length of each non-ASCII character is given by the number of leading 1 bits.

- All UCS characters can be encoded.

- The comparison order of UCS values is preserved.

Notice that UTF-8 is a transformation of UCS which is an encoding of characters. UCS is merely a table that relates values to characters and says nothing about how you should represent those values on a computer. The same could be said of ASCII, but as there is such an obvious one-to-one transformation, the issue never arises.

That's not to say that the presentation problem for characters has gone away as it needs software writers to actually use the standards: authors of tools that create Web pages are notorious for getting these things wrong.

11.3   Other Data: XDR

Another big presentation problem is the byte order of representations of numbers on different machine architectures. An integer is typically represented in a machine by using four bytes: but how those bytes are used varies.

RFC   1014

Some machines (e.g., Sparc) use a big endian format (Figure 11.1). This stores the most significant byte (big end) at the lowest machine address, less significant bytes at increasing addresses. Other machines (e.g., Intel) use the little endian format and store

Machine address	...	99	100	101	102	103	104	...	...	99	100	101	102	103	104	...
Value			00	00	00	2A					2A	00	00	00		
				Big endian								Little endian				

Figure 11.1 Endian.

the least significant byte (little end) at the lowest machine address, and more significant bytes at increasing addresses. Other arrangements are possible, too.

This is the problem: if a machine receives four bytes 00 00 00 2A, does that mean the integer 42 (hex 0000002A) or the integer 704643072 (hex 2A000000)? A typical solution to this is to pick a single representation, the *network byte order*, and always transmit bytes in that order. When a machine wants to send an integer, it converts it into network byte order. When a machine receives an integer, it converts it to its native byte order. The *de facto* network byte order as used on many networks is big endian. For a big endian machine, conversions of integers in and out of network order are trivial: nothing needs to be done. For a little endian machine, the conversions are to reverse the order of the bytes.

Typically a networking library has functions like `htonl` (host to network long) and `ntohl` (network to host long) for the programmer to use to do this swapping: when writing code we just have to make sure we are using these functions when appropriate. When a little endian machine communicates with a little endian machine, both machines should still do the reversals. This is simpler than trying to negotiate endiannesses and having separate code for the reversal and non-reversal cases.

More generally, we have the presentation problem for all kinds of numeric data. Another example is the several different representations of floating point numbers that are used. This is not simply a byte order problem, but includes details like which bits and how many bits are used to represent exponents and mantissas. Again, things are not quite as bad as they could be since most systems have plumped for the IEEE Standard for Binary Floating Point Arithmetic.

IEEE 754-1985

The IP layering model does not include a presentation layer, so presentation issues are not addressed by IP. Applications that run on top of IP must use something like the `htonl` functions or the *XDR* package if they want to interoperate between different architectures.

RFC 1832

The *External Data Representation* package is one approach to the presentation problem. It is a collection of functions that convert data to a standard network format. XDR functions see to swapping the order of bytes in integers when necessary, converting between different floating point formats and so on.

Here is a simple example of how XDR might be used. Suppose we wish to send some integers from one machine to another. The following program produces 10 XDR encoded integers on the standard output:

```
#include <stdio.h>
#include <rpc/rpc.h>

int main(int argc, char **argv)
{
  XDR xdrs;
  int i;

  xdrstdio_create(&xdrs, stdout, XDR_ENCODE);
  for (i = 0; i < 10; i++) {
    if (xdr_int(&xdrs, &i) == 0) {
```

```
        perror("xdr_int failed");
        exit(1);
      }
    }
    xdr_destroy(&xdrs);

    return 0;
}
```

The `xdrstdio_create` makes an XDR *handle* which is joined to the standard output stdout. Calls to, say, `xdr_int` will ENCODE values and write them to the standard output. At the end, to be tidy, we destroy the XDR handle which flushes buffers, frees any memory the handle used and generally tidies up.

The next program reads 10 XDR encoded integers from the standard input and prints them:

```
#include <stdio.h>
#include <rpc/rpc.h>

int main(int argc, char **argv)
{
  XDR xdrs;
  int i, n;

  xdrstdio_create(&xdrs, stdin, XDR_DECODE);
  for (i = 0; i < 10; i++) {
    if (xdr_int(&xdrs, &n) == 0) {
      perror("xdr_int failed");
      exit(1);
    }
    printf("%d ", n);
  }
  putchar('\n');

  xdr_destroy(&xdrs);

  return 0;
}
```

Now `xdr_int` DECODEs stuff that it reads from the standard input stdin.

This code will write, read and print numbers correctly, regardless of the architectures of the machines it is running on.

Similar functions exist for chars, longs, doubles, unsigned ints, and so on. Notice the symmetry of using `xdr_int` for both encoding and decoding: the direction is specified in the handle, not the function.

Lately, an XML-based alternative to XDR is beginning to be adopted for the transmission of information over the Web. See p. 225.

11.4 MIME

RFC 2045
RFC 2046
RFC 2047
RFC 2048
RFC 2049

Another approach to presentation is taken by the *Multipurpose Internet Mail Extension* (MIME). As its name suggests, it grew out of the presentation problem in email: how to ensure that various kinds of data, such as sounds and pictures, are transmitted safely in email messages. Thus it has several features that are a little unusual, such as its treatment of the end-of-line character.

The full MIME standard is long and complex, so here are a few highlights.

It works by taking raw data and regarding it as a sequence of 8 bit bytes. The bytes are encoded by one of a selection of techniques. Important ones include:

- 7bit. No transformation, the data are pure 7 bit ASCII characters.

- 8bit. No transformation, the data are 8 bit characters.

- Quoted-printable. Bytes of values less than 128 represent themselves. Values 128 and over are represented by an equals sign followed by a two digit hexadecimal value. Thus value 193 (which might represent Á) is encoded as the three characters =C1. The equals sign itself is represented as =3D (recall byte stuffing, p. 46).

- Base64. This transforms the input into a 65 character subset of ASCII: A–Z, a–z, 0–9, +, /, and the special pad character = (Figure 11.2). The 64 non-pad characters

0	A	16	Q	32	g	48	w
1	B	17	R	33	h	49	x
2	C	18	S	34	i	50	y
3	D	19	T	35	j	51	z
4	E	20	U	36	k	52	0
5	F	21	V	37	l	53	1
6	G	22	W	38	m	54	2
7	H	23	X	39	n	55	3
8	I	24	Y	40	o	56	4
9	J	25	Z	41	p	57	5
10	K	26	a	42	q	58	6
11	L	27	b	43	r	59	7
12	M	28	c	44	s	60	8
13	N	29	d	45	t	61	9
14	O	30	e	46	u	62	+
15	P	31	f	47	v	63	/

Figure 11.2 Base64 encoding.

can be represented in 6 bits. The transform takes three input bytes, regards them as four 6 bit values, then encodes and outputs those four values in four bytes. The pad is needed when the input is not a multiple of three bytes long.

Thus the message 'bit', in ASCII binary '01100010 01101001 01110100', is regarded as '011000 100110 100101 110100' or 'Yml0'. Decoding is simply the reverse of the above.

Note that there is a 33% expansion in the size of the data.

Both base64 and printed-quotable reduce the range of values used in the data in the hope that they will be transmitted correctly.

MIME encapsulation adds many headers:

- `Mime-Version: 1.0`. The version of MIME being used.

- `Content-Type: text/plain; charset=ISO-8859-15`. The original data was text using the ISO 8859-15 character set (a simple extension of ASCII).   ISO 8859

- `Content-transfer-encoding: base64`. The data is presented in a base64 encoding.

There are several others. The data follows a blank line after the MIME header. MIME also allows for a single large chunk of data to be split into several smaller pieces: this is to allow data to travel via emailers that have limitations on message sizes.

As an example, the message '£100 is about €150' could become:

```
Content-Transfer-Encoding: quoted-printable
Content-Type: text/plain; charset=ISO-8859-15
MIME-Version: 1.0

=A3100 is about =A4150
```

in quoted-printable, or

```
Content-Transfer-Encoding: base64
Content-Type: text/plain; charset=ISO-8859-15
MIME-Version: 1.0

ozEwMCBpcyBhYm91dCCkMTUwCg==
```

in base64.

11.5   The End of the Line

With all these solutions to the presentation problem it would be easy to think that it has been solved. Not so: there is still a lot to be done. For example, there is a very basic problem that *still* trips people up: *how do you represent the end of a line in a text file?*

The issue here is that:

- Unix-like systems use a linefeed (LF, character 10 in ASCII) for the end of a line;

- Windows systems use a carriage return character (CR, ASCII 13) followed by an LF;

- pre-MacOS X Macintosh systems used a single CR.

Thus if you want to copy a file from one system to another, you must know in advance whether it is text (when you should translate the end of line between the conventions) or whether it is other data (when you should leave the byte values 10 and 13 unmolested). Note that a text file might change in length as it gets copied. You can't just blindly transfer the file! For example, if you use FTP you must explicitly set binary or ASCII (text) mode before a transfer.

If it's so tricky to sort out such a simple and common problem, just think of the general case!

11.6   Exercises

Exercise 11.1 Encode your name in

- (a)   ASCII
- (b)   EBCDIC
- (c)   UCS
- (d)   UTF-8

(People with non-English names may have problems with parts (a) and (b) and should use instead MIME quoted-printable.)

ISO 8859   **Exercise 11.2** Investigate the use of multiple character sets as a solution to representing non-European characters.

Exercise 11.3 Read Jonathan Swift's *Gulliver's Travels* (in particular the adventure in the Empire of Blefuscu). Explain the relevance.

Exercise 11.4 Write some pairs of XDR programs that transmit various kinds of data, including floating point numbers, strings and more complicated data structures.

Exercise 11.5 Look at the source of Web pages from countries that use a non-Western alphabet. Classify the ways that they approach the presentation problem.

Exercise 11.6 MIME is used in many contexts. Look at the MIME encapsulation used in several applications, such as email and Web pages. What does MIME do to the size of a chunk of data?

Exercise 11.7 Decode the base64 encoded message

```
RG9uJ3QgYmUgYmxhc+kgYWJvdXQgcHJlc2VudGF0aW9uLg==
```

into the ISO 8859-15 character set.

ISO 8859

THE APPLICATION LAYER

12

12.1 Introduction

There are many applications that run over the IP. We shall only be giving the barest introduction to some of these since a proper treatment of many of them would require a complete book each:

- Telnet. Logging in to remote machines for interactive use, this first appeared in 1969. It uses TCP for reliability.

- File Transfer Protocol (FTP). A basic way of transferring files between machines. Uses TCP.

- Simple Mail Transfer Protocol (SMTP). Email, the killer application for the Internet. Uses TCP.

- Domain Name System (DNS). UDP for (most) lookups, TCP for zone transfers. See Chapter 8.

- Network File System (NFS). Allows remote disks to appear as local disks (transparent remote file access). Unlike FTP, which only transmits whole files, this allows true random access to the remote file system at the byte-by-byte level. NFS is layered over an intermediate protocol called RPC. Older versions of RPC use UDP while the latest versions also use TCP.

- HyperText Transfer Protocol (HTTP). For requesting and transferring Web pages. Web pages are encoded using HyperText Markup Language (HTML). Uses TCP.

- The Wireless Application Protocol (WAP). A variant of HTTP more suited to the lower bandwidths as supplied by mobile telephone networks.

- Internet radio. Radio broadcasting.

- Television over IP (IPTV). TV broadcasting.

- Voice over IP (VoIP). Using the Internet to transmit voice conversations.

- Many others. Finger, Whois, LDAP, X Window System, ssh, pop, IMAP, USENET news, network time synchronization, and so on. See `/etc/services` for a wide variety of standard applications.

12.2   Telnet

Telnet is really a very simple program, barely an application at all. Practically all it does is connect to a port on some server and then relay bytes back and forth between the user's terminal and the program running on that port. Thus

RFC 854

```
telnet mailhost.example.com 25
```

would (typically) connect to an SMTP mail server. You then need to know what to type at an SMTP server (Section 12.4) to get meaningful results.

More useful – and this is what most people think of as telnet – is the connection to a login service, which conventionally runs on port 23. The login server is a program that asks for your username and password, authenticates them, and logs you in if successful. You are now connected to a shell on the server machine and so the telnet application relays bytes back and forth between you and the shell, i.e., you type a command and the remote machine executes it just as if you were sitting at a terminal connected directly to the machine:

```
% telnet example.com
Trying 10.0.0.1...
Connected to example.com.
Escape character is '^]'.
Welcome to SuSE Linux 9.1 (i586) - Kernel 2.6.5-7.151-
default (7).
example.com login: rjbradford
Password:
Last login: Thu May 19 20:54:08 from fire
~:1 %
```

Telnet was one of the earliest applications developed for the Internet as its main purpose is to give remote access to machines and the original purpose of the Internet was to give remote access to machines. Note that the connection is insecure in that data in the connection (including the password when you logged in) is readable by the machines that route the packets as they travel. This means that an eavesdropper on a router could read confidential information as it goes past. For this reason telnet is deprecated by security-conscious systems managers.

These days there are more sophisticated and secure means to gain remote access (e.g., ssh, p. 232, the *secure shell*, which encrypts all data before sending), but telnet is still occasionally useful due to its simplicity and ubiquity.

12.3   FTP

RFC 959

The *File Transfer Protocol* (FTP), together with telnet and email, was one of the first applications of the fledgling Internet. One of the original design requirements of the Internet was to share data and this is exactly what FTP does.

To start, you log in to an FTP server with your username and password:

```
% ftp example.com
Trying 172.17.2.1...
Connected to example.com (172.17.2.1).
220 example.com FTP server ready.
Name (example.com:rjbradford): rjbradford
331 Password required for rjbradford.
Password:
230 User rjbradford logged in.
Remote system type is UNIX.
Using binary mode to transfer files.
ftp>
```

There are several commands available:

```
ftp> dir
227 Entering Passive Mode (172,17,2,1,247,214)
150 Opening ASCII mode data connection for directory listing.
total 122
-rw-r--r--   1 1082      100           158535 Aug 14 18:46 6month.ps
drwxr-xr-x   6 1082      100             2048 Sep  4 19:20 Misc
-rw-r--r--   1 1082      100           129761 Dec 21  2000 mrbenn.ogg
-rw-r--r--   1 1082      100             7100 Jun 20  2000 tcp.eps
-rw-r--r--   1 1082      100              216 Apr  8  1999 test.c
226 Transfer complete.
ftp>
```

Though FTP is primarily used for transfer of files:

```
ftp> get test.c
local: test.c remote: test.c
227 Entering Passive Mode (172,17,2,1,71,184)
150 Opening BINARY mode data connection for test.c (216 bytes).
226 Transfer complete.
216 bytes received in 0.0199 secs (11 Kbytes/sec)
ftp>
```

Also there is `put` to send a file.

```
ftp> bye
221-You have transferred 216 bytes in 1 files.
221-Total traffic for this session was 923 bytes in 1 transfers.
221 Thank you for using the FTP service on example.com.
```

The way files are copied seems somewhat eccentric to the modern eye. Early systems used *active mode* transfer, while *passive mode* transfer came along later.

In active mode a new reverse TCP connection is made from the server back to the client whenever data is to be transmitted. The existing connection is only used for control data. This arrangement causes problems with firewalls (Section 13.3) as the new incoming connection would likely be rejected by a security-conscious configuration. One solution is to use a clever firewall that recognizes the new connection as being related to the existing FTP connection, though this requires inspecting the contents of the FTP packets in the control connection to recognize when this is happening. A simpler solution is to use passive mode where the client initiates the data connection.

In an active FTP (Figure 12.1):

1. The client connects from some ephemeral port E to the server's FTP port, 21. This is the control connection.

2. The client issues a PORT F command, where F is an ephemeral port it is listening to and expecting data to arrive on.

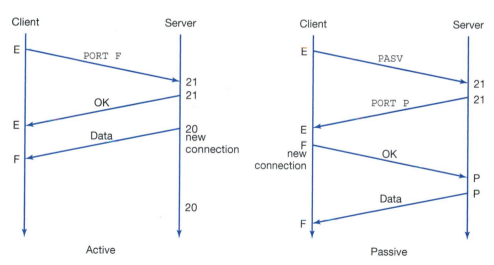

Figure 12.1 Active and passive FTP (simplified).

3. The server creates a new TCP connection from port 20 (FTP data port) to client port F, and this connection is used to pass data.

In a passive FTP:

1. The client connects from some ephemeral port E to the server's FTP port, 21.

2. The client issues a PASV command to indicate it wants a passive connection.

3. The server replies with a PORT P, where P is a port it is listening to and expecting data to arrive on.

4. The *client* creates a new TCP connection from some other ephemeral port F to server port P, and this connection is used to pass data.

So now the new connection is initiated by the client, within the firewall. This allows the firewall easily to determine whether the connection is safe or not.

Most FTP programs still support the old active mode just in case the remote host doesn't have passive mode.

The day of FTP has passed and HTTP (Section 12.8) transfers far outnumber FTP transfers. On the other hand, FTP is still widely implemented (even in Web browsers) and is still often used as it is particularly efficient for transferring large numbers of large files.

> Indeed in the emergent Grid, a modification of FTP is the protocol used to move around the huge datasets that modern big science produces.

12.4   SMTP

RFC 2821
RFC 2822

The *Simple Mail Transfer Protocol* (SMTP) is the protocol behind email: the application that initially made the Internet take off, although later the WWW took over as the killer application. A *killer application* is something that makes someone buy into a service just to get access to it. For example, buying a subscription to a TV channel because you want to see a particular show, or buying a PC because you want to use email.

Email is simultaneously one of the Internet's biggest success stories (it is so popular), but also one of its biggest problems (spam).

SMTP was developed early in the life of the Internet and uses simple human-readable messages like HELO, MAIL FROM: me@myhost. This made debugging easier and somewhat helped interoperability between different systems (recall that presentation was ignored in the IP).

A simple exchange might look like the following (lines starting with numbers are sent by the SMTP server, other lines are the client):

```
220 yourhost.bath.ac.uk ESMTP Postfix
HELO myhost
250 yourhost.bath.ac.uk
```

```
MAIL FROM: me@myhost
250 Ok
RCPT TO: you@yourhost
250 Ok
DATA
354 End data with <CR><LF>.<CR><LF>
Date: Fri, 20 May 2005 09:37:30 +0100
From: me@myhost
To: you@yourhost
Subject: sending email

This is an example email.
.
250 Ok: queued as 1BC31201B82
```

Points to note:

- Replies from the SMTP server are prefixed with numerical return codes. These indicate success or failure and other states. For example, 220 is 'service ready', 250 is 'success', while 354 is 'start mail input'. See RFC 2821 for a full list. RFC 2821

- The client starts with a HELO. More modern versions of SMTP use EHLO. Using EHLO indicates the client can use the later extensions to SMTP. The hello identifies the name of the client (which may be checked against where the connection is actually coming from).

- MAIL FROM identifies the sender of the email.

- RCPT TO identifies the one or more intended recipients of this email.

- DATA marks the start of the email itself. The text up to this point is called the *envelope* of the email.

- The email contains its own conventional header containing From, To, Subject, CC, and so on. Addresses in the data section need not correspond to the envelope. The email is delivered to the addresses in the envelope.

- The end of the email is marked by a lone full stop or period. If the email itself contains punctuation like this it is prefixed (i.e., encapsulated) by an extra full stop. On receipt, full stops at the start of lines are stripped.

- To be safe, only ASCII-encoded messages should be used. Some early mailers got into terrible problems with anything more sophisticated. To send more interesting data, a MIME (Section 11.4) encoding should be used. RFC 2045

Email has been hugely successful, with millions being sent every day. Unfortunately, its success has also been part of its downfall. At the time of writing, it is estimated that over 80% of email being sent is *bulk unsolicited commercial email*, or spam as it is popularly known. Since email was developed in a trusted academic environment, no thought to authentication was given. This means that when you receive an email, you have no idea where or who it came from: the 'From' address is no help as it can be set to anything the sender wishes. Spammers use this openness to their advantage: because sending email is so cheap they only need a tiny fraction of a percent response to make it profitable, no matter if their product abuses and annoys 99.9% of the public.

If spam alone wasn't bad enough, MIME enables executable code to be emailed: this allows worms and viruses (collectively called *malware*) to propagate. Many tools and techniques have arisen to combat the problems of spam and viruses. In particular there are:

- Virus filters: emails are checked for malicious code before they are delivered to the recipient. These filters need continual updating with the patterns they require to recognize the latest viruses.

- Spam filters: emails are checked to see if they are likely to be spam. Spam messages share many distinguishing features as they all have the same purpose: get as many emails to as many people as fast as possible. This makes them amenable to various analyses, such as the email envelope, their source, the layout of the content, the nature of the content, and many others. Spam filters are quite good these days, but they need constant updating as the spammers change their tactics.

- Laws against spam: these have spectacularly failed to make any impact on the volume of spam. If anything, laws have only convinced spammers to go underground and use even more dubious techniques.

RFC 3207
There are secure versions of SMTP, namely *Secure SMTP* (SSMTP or SMTPS), which is SMTP layered over SSL/TLS (Section 13.6) and its update STARTTLS. While this makes email secure against being read while in transit, it does nothing for the spam problem.

Proposed defences against spam are many and varied:

- Blacklisting: keep a list of IP addresses associated with spammers and refuse to accept email from them. This can be made efficient by using DNS and *Realtime Blackhole Lists* (RBL, p. 152) to look up IP addresses.

- Whitelisting: keep a list of IP addresses associated with people you trust and only accept email from them. This works reasonably for individuals, but not for companies that want to receive email from new customers.

- Greylisting: keep a whitelist, but if an email arrives from a new address, return a temporary delivery failure message and put the address on the whitelist (with an expiry date). The normal action for the sender would be to retry a little later and then their email would be accepted. But as spammers rarely use RFC-compliant emailers and are in such a rush to send as many emails as possible, it is unlikely the spammer will retry.

- *Sender Policy Framework* (SPF, aka *Sender Permitted From*) can help against the forging of 'From' addresses. This again coopts the DNS, this time to look up whether the From address is permitted to send from the actual IP the email came from. If not, the email is likely spam. Another technology with similar results is *domain keys*, which uses the DNS to store public encryption keys that can be used to check signatures on emails.

- Analysis of the email headers. You might specifically accept or reject an email RFC 3028 according to the 'From' header, or 'Subject's that you don't like. As headers can be set to whatever the sender wishes this is not a strong defence against spoofing.

- Analysis of the email content. For example, email with certain words and phrases like 'click here'; email with few words but a large picture; emailxt that uses HTML; email that uses text colour the same as the background colour; and so on for a large number of features that would not be natural for a normal email written by a human. Each feature can be given a score and if the sum of the scores is large, this email can be marked as spam.

Another approach is to fix SMTP itself. By changing SMTP we could:

- Require computational challenges: to reduce the ferocious rate that a spammer can send emails, it is suggested that part of the protocol would require the sender to complete a time-consuming computational challenge posed by the receiver. This would reduce the rate of sending so much as to make it uneconomic for the spammer.

- In a similar way, charge a small amount of money for each email, say a tenth of a cent; this would destroy the economics of sending millions of emails.

There are so many problems with SMTP that some people have recommended that trying to patch it up is pointless and it should be scrapped completely and be replaced by something designed to match the way the modern Internet is used. No real alternatives have yet arisen and the logistics of introducing any new system would be immense.

Much more could be said about email, but as most people have direct experience, we shall stop here.

> As spammers have found that using legitimate means of sending email has become more difficult for them, they have started using large networks of cracked machines to send email instead. There are hundreds of thousands, perhaps millions, of vulnerable machines out there waiting to be taken over and used to pump spam out into the world.
>
> Never think that nobody would be interested in your machine so it's pointless spending any time securing it. Your machine is *exactly* what they are looking for!

12.5   RPC and the Portmapper

RFC 1094
RFC 1813
RFC 3530

Sun's *Network File System* (NFS) is an approach to providing *transparent* file sharing between machines. By 'transparent' we mean that a program will be unaware whether a file it is using is local to its machine or is actually on some other machine elsewhere across the network. Other file sharing systems exist (e.g., AFS, InterMezzo and SMB, also known as CIFS) but NFS is by far the most widely adopted system and their principles are broadly similar.

RFC 1831

Firstly, though, we must address the topic of *Remote Procedure Call* (RPC) as NFS relies on RPC for its function. Sometimes we wish to execute a function or program on some other machine (a *remote server*), perhaps as part of a distributed program, or perhaps to gather information from the remote server. RPC is an abstraction layer (also invented by Sun) designed to make calling functions on remote machines more or less as simple as calling functions on the local machine. In practice it's not as quite as easy as that!

RPC could be used to support parallel programs where a single program uses the resources of many machines, but in practice there are better ways (e.g., MPI or PVM) as RPC was really designed to support remote services like NFS.

RPC is typically layered on top of TCP or UDP, though theoretically it can use any transport layer. If a program on the local machine wants to call a procedure on the remote machine (Figure 12.2), this is what happens:

1. The local function calls a function called the *client stub*.

2. The client stub is a piece of code (either written by the programmer or taken from a standard library) that collects the arguments of the function call and packages them into a network message which it sends to the server together with enough information to describe which function we want to call on the server.

3. A *server stub* on the server receives the message, decodes it and calls the function we wanted, the remote procedure.

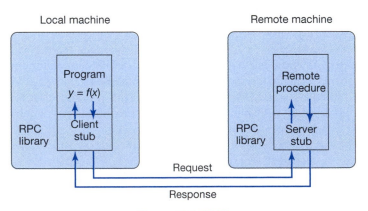

Figure 12.2 RPC.

4. The results are similarly packaged by the server stub and sent back to the client.

5. The client stub receives the results message, unpacks it and returns the results to the original calling function.

When complicated data structures need to be passed through RPC, the program `rpcgen` can be used to help write the appropriate code. This takes specifications of data structures and produces C code that implements the client and server side stubs for those data structures. This code can then be linked into the user's program.

From the programmer's point of view a function was called and some results were returned. The details of the networking are hidden, in particular things like timeouts and retransmits over UDP, presentation issues (RPC does XDR translations for us, Section 11.3), and so on.

One particular RPC service is called the *portmapper*. This purpose of this service is to the provide a mapping from RPC services to the UDP/TCP port number. If a program wishes to contact, say, NFS it must know the port number that the service is running on. When the NFS server program starts it registers itself with the portmapper (i.e., tells it that it is running) and supplies the portmapper with its port number, 2049 say.

Now when a client wants to find the NFS program on our server it first contacts the portmapper (which always runs on port 111) saying 'where is NFS?' and gets the reply 'port 2049'. Now the client can directly contact the NFS server.

This rather roundabout way of doing things allows for a dynamic configuration where services come and go and listen on a variety of port numbers. All this works as long as the portmapper is running!

A portmapper service is identified by a triplet of numbers:

1. Program number. This is a number which tells us which service we want. For example, NFS has assigned number 100003.

2. Program version. There can be different versions of the same service, perhaps with different protocols. For example, versions 2 and 3 of NFS are both commonly used. Note that we can provide more than one version of a service simultaneously as this number will tell us which version is required.

3. Procedure number. A service can offer several operations. For example, NFS allows us to create, delete, read, etc., files and this number chooses which of these to do.

The `rpcinfo` program will give details of the RPC services available on a machine. Try `rpcinfo -p machine`. Also `/etc/rpc` lists the program-number-to-program-name association.

As XML (p. 220) grows in importance, new RPC-like protocols are emerging. These include XML-RPC and the *Simple Object Access Protocol* (SOAP, p. 225). These enable remote procedure calls to be made over the WWW. Both these protocols essentially replicate the functionality of RPC, but communicate using messages encoded in XML, which uses HTTP (Section 12.8) as a transport layer.

12.6 NFS

NFS (Figure 12.3) allows us to use a file on a remote machine just as if it were on our own machine. The only perceivable difference is that the speed of access is a little lower.

NFS is implemented using RPC. When NFS starts on a client it uses an RPC call to the server portmapper to determine where the server NFS program is running. After this, the client sends RPC requests directly to the NFS program.

The actions of NFS are similar to the remote procedure call, above. For example, if a program on the local machine wishes to read bytes 10–20 from file `foo` it executes a normal `read` function. The local operating system finds that `foo` lives on a remote machine and assembles an RPC request to send to it. This request is essentially (though not actually) 'give me bytes 10–20 from file `foo`' and it makes the RPC call to the NFS service with the appropriate version number, and with the `read` procedure number. The remote machine gets this request and responds with the data from `foo`. The local operating system receives the bytes and passes them up to the original program as the result of the original `read` function call.

All this is transparent to the user program, except, possibly, for the speed: a remote file access can be many times slower than a local file access. The NFS takes care of:

- presentation issues by using XDR;

- composing and sending the RPC;

- receiving the reply;

- unpacking the results and passing them back to the caller.

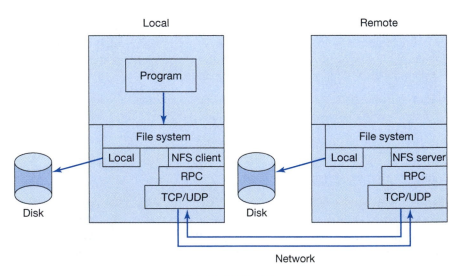

Figure 12.3 NFS.

Traditionally, NFS uses RPC over UDP. UDP was originally chosen for its extra speed over TCP. This means that NFS has to worry about lost and out-of-order packets and making retransmissions wherever necessary. Fortunately, NFS actions are mostly *idempotent*, meaning that they can be done more than once and get the same answer each time. Thus, if a 'read bytes 10–20 from file `foo`' packet gets lost, we can simply resend it.

NFS servers are *stateless*, meaning that no information is kept about past NFS requests. The benefit of being stateless is as follows. Suppose a client makes an NFS request to a server. The server chooses this moment to crash. The client gets no reply and resends its request, probably several times. Meanwhile, the server reboots. A request eventually gets through to the server, which can immediately service it. The client is now happy, though it did have to wait a bit. If the server kept client information, say, which files the client had open or where in those files the client had read up to, this would never work. This is why a request is 'read bytes 10–20 from file `foo`' and not simply 'get me the next 11 bytes' while hoping the server knew where you were in which file. Of course, this means that every request contains a lot of repeated information, but it is this redundancy that makes NFS robust to crashes.

Versions 3 and onwards of NFS can also use TCP. This is appropriate now that TCP has been tuned so well that UDP's speed advantage is minimal for large files or over WANs. NFS over TCP can benefit from TCP's sophisticated flow control and retransmission strategies rather than having to implement them for itself over UDP. There are complications, of course, that arise from TCP being stateful while NFS is stateless: if the server crashes a new TCP connection has to be created and if the client crashes it leaves a connection dangling on the server which may eventually be cleared up by a keepalive.

NFS has been hugely successful and is widely deployed even though its design is lacking in various respects, particularly security and raw speed. Successive versions of NFS have partially addressed some of these problems but there are performance limits inherent in its stateless nature. While other remote file systems like SMB and AFS (or its open cousin OpenAFS) may have occasional technical advantages, their proprietary nature means that they lag well behind NFS in use in real systems.

12.7   Storage Area Networks

NFS is a *Network Attached Storage* (NAS) system, providing a file-based interface to remote disks (in this context local disks are deemed *Direct Attached Storage*, or DAS). An alternative to this is *Storage Area Network* (SAN), which provides a disk-block-based interface. An SAN aims to join together many disks by a network and present them to a host as a single, somewhat large, but otherwise ordinary disk. While NFS (and CIFS and friends) seek to present the illusion of a local file system (files, directories, access permissions, and so on), an SAN is just a 'disk' that gives you access to blocks of data. A file system can be provided by a higher layer, if needed. This block-oriented access is preferred by high-performance systems like databases where a file system just gets in the way. Additionally, SANs have much lower overheads than NFS with its XDR and RPC and so on.

If an SAN is a virtual disk, then you need to access it by issuing disk-like commands rather than file-like commands such as `read` and `write`. The popular *Small Computer System Interface* (better known as SCSI) is used in two SAN systems, *Fibre Channel* and *Internet SCSI* (iSCSI). SCSI commands are things like 'get block number such-and-such', and 'write this data to block so-and-so'.

ANSI
X3.230-1994
ISO 14165-1

Fibre Channel is a 4Gb/s and faster network that uses its own network layer protocols over its own specification fibres and switches. It encapsulates SCSI commands and simply delivers them from host to network disk. While the SCSI disks are commodity, the FC infrastructure is specific to FC.

RFC 3720

iSCSI, on the other hand, runs over commodity IP networks (Figure 12.4). Thus, its speed is determined by whatever network you are using. For example, iSCSI on a Gigabit Ethernet is quite comparable to FC. Like FC, iSCSI encapsulates SCSI commands. Unlike FC, it is layered over standard TCP and so can benefit from its flow control, retransmission strategies, and any improvements in TCP that may appear in the future.

iSCSI has several advantages over FC:

- FC uses relatively expensive specialized equipment while iSCSI uses common Ethernet.

RFC 3821
RFC 4172

- While standards exist for *Fibre Channel over TCP/IP* (FCIP) tunnelling and *Internet Fibre Channel Protocol* (iFCP) which does protocol translations between FC and TCP, these still require some FC equipment, while iSCSI can use an existing network.

- FC networks are harder to maintain (if for no other reason than unfamiliarity), while IP networks are already widely understood by systems administrators.

- FC has had some intervendor interoperability issues while IP interoperates every-where.

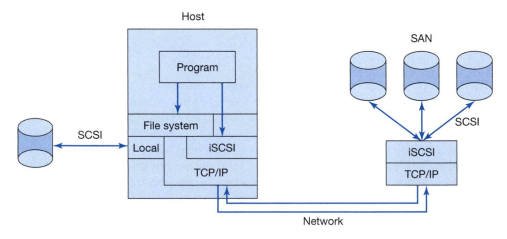

Figure 12.4 iSCSI.

- FC speeds are slowly being increased through new FC standards, while iSCSI rides on the back of Ethernet which is 10Gb/s and more. Similarly, iSCSI can benefit from any IP-related feature, such as QoS.

- FC networks are limited to 10 km, while IP has no problem with much larger distances. This is important for remote data replication and data recovery.

- SCSI is not limited to disks. In particular there are also SCSI tape drives: iSCSI also works with these. Network-attached tape drives are particularly important for centralized or remote system backups.

In contrast, FC has one big advantage over iSCSI: it exists, it works and it is in the market, while iSCSI has only just finished standardization. A strong market presence can often outweigh technical superiority and FC will be around for many years to come.

> There also exist special iSCSI network cards (*host bus adaptors* or HBAs, aka *TCP/IP offload engines*, TOEs) that implement the TCP/IP stack themselves, thus offloading work from the host processor. However, buying one detracts somewhat from the price advantage of iSCSI and initial evidence seems to imply that the benefit of hardware over a well-tuned IP implementation is not as great as you would think.

Another challenger in the NAS arena is HyperSCSI. This runs SCSI directly over raw Ethernet. Its advantage is that this avoids the overheads of TCP/IP and so gains a boost in speed over iSCSI. On the other hand, it also has a few disadvantages since it doesn't have the support of IP to do routing, or the support of TCP for a guarantee of delivery, flow control and error resilience.

We also note that there is also an *ATA over Ethernet* (AoE) standard that layers ATA disk commands directly over Ethernet. This is a lightweight protocol that doesn't need a TOE and has low encapsulation overheads, but again can't take advantage of IP features, in particular routing.

On the other hand, proponents of HyperSCSI and AoE point out that few disk installations actually run over anything other than the local network and so the features (and overheads) of IP are not often required.

To add to the fun, there is even a standard for IP over FC! RFC 3831

12.8   HTTP

The World Wide Web (WWW) is what many people (wrongly) think is the Internet. The fact that most of the public believe this is a reflection of how the growth of the WWW was the major driving force behind the commercialization and general acceptance of the Internet. HTTP is the protocol that drives the WWW. RFC 2616

The WWW is, at base, a very simple thing. A client requests a document (page, picture, sound or whatever) and the server delivers it. Thus the *HyperText Transfer Protocol*

(HTTP) started as a simple request–response protocol. To make it easy to debug, the protocol is human readable.

A request for a Web page could be

```
GET /home.html HTTP/1.0
Host: wibble:80
```

(There is a blank line at the end of this.) This is an example of HTTP version 1.0 for simplicity; generally people currently use version 1.1.

This requests the file `home.html` from the server `wibble`. The client is using HTTP version 1.0: later versions of the protocol have more features and so this value is an indication of what features the client expects. The host field indicates which server the client thinks it is connecting to: this allows a single machine to appear under several different names and potentially give different responses to each. It also allows HTTP *proxying* (see below).

The 80 is the conventional port number that a Web server uses. The blank line ends the HTTP header. Sometimes additional data follows when the client needs to send more information to the server.

A reply from the server could be:

```
HTTP/1.0 200 OK
Server: Wombat Server 1.0
MIME-version: 1.0
Content-type: text/html
Content-length: 81
Expires: Tue Feb 14 22:57:29 2006

<html>
<head>
<title>Example</title>
</head>
<body>
Hello world.
</body>
</html>
```

The data (some HTML in this case) starts after the blank line after the header. The header includes lots of useful information about the data:

- `HTTP/1.0 200 OK`. The server is willing and able to talk HTTP version 1.0 and 200 is a code that indicates success.

- `Server`. The name of the program that served the data.

- `MIME-version` (*Multipurpose Internet Mail Extensions*, Section 11.4). This encapsulates the data and allows a Web browser to figure out what to do with the data that follows (display it, play it, etc.). The following headers are part of the MIME encapsulation.

- `Content-type`. Some HTML follows.

- `Content-length`. The data is 81 bytes long.

- `Expires`. The lifetime of the data. Some Web pages change rapidly, some remain for a long time. This indicates which and is used when we cache Web pages to know when a page should be re-fetched rather than read from the local cache.

- The blank line ends the header and the data follows.

In early versions of HTTP (before version 1.1) a new TCP connection was created for each HTTP request. A Web page can easily require dozens of requests (one for the page and one for each image on the page) for files that are typically fairly small. Thus the TCP setup and closedown overhead is relatively large and flow control does not get up to speed, which means that we do not get as good a throughput as we might expect. One suggested solution is to use T/TCP (Section 10.15.1) to reduce the overhead, but the generally recognized solution was introduced in HTTP version 1.1, namely *persistent connections*.

A persistent connection is a TCP pipe that stays open and is used for more than one HTTP request, thus amortizing the setup overhead. Also, the TCP flow strategies get a better chance to increase throughput. Persistent connections are a little harder to implement than one-shot connections (we need some way to identify when one document ends and the next one starts in the TCP stream) but the benefits are worthwhile.

Another useful feature is HTTP *proxying*. A host may not have a direct connection to the Internet; perhaps for security reasons it is behind a firewall (Section 13.3). A *proxy server* can be set up that has access to the Internet which relays HTTP requests from the client to the WWW. The client's Web server must be configured to send all HTTP requests to the proxy, but the HTTP header contains the information (in particular the server host name) for the proxy to forward the request to the right server. The proxy host also relays the returning data back to the original client.

Proxying has various features:

- Security: administrators can focus on the proxy server and make it as secure as possible. This reduces the pressure of having to ensure that all the clients are 100% secure from external attack.

- Monitoring: the proxy server can record all the HTTP requests that it passes on.

- Control: the proxy can be configured by the systems administrator to refuse to connect to certain WWW sites.

A variant of HTTP is called HTTPS, or secure HTTP, and is used to retrieve Web pages when it is important that their contents can't be read by an eavesdropper on an intermediate machine on the transmission path. This is just HTTP run over an encrypting secure socket layer SSL/TLS (Section 13.6). In contrast, SHTTP is an extension to the HTTP protocol   RFC 2818 to include security and authentication. HTTPS is used far more in the real world, possibly because it uses an existing encryption layer and does not require setting up a configuration that replicates existing security functionality.

12.8.1   HTML and XML

W3C HTML
4.01

ISO 8879

HTML is the 'language of the Web' and is used to describe how a Web page should look. As a language it is too large and complex to detail here, even though it is based on a 'simplified' version of the more general *Standard Generalized Markup Language* (SGML), but we shall just hint at it.

> HTML, XML, and various supporting languages are defined and controlled by the World Wide Web Consortium (W3C). In an ideal world the standards would be followed to the letter, but unfortunately many companies take liberties in their servers and implement languages that are not quite true HTML. This causes all kinds of compatibility problems across browsers from different vendors. For example, many people write to a version of HTML that suits Microsoft browsers, ignoring the fact their document displays poorly in other browsers. The presence of the phrases 'best viewed in such-and-such browser' or 'site optimized for …' is a sure sign that the author has written poor or incorrect HTML: HTML is supposed to be browser *independent*. In most cases writing W3C-conformant HTML would actually improve Web pages for everybody, including the author.

HTML uses *tags* like <b> and </b> to mark areas of text that should be displayed in a special way, so <b> and </b> indicate **boldface**; <hr> draws a horizontal rule across the page; and so on for very many kinds of tags.

The major feature of HTML is that it has *anchor links* such as

```
Time for <a href="http://news.bbc.co.uk">the News</a>.
```

to include hypertext references to other documents. This might appear in a Web browser as

Time for the News.

The browser will fetch the named document when the user clicks on the link. This is what makes it a 'Web': documents are joined to documents in an immense and complicated network.

Here, a larger example:

```
<!DOCTYPE HTML PUBLIC "-//W3C//DTD HTML 4.01 Transitional//EN">
<html>
<head>
<title>Evening News</title>
</head>
```

```
<body>
<h2 align="center">News: Evening Edition</h2>

News for the twilight hours
<p>
Last updated: Tuesday, 31st May, 2005, 16:23 BST<br>
Copyright: Acme News Corporation
</p>

<h2>World Peace Achieved</h2>
Officials were stunned when peace spontaneously broke out this
morning.
<a href="http://www.acmenews.com/news/item1234.html">Link</a>

<h2>Aliens visit the Taj Mahal</h2>
The space travellers
from Betelgeuse continue on their world tour.
<a href="http://www.acmenews.com/news/item2134.html">Link</a>
</body>
</html>
```

could look like:

News: Evening Edition

News for the twilight hours

Last updated: Tuesday, 31st May, 2005, 16:23 BST

Copyright: Acme News Corporation

World Peace Achieved
Officials were stunned when peace spontaneously broke out this morning. Link

Aliens visit the Taj Mahal
The space travellers from Betelgeuse continue on their world tour. Link

---

Many Web browser supply a 'view page source' option which will reveal how HTML is used in the real world and will show the horror of the HTML that is generated by automatic tools such as word processors.

What is turning out to be just as important as HTML is the *Extensible Markup Language* (XML). This is a markup language framework in the style of HTML and SGML, but the data it marks up is not just text. While HTML markup is concerned with the layout of a document, XML markup is there to describe what the data means.

A simple example is *RDF Site Summary* (RSS, aka *Rich Site Summary*), a lightweight XML markup that is primarily used to provide news headlines on the WWW. RSS is part of the *Resource Description Framework* (RDF):

W3C XML
1.1

W3C RSS 1.0

W3C RDF

```
<?xml version="1.0" encoding="ISO-8859-1"?>
<?xml-stylesheet href="http://www.acmenews.com/rss/rss.css"
type="text/css"?>

<!DOCTYPE rss SYSTEM "http://www.acmenews.com/rss/rss-0.91.dtd">
<rss version="0.91">
<channel>
<title>News: Evening Edition</title>
<link>http://www.acmenews.com/home.html</link>
<description>News for the twilight hours</description>
<language>en-gb</language>
<lastBuildDate>Last updated: Tuesday, 31st May, 2005,
16:23 BST</lastBuildDate>
<copyright>Copyright: Acme News Corporation</copyright>

<docs>http://www.acmenews.com/news/</docs>

<image>
  <title>Acme News</title>
  <url>http://www.acmenews.com/pics/eve_news.gif</url>
  <link>http://www.acmenews.com/home.html</link>
</image>

<item>
  <title>World Peace Achieved</title>
  <description>Officials were stunned when peace sponta-
neously broke
  out this morning.</description>
  <link>http://www.acmenews.com/news/item1234.html</link>
</item>

<item>
  <title>Aliens visit the Taj Mahal</title>
  <description>The space travellers from Betelgeuse con-
tinue on their
  world tour.</description>
  <link>http://www.acmenews.com/news/item2134.html</link>
</item>

</channel>
</rss>
```

Associated with this is the *Document Type Definition* (DTD) which describes what are legal elements in this markup and how they can be nested. More importantly, a DTD allows *verification* of an XML application: it is easy to see if a document is *well formed* as we can go through and check the syntax and ensure all elements are properly paired.

This doesn't tell us, though, that the content is meaningful. This is what the DTD does for us by giving a specification for the content. With the DTD we can tell if the document is *valid*, i.e., satisfies the relevant specification.

The DTD can contain data like

```
<!ELEMENT item (title | link | description)*>
<!ELEMENT title (#PCDATA)>
```

This tells us about the item and title elements and says that title, link or description (and only these) can be nested inside an item. A title can contain only data ('parsed character data'). A more sophisticated way of defining XML document structure is to use XML *Schema* which allows the mixing of elements from several different applications.

XML is primarily intended for the transmission of information, but in those cases where we want to display an XML document there will be associated with that document a *Cascading Style Sheet* (CSS) which describes how to render (i.e., display) an XML document. It is 'cascading' as more than one style sheet can be applied to a page and priority rules determine how styles are combined. W3C CSS2

The CSS informs a browser how to display elements such as title:

```
item title {
  display:block;
  font-family:"Verdana",sans-serif;
  font-size:large;
  font-weight:bold;
  text-align:left;
}
```

This says that a title within an item should be shown in a large bold Verdana font aligned to the left on the page.

CSS has many other tricks:

```
item link {
  display:block;
}
item link:before {
  content: "Link: <";
}
item link:after {
  content: ">";
}
```

This puts the text Link: < before a link inside an item and the text > after.

So the above XML document might be rendered as follows:

News: Evening Edition

News for the twilight hours

Last updated: Tuesday, 31st May, 2005, 16:23 BST

Copyright: Acme News Corporation

World Peace Achieved

Officials were stunned when peace spontaneously broke out this morning.
Link: `<http://www.acmenews.com/news/item1234.html>`

Aliens visit the Taj Mahal

The space travellers from Betelgeuse continue on their world tour.
Link: `<http://www.acmenews.com/news/item2134.html>`

W3C XSLT 1.0

Closely related to CSS is the *Extensible Style Language* (XSL). This has a similar role to CSS in that it tells us how to display an XML file, but it differs in a couple of ways. Firstly, the XSL styles are written in XML while CSS has its own language (see the example above). Secondly, XSL *transforms* the XML using the *XSL Transformations* (XSLT) language into, say, HTML plus CSS which can then be displayed. CSS, on the other hand, simply tells us how to display the original XML or HTML.

The W3C have this motto: 'Use CSS when you can, use XSL when you must.' CSS is much easier and simpler to use and therefore to maintain, but occasionally you need the power of XSL. Note that XSL does not work on HTML as HTML is not strict XML. CSS works with both HTML and XML. While CSS is reasonably well supported by current browsers, XSL is very much less so.

The most important aspect of XML is that an XML document can be easily parsed to extract the information it contains. The CSS and rendering are really a secondary aspect. It is straightforward to extract the headlines in the above example: they are given by `title` elements within `items` (and are nowhere else). Compare this to the HTML page of news where there is no particular indication where the headlines are: HTML is all about display, not about the content. Similarly, finding the copyright in the XML example is trivial as it has its own marker. Finding the copyright in the HTML example is fraught with danger: simply looking for the word 'copyright' is not enough as there might be a news article on copyright abuse. The act of reading though HTML and trying to reconstruct information like this is sometimes called *scraping* and is never foolproof.

This facility means that XML is being used to mark up all kinds of information. The *Organization for the Advancement of Structured Information Standards* (OASIS) is a consortium of companies that devises and publishes XML DTDs for various e-commerce activities. It is to everybody's advantage that widely accepted XML standards are used to maximize the interoperability of data exchange between institutions.

Here is a random selection of examples. Many are standardized by OASIS or are available through the OASIS Website:

- An important XML application is the *Simple Object Access Protocol* (SOAP). This is designed to be part of an RPC mechanism (Section 12.5) that can be carried within HTTP and thus over the Web. The idea is to use the ubiquity of the Web to provide an equivalent ubiquity for processing. XML elements are defined for integers, floats, strings and other data types and a protocol is defined to call remote procedures, *W3C SOAP 1.2*

- Web Services Description Language (WDSL). This specifies the location of a service and the operations the service provides, somewhat like the portmapper (Section 12.5), but not restricted to a single server. This ties in with SOAP, which is used to transport the data to the services. *W3C WDSL 1.2*

- Mathematical Markup Language (MathML). This is to describe mathematics in such a way that its meaning is easy to extract. The intention is that MathML is for the delivery of mathematics just as HTML is for the delivery of text. *W3C MathML 1.01*

- Open Financial Exchange (OFX). A specification for the exchange of financial data among financial institutions, business and consumers. *OASIS OFX 2.0*

- XML User-interface Language (XUL). A language for describing user interfaces. For example, the layout of a browser (the 'chrome' of the interface) can be defined in XUL. *OASIS XUL 1.0*

- Astronomical Markup Language (AML). For controlling astronomical instruments. *OASIS AML*

- Wireless Markup Language (WML). A version of HTML for low-rate telephone links. See Section 12.8.2. *WAP 2.0*

- Scalable Vector Graphics (SVG). For describing two dimensional vector graphics. *W3C SVG 1.0*

- MusicXML. A collection of DTDs to represent (Western notation) musical scores, sheet music, and so on. *OASIS Music*

- Voice Extensible Markup Language (VoiceXML). For voice user interfaces. VoiceXML controls synthesized speech and recognition and recording of spoken word input. *W3C VoiceXML 2.0*

- Product Data Markup Language (PDML). To support the interchange of product information among commercial systems. *OASIS PDML*

- Log Markup Language (LOGML). This describes log reports of Web servers. Good for mining Web access data. *OASIS LOGML 1.0*

- DocBook. For books, papers and documentation. It has elements to mark chapters, sections, titles, and so on. The advantage of using DocBook is that there are tools to convert DocBook documents to HTML and also to more traditional typesetters like LaTeX so that the same document can be presented in many media. *OASIS DocBook 4.1*

- Open Document. For office applications, such as documents, spreadsheets, presentations, and so on. This is in direct competition with Microsoft's proprietary formats for the same applications. *OASIS Open Document v1.0*

W3C SMIL 2.0	• Synchronized Multimedia Integration Language (SMIL). For controlling and synchronizing multimedia applications such as streaming video with graphics, text and sound.
OASIS SAML v2.0	• Open Security Assertion Markup Language (SAML). A standard for the exchange of authentication and authorization data. You should be able to sign on to one Website and have that authentication passed across to other related Websites ('single sign-on').
OASIS LI-XML	• Lawful Intercept XML (LI-XML). A standard for the rapid discovery and sharing of suspected criminal and terrorist evidence by law enforcement agencies. This will include names, telephone numbers, email addresses and *Global User Identifiers*.
RFC 3920	• Extensible Messaging and Presence Protocol (XMPP). For instant messaging.
	• Gastro Intestinal Markup Language. Huh?!
W3C XHTML 1.1	• There is even a DTD for XHTML, an XML markup that looks very much like HTML. It is intended that XHTML will replace HTML as all the XML functionality and tools are then applicable to Web pages.

And hundreds more. Anyone can make up a DTD for an application, but its use will be fairly limited until it gets wide acceptance, which is why recognition by a standards body such as OASIS is so important.

12.8.2 WAP and WML

WAP 2.0

The *Wireless Application Protocol* (WAP) is used for the delivery of Web content to mobile telephones (Figure 12.5). Defined by the *Open Mobile Alliance* (OML, formerly the WAP Forum), WAP is analogous to HTTP, while the role of HTML is played by *Wireless Markup Language* (WML), another instance of XML.

The idea is to tap into the information content provided by the WWW, whilst recognizing the many limitations when using mobile devices:

• slower interconnect speeds;

• limited resolution of display;

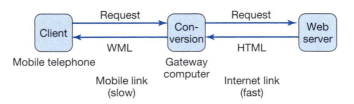

Figure 12.5 WAP.

- limited computational ability;
- limited memory.

It is pointless downloading 750KB's worth of 1600×1200 pixel, 16 million colour image over a slow link if you have a 100×100 pixel black-and-white display. Instead of communicating directly with a Web server, a WAP client talks to a *WAP gateway*. The gateway makes an HTTP request to the relevant server and receives the reply. If, as is increasingly popular, the Web server can deliver WML directly, this is compressed by the gateway to a compact bytestream which is then streamed to the mobile device. The device interprets the stream and displays it appropriately.

If the Web server returns an HTML page, the gateway can attempt *content conversion*. This includes transforming from the server's HTML to WML and compressing images. Compressing an image might involve converting to black and white and reducing the resolution to 100×100 pixels. This very much smaller version of the original (maybe a few kilobytes) is sent over the slow link to the client. The client benefits since this is very much faster than downloading the original and then downgrading it itself.

Also a WAP client can run WMLScript, analogous to JavaScript. The gateway compiles the WMLScript code into a compact bytestream which the client then executes.

WAP has taken a long time to gain any level of acceptance. Only with the emergence of GPRS (Section 5.2.5) has the number of page hits even started to take off. GPRS charges per byte downloaded rather than on connection time (as GPRS is 'always connected') and it appears that the ability to download polyphonic ringtones for phones has been one of the driving forces in the uptake. Perhaps, previously, low download rates, high cost and over-hype of WAP by phone companies had suppressed demand.

12.9 Internet Radio

Digitized sound is data, so it makes sense to deliver sound over the Internet. As the data rate needed for a passable sound quality is fairly small (AM radio quality is possible over a 56Kb link, while CD quality and beyond is achievable on broadband), this has been a highly successful application. There are a huge number of Internet radio stations currently broadcasting, providing all kinds of music and speech from both traditional broadcasters, such as the BBC, and Internet-only individual Webcasters. The reach of such a radio station is huge, namely the entire Internet-connected world, so anyone anywhere can always find something to their taste.

Streams are supplied in a variety of formats (MP3 is a popular choice), always compressed to reduce bandwidth requirements. Very little is needed to provide a stream as long as you have sufficient bandwidth to keep the bits flowing steadily, and even HTTP can be used as a transport. Only when more than a few clients want to be served does the system have to be sophisticated, employing management protocols such as the *Real Time Streaming Protocol* (RTSP) allied with the *Real-Time Transport Protocol* (RTP) to keep things going smoothly.

RFC 2326
RFC 3550

Most of the problems of Internet radio are economic:

- How to fund a radio station? Streaming radio consumes a large amount of bandwidth which must be paid for. Subscription is not popular with consumers and adverts are problematic as the Internet is worldwide and few advertisers like targets that are so diffuse.

- The infrastructure needed to support a large number of clients is expensive, so only large companies can reach a large number of customers.

- Paying for performance rights is a further cost that must be taken into account and the rights holders are still uncomfortable with the idea of Internet radio.

- Large-scale broadcasts would ideally use multicasting, but unfortunately the support for multicasting in current domestic networks is very weak, so providers are having to rely on unicast.

Small broadcasters often turn to radio aggregators like Shoutcast and Live365, which are companies that (for a price) provide the infrastructure needed.

Despite its problems, Internet radio is an unqualified success.

12.10   Television over IP

In their enduring quest to find ever more ways of getting TV to the consumer, some TV broadcasters are looking at IP. The term 'IPTV' means many things, but it generally covers the several ways of broadcasting TV over the Internet. At the time of writing, it is still an immature technology, with several companies holding trials and tentative initial roll-outs to see what is the best way of proceeding. Vision and sound compression protocols like MPEG2 (as used on DVDs and traditional digital TV) and MPEG4 including H.264 are being employed to squeeze what is hoped to be sufficient quality pictures down the last mile (Section 5.3) to the consumer. The current drift towards high-definition (HD) TV just makes the problem worse: an HD TV stream can require several times the bandwidth of a standard definition stream.

ISO 13818
ISO 14496
ITU-T H.264

An IPTV program can be *streamed*, i.e., viewed on-the-fly as the data arrives, or sometimes simply downloaded and watched at the viewer's leisure. Program makers tend to prefer streaming as they don't like the idea of copies of their work being in the hands of consumers. The issue of control of data (*digital rights management*, or DRM) is simply too difficult and contentious to go into here.

Advantages of IPTV for the consumer include:

- personalized TV channels (sometimes called *narrowcasting*);
- the ability to control delivery (pause, rewind, and so on);

- being able to choose when to view a programme (video on demand) as well as having live programming;

- having interactive services, such as taking part in quizzes or being able immediately to buy items seen in programmes or in adverts;

- having a larger range of programmes and (eventually) programme providers available.

Advantages of IPTV for the broadcaster include:

- being able to profile individual customers and target advertising at them;

- being able to charge differential rates for TV programmes;

- increasing revenue by sell-through from programmes and adverts;

- ending the reliance on expensive broadcasting equipment (transmitters and the like);

- being able to reshow (i.e., resell) the large back catalogue of old TV programmes and films.

The downsides include the following:

- As for radio, live IPTV would naturally use multicasting, but the support for multicasting in current domestic IP networks is poor.

- IPTV also needs a good deal of bandwidth, perhaps a few megabits per second for a picture quality comparable to existing TV.

- To maintain picture quality in a streamed broadcast, the service really needs a guaranteed bandwidth to ensure smooth delivery of the data, so requiring technologies like QoS (p. 51), which again is currently poorly supported in mainstream consumer IP networks. Some providers only sell IPTV bundled with a broadband connection so they can control the data path between source and consumer.

- TV has all the funding and rights issues of radio writ large.

Only when the infrastructure is solid will IPTV be a realistic proposition as the customer will not pay for a small, blocky, unreliable TV image while conventional TV (over the air, cable or satellite) is cheaper and better. Perhaps the short-term growth will be in IPTV to mobile devices, such as phones, whose small displays only require a moderate amount of bandwidth.

12.11   Voice over IP

Possibly the next big growth area in the use of the Internet is *Voice over IP* (VoIP), or Internet telephony. As might be guessed, this is transmitting voice conversations over IP.

As use of the Internet has only a tiny marginal cost, while long-distance telephone calls are very expensive, it is only a short leap of imagination to digitize voice and send it over the Internet. This means that you can get essentially free worldwide communications for minimal outlay (the cost of a microphone headset). IP-to-IP calls are now widespread, while for those still using old technology, IP-to-telephone and telephone-to-IP calls are building in popularity.

There are several VoIP systems in use, with both free and paid-for, hardware- and software-only, solutions on offer. The protocols they use are not always published, but things like the *Session Initiation Protocol* (SIP), the ITU-T H.323 teleconferencing protocol, and the *Real-Time Transport Protocol* (RTP) are often involved. They use a mixture of UDP and TCP, with UDP being preferred for data and TCP for control. Current implementations work well over broadband connections, but their quality over a 56Kb link can be fine, too.

RFC 3261
ITU-T H.323
RFC 3550

The ITU *Electronic Numbering* (ENUM) standard hopes to bring together the worlds of telephone numbers and Internet domain addresses. A number, such as +1 555 123 4567, becomes the E.164 address `7.6.5.4.3.2.1.5.5.5.1.e164.arpa`, which then refers to the relevant VoIP endpoint. Not all VoIPs use IP addresses, though, some preferring to use their own style of address which they convert to IP endpoints in their own special way. In this case, looking up a DNS *Naming Authority Pointer* record (NAPTR) for the above address will return (say) the corresponding native SIP address.

ITU-T E.164
RFC 3761

RFC 3762
RFC 3764
RFC 3401
RFC 3402
RFC 3403
RFC 3404

Consider the irony of using VoIP over a telephone line! Many telecoms companies regard this irony as too much to bear and are actively trying to get into VoIP in order to retain control of their market.

One of the current obstacles to VoIP is the poor interaction between many VoIP protocols and firewalls. In particular, RTP does not work well with NAT. This can often be overcome by using the *Simple Traversal of UDP through Network Address Translators* (STUN) protocol, which uses an external server to monitor the address translation, but this is not a complete solution.

RFC 3489

As firewalls become more aware of VoIP these problems should fade.

12.12   More Applications

The range of applications is ever growing. Here are brief descriptions of just a few:

RFC 1288

- Finger. A program to see who is logged in to a remote machine. Often not enabled so as not to hand information to potential crackers.

RFC 3912

- Whois. A service run by DNS providers that gives information on DNS names and IP addresses:

```
% whois bbc.com
...
Registrant:
 BBC Internet Services
 Kingswood Warren
 Tadworth, Surrey KT20 6NP
 UK

 Domain name: BBC.COM

 Administrative Contact:
 ...

 Domain servers in listed order:
    NS0.THNY.BBC.CO.UK
    NS0.THDO.BBC.CO.UK

...
```

- LDAP, *Lightweight Directory Access Protocol*. A *directory* is simply a collection of useful information, such as usernames, passwords, email addresses, even telephone numbers. The distinction between directories and databases is that a database is optimized for multiple concurrent reads and updates while a directory is specialized for reading with only the occasional update. RFC 2251 RFC 3377 RFC 3771

  LDAP is 'lightweight' as it is a simplification of the much more heavyweight X.500 directory services protocol, a protocol that never really gained much ground due to difficulty of implementation. On the other hand, LDAP is widespread.

  LDAP shares many properties of the DNS. It can be distributed: items of data can be on different remote machines. It can be replicated for resilience and speed: the same item of data can be on more than one machine. The directory is hierarchical, though keys can be more general than simple DNS labels. Lookup can use complex filters such as 'find all people with names starting with "R" and date of birth before 1970' (suitably expressed in the LDAP language!).

  Furthermore, the data stored in an LDAP directory is not limited to IP addresses but can be arbitrary data chunks. It should be possible to replace DNS with LDAP with a modest loss of efficiency, but that is unlikely to happen as everybody prefers the more specialized (and incumbent) system. RFC 1279 RFC 2307

  LDAP is important in the administration of large networks where there are many machines and many users. User passwords, for example, can be kept in an LDAP directory rather than in a separate file on each host. When a user logs in, the password verification refers to the LDAP server. Also, administration (such as RFC 2307 changing the password) is merely a matter of updating the LDAP server rather than the hundreds of separate password files. Microsoft's Active Directory and NDS, Novell's directory service, both build on LDAP.

RFC 1013

- **X Window System.** A network-transparent graphical interface system. This separates where a program runs from where it displays its results. Such a mechanism is very useful as it means that a graphical program doesn't have to run on the machine you are sitting in front of: the program can run where it is most suitable and it can display where it is most suitable. Thus, for example, a numerically intensive program might be running on a large mainframe in Canada while the results are appearing on a laptop in England. Or a Web browser can be running on one machine but displaying on another.

- **ssh,** *Secure Shell.* One of the problems of telnet is security: when a user logs in on a remote machine their password is transmitted over the network in the clear. A sniffer program en route could pick this up and so allow a cracker access. And what's more, all subsequent data traffic between the user and the remote machine is also readable, which is a problem if the data are confidential.

  The ssh application was developed to fix this. Using clever public key encryption technology it ensures that no data or password is ever transmitted unencrypted. This is much more complicated than the simple telnet, but is always to be preferred if available. Some administrators disable the use of telnet (i.e., they do not run the login program on port 23) on their machines for precisely these security worries.

- **POP and IMAP.** While SMTP is for *sending* email, POP and IMAP are for *fetching* email.

  Originally email was sent to a specific user on a specific machine. That was fine in the early days of the Internet as there were relatively few machines and a user would typically use just one. These days, though, users often switch between machines, or even the machines themselves move about (laptops!).

  So it is not so convenient for email to end up on a per-user basis. Instead, it is better for email to be stored in one place that can be easily accessed from any other machine. This is the 'post office' idea: a user's email is collected in a single place, but the user can connect to their email from wherever they happen to be.

RFC 1939

  The *Post Office Protocol* (POP) is a protocol designed to do just this. It allows the user's local machine to interrogate the post office machine and retrieve email headers and then selected emails themselves.

RFC 2060
RFC 2061

  A more flexible protocol, the *Internet Message Access Protocol* (IMAP), is now commonly used. This fixes some deficiencies of POP, such as having multiple simultaneous open sessions with the post office machine and having more advanced message manipulation facilities.

Because emails can be sensitive there are secure versions of POP and IMAP, namely SPOP and SIMAP (aka IMAPS), which are POP or IMAP run over an encrypting secure socket layer SSL/TLS (Section 13.6).

RFC 2595

A complete email system has four parts:

– a *Mail User Agent* (MUA), the program that interfaces to the user;

– a *Mail Transport Agent* (MTA) that sends the email (this would probably use SMTP);

– a *Mail Delivery Agent* (MDA) that delivers the email to the appropriate user;

– a *Mail Access Agent* (MAA), the program that interfaces to the user (e.g., your favorite email reader).

- USENET, *User Network*. This was developed from the bulletin boards of the early Internet, itself a model of notice boards where you can pin up notices and read notices that others have pinned up. Bulletin boards and USENET are simple collections of messages organized (if that is not too strong a word) by topic. Each topic is called a *newsgroup*. Users read and post messages in the newsgroups.

RFC 1036

Use of USENET has been in decline since the advent of the WWW, but there are many tens of thousands of newsgroups. Most hosts only choose to subscribe to and receive a limited subset of all those possible. USENET employs the NNTP (*Network News Transfer Protocol*) to manage the propagation of articles between participating hosts. The network of machines passes new articles amongst themselves: eventually an article reaches all hosts that want it.

RFC 977

There is very little oversight of USENET and new groups can be created more or less at will. This has led to what is called *newsgroup anarchy* where all kinds of unrestricted behaviour rule. Google keeps a searchable archive of just about all the important parts of USENET going right back to its inception. It provides a valuable source for researching the early Internet. See `http://groups.google.com`.

- NTP, *Network Time Protocol*. This is a hierarchical system to ensure the clock on your computer is correct. A primary or *stratum 1* NTP server is a machine that carries a high-precision timepiece such as a radio or caesium clock. Access to these machines is generally limited to stratum 2 servers which are the main means of disseminating time. An institution might implement a stratum 3 server, which gets its time from a stratum 2 server and so on. The hierarchical arrangement spreads the load across many machines.

RFC 1305

An end client will periodically connect to a suitable stratum server using NTP, get the current time and update its own clock as necessary. However, NTP is actually quite sophisticated as it has to compensate for the variable delays introduced by the network. Roughly speaking, an NTP client makes several requests to a server, computes the round-trip time from timestamps on the requests, and uses this as an offset to the time reported by the server.

- And so on. The range of things that may be done with a network is limited only by our imagination.

12.13   Exercises

Exercise 12.1 Telnet allows us to discover the protocols that are used by various applications. For example, `telnet wwwhost 80` will connect to a Web server. Experiment with HTTP.

Exercise 12.2 Some files are available both via the Web and via FTP. Determine by experiment which is the more efficient at transmitting (a) large files, (b) small files.

Exercise 12.3 Use `rpcinfo` to discover the RPC services available from various machines. Find out what these services do.

Exercise 12.4 Measure the difference in time it takes to read a large file from a local disk (on your machine) and from an NFS disk. Repeat for any other remote file system you have access to. What is the rate of slowdown? Relate this to the speeds of the network connections.

Exercise 12.5 Read up on XML and its related technologies (CSS, XSL, XSLT and the like). Why do you think that XML has proved so popular?

Exercise 12.6 Look into using `ssh` (aka `putty`). What means of authentication and security does it use?

Exercise 12.7 Investigate the way you normally read email. What protocol is used? Is it secure? Repeat for how you *send* email.

Exercise 12.8 Write down and make notes on as many applications that use networks as you can. Concentrate on the protocols they use.

Exercise 12.9 'Layering models are useless. TCP/IP is nothing like the ISO model, and because of ICMP it doesn't even fit its own model.' Discuss.

13 ISSUES OF SECURITY

13.1   Introduction

IP was originally developed in a 'safe' academic environment. As such, no real attention was paid to security or authentication in the protocol. Also, some of the original implementations left a lot to be desired in terms of good programming habits. On the one hand, the quick development of code meant that IP was soon out in the real world, which contributed to its huge success. On the other hand, it meant that experimental and imperfectly tested code was rapidly incorporated into a wide variety of services.

Thus there tends to be generic bugs that appear in many companies' IP code. Some of these bugs are benign (like the use of TTLs as a hop count), but some can be exploited to maybe

RFC 2525

- crash the machine;

- tie up the machine with so much bogus traffic that real traffic can't get serviced – this is called *denial of service*;

- gain unauthorized access to the machine. This could be reading, writing or deleting files that should be private, or running unauthorized programs on the machine, such as sending spam email (Section 12.4). One popular use is to use the machine as a base to attack further machines.

Today the Internet is no longer a safe place. Due to its ubiquity in modern life, there are many people out there seeking to use it for monetary, political or other gain, or simply wanting to make a nuisance of themselves. So in the modern Internet we must seek to address these issues and protect ourselves from those who would do us harm.

Now, the technology and psychology of Internet security is a *huge* topic and there is no way we can cover more than the merest hint of the problem here. As usual, we shall look at just a few examples.

13.2   Network Attacks

Here we outline a few of the simpler ways IP networks can be attacked.

13.2.1   SYN Flooding

This is a denial of service attack. A TCP connection starts with a SYN from the client. The server notes this and ACKs with its own SYN. Also, the server saves a chunk of information about this potential new connection (e.g., information to recognize the corresponding final ACK of the three way handshake and the facilities, like SACK, negotiated in the optional header). A SYN flood is where the attacker sends very many active open SYN segments and never completes the three way handshake. Each SYN consumes resources on the server that are not released until a suitable timeout period has passed. The server can run out of memory space and thus is unable to service real TCP connection requests.

There have been several solutions suggested. When resources are low we can start dropping half-open requests in some sensible manner, e.g. oldest first, or at random. A real connection request may be dropped, but the probabilities are that it will get accepted eventually.

An alternative is to use *syncookies*. This scheme stores no information about the putative connection on the server, but cleverly encodes it in the server's initial sequence number for this connection. When the second ACK comes back, its ACK field can be decoded to tell us which connection it refers to. This method is good as the server can never run out of resources, but is tricky to get right as 32 bits of sequence number is not a lot to work with, and the value must be carefully encrypted or else the connection will be open to spoofing.

Another problem is that syncookies do not provide enough bits to encode all the possible options (like SACK, timestamps, etc.) that get negotiated in the initial SYNs. Therefore syncookies are only used when we start to get SYN overload and such optimizing features are not enabled during a flood: the loss of SACK and the like is not a big deal when we have to cope with a SYN flood.

The idea of using cookies to protect against flooding was adopted by SCTP and is a mandatory part of its setup handshake. See Section 10.15.2.

13.2.2   Distributed Denial of Service

This is a way to SYN-flood. Many thousands of poorly protected hosts are subverted by crackers: these hosts are called *zombies*. At a signal all zombies send (SYNs for) HTTP requests to the victim server. This overload severely reduces the level of service for other users, often down to zero. This is now being used to overload hosts that the crackers dislike for some reason (often political) or as part of an extortion attack against a commercial host (e.g., a betting site) to get it to pay a ransom.

You do not always need high technology to mount a DDOS. The Website for the World Trade Organization meeting at Seattle in 1999 was overloaded in a similar way, but the zombies were hundreds of actual people clicking away at the Web page.

13.2.3 Implementation Attacks

Many implementations of the IP have bugs. These bugs can sometimes be exploited by those wishing to cause mayhem. For example, some machines were vulnerable to oversized ping packets in an attack called the *ping of death*. These packets were much larger than the MTU and overflowed internal buffers when the host tried to reassemble the fragments: the writers of the code never expected ICMP packets to be that large. The usual result is a crash.

We can also generate this by constructing a fragment of length (say) 1000 and fragment offset 65400. This would imply a packet of length greater than 65535 bytes, which is the longest a packet can be (16 bit header field).

The easiest solution is to ignore ICMP packets that are larger than the MTU. Real ICMP packets are never large enough to require fragmentation, so we can safely drop ICMP fragments. Of course, you could fix the reassembly code, too.

In a similar vein, some systems could not cope with *fragment bombs*. This is when a large number of packets' fragments are received, but all the packets have fragments missing and therefore cannot be reassembled. Again, a lack of resources needed to store the fragment leads to problems.

There have been many others. Modern IP implementers should be aware of these problems and be able to avoid them. They are mostly problems with making invalid assumptions in the IP processing code that packets are benign and correctly formed.

Others have included:

- Jolt (aka sPING). Fragmented ICMP packets.

- Land attack. The source IP addresses on TCP SYNs spoofed to be same as the destination's. The destination tries to respond to itself.

- Teardrop. Overlapping fragments cause problems on reassembly.

- New Teardrop (aka Bonk, Boink, Teardrop2). Overlapping fragments of a UDP packet reassemble to form a whole packet with an invalid header.

- Bandwidth attack. Simply send so much data that the destination cannot cope, e.g., Smurf. A ping packet is sent to the broadcast address of a victim network. The replies flood the network. The source address is set to some other victim: the replies flood back there, too.

- Zero length fragments. In some implementations these were saved but never used and eventually used up all memory.

And so on. It's not easy writing a robust IP implementation.

13.2.4 Malware

Quite often writers of software seek to enhance their application by adding features like the ability to send or execute code across the Internet. Unfortunately, quite often this is a very bad idea. The biggest example is the ability for email to transport malicious code: code that can take over an unsuspecting machine.

Malicious code, or *malware*, comes in several guises:

- Viruses: code that attaches itself to other programs.

- Worms: code that is independent, but seeks to transmit itself from machine to machine.

- Trojans: code that pretends to be something else in the hope you will execute it by mistake.

Another way into a machine is when the application does insufficient checking of received data. In the *buffer overflow* attack a server sends a large amount of carefully crafted data that the client fails to check. This overflows the memory buffer that the client has allocated for the data and the result is that the client starts executing the received data, which, of course, does something to the advantage of the server and the detriment of the client. Web browsers, being large and complex pieces of code, are particularly susceptible to this kind of problem.

The psychology behind the authors of such code is moot, but the effect has been felt worldwide. The Warhol worm (p. 157) is a case in point: a simple piece of code that exploited a hole in a database server and brought large chunks of the Internet to its knees in under 10 minutes. The only defences against such things are (a) ensuring your virus protection is up to date; and (b) using consumer pressure against vendors of applications to ensure they do not have exploitable loopholes. The legal approach of making vendors liable for problems with their code remains strangely unexplored.

> In early 2005 experiments showed that a newly installed Windows machine placed unprotected on the Internet would be attacked in an average of about 3 minutes.

13.2.5 Social Engineering Attacks

This is an ancient form of attack that has found a new lease of life in the Internet era. When applied in real life this is often called a *confidence trick*.

If the machine is too hard to break, attack the user instead. Many people find social engineering attacks much easier than machine attacks. The simplest form involves phoning up a systems administrator and persuading them to give you a password to their machine. This can involve you pretending to be their superior and threatening to sack them; pretending to be a distraught user who has forgotten their password; or any other kind of pretence to unbalance them or get their sympathy. This is much easier and faster than trying to crack a password by brute force!

Another growth industry is *phishing*. This is a form of identity impersonation to try and convince the victim to hand over valuable information, such as bank account numbers or credit card numbers.

A typical phishing attack is:

- The victim receives an email purporting to be from their bank asking them to update their personal details. The email provides a convenient link to take them to a Website to do this.

- The Web page they get to looks plausibly like their bank's.

- The victim enters their bank details and sends them off.

Of course, both the email and the Web page are fakes and the personal details are now in the hands of criminals.

Reliance on people's greed is another way. The 419 or Nigerian fraud is named after the South African police code used to identify this particular approach and the country where it seems to originate from:

- The victim receives an email with a story of woe about someone who has a large amount of money or gold or diamonds they want to transfer out of their country, but some regulation or law is preventing them doing so.

- The email offers the victim a percentage of the money if they would help, but first the victim must secure their involvement by paying a fee upfront or maybe just sending their bank details in order to enable the transfer.

A similar attack is to imply the victim has won the lottery and bank details are required to transfer the winnings.

Social engineering attacks have existed since before the Internet: the 419 attack used to be perpetrated using normal letters and faxes. As a society we have developed ways of spotting real-life cons: to live in the Internet age we must do the same for online cons.

13.3   Firewalls

One way to reduce the danger of attack is to prevent bad packets from reaching the host in the first place.

A *firewall* is a router that sits between a private network and the wider Internet and tries to protect the private network from attacks from the outside world by looking at each packet as it goes through and making a decision on what to do with it (Figure 13.1). This might be to:

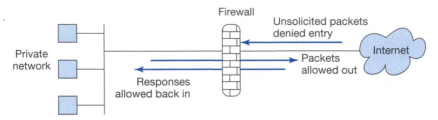

Figure 13.1 Firewall.

- pass the packet through unchanged;

- pass the packet through but modified in some way, perhaps with the TOS bits changed, or see Section 6.7 for Network Address Translation (NAT);

- drop the packet and send some ICMP notification back to the sender, e.g., 'port unreachable';

- silently drop the packet

amongst other possibilities. Dropping the packet silently is a good defence against probes from malicious sources looking for vulnerable services. The normal response to a packet sent to a closed UDP port is to reply with an ICMP 'port unreachable'. This is a signal to the sender that the machine is up and running and worth probing further. Silence can make the sender believe that there is no machine there at all!

Firewalling can be applied at any layer. The most common and useful are:

- *packet filters*, which work at the data link, network and transport layers at the individual packet level, making decisions based on protocols (UDP, TCP, etc.), source and destination addresses, ports, TOS bits, and so on; and

- *application proxies*, which work at the application layer and can use information that applications use, such as HTTP proxies (p. 219), which can choose to allow access at the individual Web page level.

Packet filters are fast, efficient and invisible to the application, but do not have the same degree of discrimination as application proxies. On the other hand, application proxies are relatively much slower and often require configuration in the application (e.g., setting up a Web browser to use the proxy server).

Firewalls can be used to control access to services. For example, suppose we wish to disallow FTP connections to machines on the private network: perhaps we are uncertain if FTP servers can be made safe from external hacking. The firewall can be instructed not to relay TCP packets to the private network that have destination port 21, the FTP port. So even if an FTP server is running on a private machine, no machine outside the firewall can connect to it as the packets simply never get there. Note that other machines *inside* the firewall *can* connect as their packets do not go through the firewall.

Conversely, there can be outward or *egress* filtering. For example, we may wish to prevent a potentially virus- or worm-infected machine from connecting to another machine to replicate itself. This could be achieved by blocking transit for outbound packets going to certain ports. Outward filtering can be also used to enforce policy, such as barring connections to filesharing programs like Napster, blocking packets with destination port 80 to force the use of an HTTP proxy, or stopping connections to external email servers in order to restrict the possibility of spamming.

Configuring a firewall correctly is a difficult business and is not something to be taken lightly: it is easy to convince yourself you have a secure firewall just when you have overlooked some unusual combination of source and destination and service.

Firewalling in conjunction with NAT and NAPT (see Section 6.7) is a particularly powerful combination.

13.4 Security and Authentication in IP

The IP was not designed with an eye on security. An email message is readable as it progresses hop by hop to its destination. Some liken (unencrypted) email to sending postcards: everyone who handles a postcard can read it. In fact, it is much worse than this simile might indicate, as it is easy to implement programs that automatically trawl through huge numbers of emails or other data in a fast and transparent manner.

> The Regulation of Investigatory Powers Act (RIPA) in the UK allows the police or government to install monitoring equipment in any ISP, and requires large ISPs to keep records of every Web page visited by all users.

These days, things are very different as a lot of valuable and sensitive data are transmitted over many and varied networks, so some effort has been spent trying to patch up the IP. Security can be applied at any layer. For example, take the IP model:

- Application. The application provides security by encrypting the data itself. For example, you (or your email application) might encrypt an email using PGP before sending it. Similarly, SHTTP (p. 219) is encrypted HTTP.   RFC 2440

- Transport layer (TCP/UDP). SSL and TLS are described in Section 13.6. If trusting the user or application to encrypt messages is too problematic, we might get the transport layer to encrypt for us. The SIMAP (p. 233) protocol is just IMAP running over SSL and HTTPS (p. 219) is HTTP over SSL/TLS.   RFC 2595

- Network layer (IP). Even lower, we have IPSec, as discussed in Section 13.5.2.   RFC 2406

- Data link. We can use security even in the data link layer. For example, WEP (Section 5.2.4) is used to obscure wireless communications.   IEEE 802.11

Encryption is just a small part in making a system secure as many other factors must be taken into account, particularly human factors (see Section 13.2.5). There is no point using military-grade encryption software if you have an easily guessable password. Furthermore, there are actually two problems to address: secrecy and authentication. While most people are familiar with secrecy, authentication is possibly more fundamental. Secrecy is 'make sure the contents of this email are not readable by anyone other than the recipient' while authentication is 'make sure the recipient is really the person I think they are'. It is no use sending a strongly encrypted message only to find you sent it to the wrong person. A typical example is buying over the Web: perhaps you want to send your credit card details to someone who appears to be the Acme Widget Company. So you negotiate a military-grade encryption key with them to encode your credit card number and send it off, happy in the knowledge that no one else can read it. Only later do you realize that the Web page was a scam and has nothing to do with Acme Widgets.

You must have some way of determining if a person or Website is who they say they are. In the real world we use documents like passports to certify people; in the Internet world we do the same, except now the certificates are chunks of data whose veracity we can check mathematically.

13.5   Link and Network Layer Security and Authentication

In Section 13.6 we shall look at security and authentication in the transport layer. We have briefly touched on link layer security in wireless networks (WEP, Section 5.2.4). But first we are going to consider a few network layer methods, namely PPTP, L2TP, and IPSec. IPSec is clearly a network layer protocol, though the other two are more properly thought of as link layer protocols, even though PPTP and L2TP layer over IP. Whatever their classification, we treat all three here.

13.5.1   PPTP and L2TP

RFC 2637
The *Point-to-Point Tunneling Protocol* (PPTP) was devised by Microsoft to support *Virtual Private Networks* (VPNs), namely allowing a remote machine to appear to be on another network by tunnelling (Section 2.4) IP traffic between them over the Internet. The 'private' refers to the fact that the tunnelled traffic is supposed to be secure in transit so that intermediate routers cannot read it.

All traffic from the host travels through the VPN tunnel to the remote network before being routed from there as if it had originated on that network. Thus all the services (such as file systems) that are available on the network are available directly to the remote host. This is particularly convenient for teleworkers who want to use their company's computers while at home or while travelling.

The PPTP (Figure 13.2):

IP header	GRE header	PPP header	PPP payload (tunnelled IP packet)

Figure 13.2 PPTP encapsulation.

- tunnels IP over PPP over the *Generic Routing Encapsulation* (GRE) protocol over IP and sends connection control messages over a separate TCP connection;   RFC 2784

- layers only over IP networks;

- can encapsulate other network protocols, such as IPX and NetBEUI;

- uses the same authentication mechanisms as PPP (Section 4.4.2);

- can use *Microsoft Point-to-Point Encryption* (MPPE) for privacy when combined with MS-CHAP authentication;

- is simple to set up.

On the other hand, PPTP is regarded as insecure as the authentication mechanism (MS-CHAP) can be spoofed. A later version (MS-CHAPv2) fixed a major hole, but left unaddressed some of the other problems.

The Layer Two Tunneling Protocol (L2TP) combines features from PPTP and *Layer Two Forwarding* (L2F) developed by Cisco Systems, Inc.   RFC 2661

The L2TP (Figure 13.3):

- tunnels IP over PPP over UDP;

- is intended to be used over ATM, Frame Relay and X.25 networks, though currently only L2TP over IP networks is defined;

- has no native encryption and must rely on, say, IPSec for secrecy;   RFC 3193

- uses the same authentication mechanisms as PPP or can use IPSec's ESP (see below);

- is believed to be more secure than PPTP;

- is simple to set up.

The last may seem an unusual comment until you compare setting up PPTP/L2TP to setting up IPSec, which is notoriously difficult.

IP header	UDP header	L2TP header	PPP header	PPP payload (tunnelled IP packet)

Figure 13.3 L2TP encapsulation.

> Note that tunnelling TCP over TCP is usually a bad idea. Each TCP has its own idea of timeouts and retransmits and they get out of sync very easily and start fighting each other. This can cause a big drop in throughput.

13.5.2 IPSec

RFC 2401

PPTP and L2TP create point-to-point VPNs. IPSec does the same, but it can also manage the secrecy and authentication of individual connections. There are several protocols involved. Secrecy is implemented by *Encapsulating Security Payload* (ESP), while authentication is achieved by *Authentication Header* (AH). Keys are managed by *Internet Key Exchange* (IKE) which runs separately using the *Internet Security Association and Key Management Protocol* (ISAKMP).

RFC 2406

RFC 2402
RFC 2409
RFC 2408

Good encryption produces data that do not compress, which can be a problem on slower connections like telephone lines where compression is used to improve throughput. IP Payload Compression (IPComp) can be used in these cases before ESP is applied.

RFC 3173

IPSec authenticates connections, not users. You do not use the authentication to log in, but rather to ensure that the remote host really is Acme Widgets before you send money to it. Both ESP and AH require a secret shared key to work. This key can:

- be pre-agreed by the hosts (*manual keying*), or

- be negotiated by IKE.

IKE itself can use a pre-agreed secret key to deliver the AH/ESP key, but can also use a public-key certificate mechanism. Typically a single per-system IKE process manages all the exchanges for a host. When a new IPSec/IP connection is started, an IKE exchange will take place before the IPSec/IP can continue: this may take an appreciable amount of time.

> Sometimes many seconds. This may cause a timeout in the TCP handshake on slow machines.

RFC 2367

> IKE uses a `PF_KEY` socket.

IPSec (Figure 13.4):

- is directly within the IP layer, so TCP and UDP (or anything else) are easily layered on top;

- clearly only applies to IP;

- lets AH do the authentication, while ESP does encryption *and*, optionally, authentication (Figure 13.5): originally, ESP did not have authentication but this was shown to be vulnerable to all kinds of impersonation attacks (rather than layer AH with ESP it was felt that adding authentication directly to ESP was the better route; encryption without authentication is not recommended);

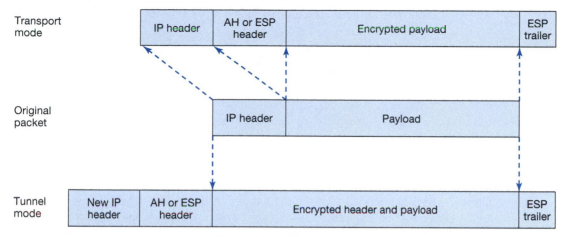

Figure 13.4 IPSec modes.

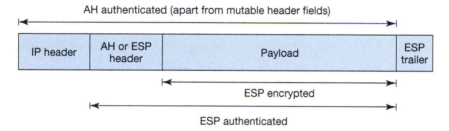

Figure 13.5 ESP and AH authentication.

- has separate transport and tunnel modes: transport for direct connections and tunnel for VPNs; in tunnel mode the packet payload is the entire original packet, IP header and all, but in transport mode the ESP or AH headers follow directly after the IP header (and the payload is encrypted);

- has ESP as a trailer as well as a header if authentication is employed; this can also contain padding to conceal the length of the original packet;

- lets ESP authenticate only the ESP and the payload, while AH authenticates all the original packet, excepting the *mutable* header fields like fragmentation and TTL which change as the packet travels;

- applies equally to IPv4 and IPv6.

Use `setsockopt` in transport mode. Tunnel mode should be transparent to the application.

IPSec is slowly gaining in popularity. Difficulties include:

- the initial connection overhead is high (not such a problem in an IPSec VPN as the tunnel gets authenticated just once);

- it is tricky to set up: managing it is difficult to get right (or, rather, no one has automated the process well enough, yet).

Opportunistic encryption is a way to use IPSec without so many of the management overheads. When set up, it can make connections from a host secure whenever it is possible to do so. When a new connection is made, it automatically looks up DNS KEY and TXT records which should contain the relevant public keys of the remote host, presuming, of course, that the remote host has published them in this way. If not, the connection falls back to an unencrypted session. All of this happens transparently to the application. Such an approach avoids the tedious management of public keys that a traditional IPSec session requires, but does need a secure DNS to prevent spoofing (p. 151) of the public keys.

Generic problems of VPNs include:

- there is extra overhead in every packet which might be a problem (and may cause extra fragmentation);

- there is extra overhead in the time taken to encrypt or authenticate the packets;

- strongly encrypted packets do not compress, which can be an issue on slow links such as modems;

- some routers make decisions based on the type of traffic, e.g., video or FTP. Encryption hides this and so makes efficient routing harder.

In VPNs performance is secondary to secrecy and convenience, but is nonetheless important since people will not use VPNs if they are desperately slow. This means that ideas like using IPComp to offset the cost of the large headers of IPSec are quite important. As machines and networks get faster these reasons not to use VPNs should fade.

Many other VPN solutions exist. For example:

- *Crypto IP Encapsulation* (CIPE) is a lightweight point-to-point protocol that layers over UDP.

- The remote login protocol ssh (p. 232) has a VPN mode, though this runs over TCP.

- *OpenVPN* tunnels IP over the transport layer encryption systems SSL/TLS (see Section 13.6) and so can benefit from their features. On the other hand, this means that we are running IP over SSL/TLS over TCP or UDP over IP, which is another layer of encapsulation. (This turns out to be about a 10% overhead in practice.)

The cryptographic robustness of these solutions varies widely. For example, CIPE is generally judged to be not much better than PPTP.

13.6 Transport Layer Security and Authentication

Just as in the network layer, security and authentication can be applied at the transport layer. Protocols like *Secure Socket Layer* (SSL, developed by Netscape) and *Transport Layer Security* (TLS), an evolution of SSL, exist to do this.

RFC 2246

There have been a couple of updates of SSL, and versions 2 and 3 are the most common. However, SSLv2 has flaws which can lead to possible breaks in the security. You should only use SSLv3, or better still TLS, which are believed secure.

The SSL/TLS layer (Figure 13.6) sits on top of TCP and provides security (encryption) for the data and authentication of the remote host. After a TCP connection has been established an SSL/TLS *handshake* authenticates the connection and negotiates a secret key. Subsequent transmissions use the secret key to encrypt the data.

Authentication in the handshake is achieved through the use of public-key certificates. The client receives a certificate from the server which it can verify in a number of ways. For example, Web browsers often contain a collection of certificates from *certification authorities* that it can use to check the certificate from the server. Similarly, if it wishes, the server can request a certificate from the client and verify it in the same way. This can be used to restrict services to those authorized to use them.

Transport layer security is good, but requires the application programmer to understand and instigate the function calls to set up the certification checking and to start the handshake. Compare this to IP layer security of which the programmer can be quite ignorant. On the other hand, transport layer security assures the programmer that security is in their control, and not at the whim of the operating system or its administrator.

> IP security is in the OS kernel, while TLS is in user space. There is no deep reason for this; it is only because generally IP is in the kernel and anything above TCP is in user space. TCP and UDP connections use machine resources (e.g., ports) that are shared amongst all users of a machine, so we can't really let them be managed by programs that can abuse them, either by accident or intent. Keeping the resources managed by the kernel ensures they are always allocated fairly.

There are overheads in using SSL/TLS just as in IP layer security: the initial connection takes time to authenticate and negotiate a secret key, and then there is the overhead of time taken to encrypt the data and the overhead of the SSL/TLS headers taking bandwidth. If a client makes repeated connections to the server (such as happens for Web pages) the SSL/TLS protocols include a certificate renegotiation facility to reduce the connection overhead. This lets the client and server reuse a previous certification rather than go through the entire procedure again and again.

Figure 13.6 SSL/TLS encapsulation.

RFC 2818 SSL/TLS is used widely in the WWW (in particular HTTPS, p. 219) to prevent eaves-droppers from sniffing personal details like credit card numbers and to authenticate Web-sites.

13.7   Exercises

Exercise 13.1 Find out the security policy for your local network. If there is none, formulate one.

Exercise 13.2 Find out from your systems administrator how many attacks per day your network is getting and what defences they have against them.

Exercise 13.3 Make a list of worms and viruses that are current on the Internet. Ensure your machine is safe against them by upgrading your virus protection and ensuring your firewall is secure. Instigate a regular date in your diary to repeat this exercise.

Exercise 13.4 The next time you buy something over the Internet check the authentication of the Web server. Is their certificate what you should expect?

Exercise 13.5 Read up on social engineering attacks. *The Art of Deception: Controlling the Human Element of Security* by Kevin Mitnick is a useful place to start.

Exercise 13.6 Get a newly installed machine and put it unprotected onto the Internet. Time how long it takes to it to be attacked and taken over. Repeat for various operating systems.

Exercise 13.7 Set up a secure VPN between a pair of networks (e.g., home and work). Write notes on the procedure involved and the quality of the connection obtained.

Exercise 13.8 Read up on algorithms and protocols for secrecy and authentication in Bruce Schneier's book *Applied Cryptography*.

Exercise 13.9 Read up on why PPTP is considered insecure. Discuss how L2PP differs.

Exercise 13.10 Investigate why SSLv2 is not advised.

Exercise 13.11 Find the various versions of SSL and TLS that your Web browser supports. Also find the list of certification authorities it contains.

Exercise 13.12 Investigate how to program the SSL/TLS layer.

EXAMPLE PROGRAMS

The gap between theory and practice is not large, but is significant enough that it is not obvious how to write programs that actually network, so here we give C code for simple clients and servers that connect using TCP and using UDP. This shows how to write programs using the *socket API* (Application Programming Interface).

There are many points to note:

- The API was designed not to be specific to IP but to apply to many kinds of protocol, so there are the occasional casts to `struct sockaddr`, a generic socket address type.

- An IP address (address, port) is held in a `struct sockaddr_in`.

- In general, a server creates a socket and then listens on it for data to arrive. The local port number is either specified or can be chosen by the operating system.

- The server can additionally restrict the addresses it will allow connections from, but generally we want to accept connections from anywhere.

- Sockets are created with no associated address; the `bind` function associates an address with a socket.

- You must be careful about using network byte orders in structures.

- The function `inet_aton` converts a string such as `"10.0.1.2"` into its binary equivalent, while `inet_ntoa` does the reverse.

- These programs do not take presentation issues into account. If we were to connect, say, an ASCII machine to an EBCDIC machine we would get nonsense.

A.1 TCP Server

This listens on a TCP port for a connection and sends a simple message:

- A TCP socket is called a `SOCK_STREAM`.

- Before it will accept connections a TCP socket must be put in the LISTEN state using `listen`. The second argument to `listen` is a *backlog* parameter. This indicates to the operating system how many pending connection requests it should keep; if the queue grows too long it should start refusing new connections. This prevents overloading if large numbers of clients are simultaneously trying to open a connection to the server.

- The `accept` function moves a connection into ESTABLISHED. It returns a new file descriptor and a structure that contains the address of the client that has connected. The file descriptor can be used just like we were `reading` or `writing` to a file, but really our data goes across the TCP connection. A socket is bidirectional and we can both read and write to it.

- The original socket is still listening for new connections: we can choose to `accept` more connections as before, or `close` the socket if we do not want any more connections.

```c
#include <stdio.h>
#include <unistd.h>
#include <stdlib.h>
#include <sys/types.h>
#include <sys/socket.h>
#include <netinet/in.h>
#include <arpa/inet.h>
#include <string.h>

#define PORT 12345
#define MESSAGE "hello"

int main(void)
{
  int sock, conn, clilen;
  struct sockaddr_in server_addr, client_addr;

  /* create a STREAM (TCP) socket in the INET (IP) protocol */
  sock = socket(PF_INET, SOCK_STREAM, 0);

  if (sock < 0) {
    perror("creating socket");
    exit(1);
  }

  /* create server address: this will say where we will be
     willing to accept connections from */

  /* clear it out */
  memset(&server_addr, 0, sizeof(server_addr));
```

```c
    /* it is an INET address */
    server_addr.sin_family = AF_INET;

    /* the client IP address, in network byte order */
    /* in this example we accept connections from ANYwhere */
    server_addr.sin_addr.s_addr = htonl(INADDR_ANY);

    /* the port we are going to listen on, in network byte order */
    server_addr.sin_port = htons(PORT);

    /* associate the socket with the address and port */
    if (bind(sock, (struct sockaddr *)&server_addr,
      sizeof(server_addr)) < 0) {
      perror("bind failed");
      exit(2);
    }

    /* start the socket listening for new connections */
    if (listen(sock, 5) < 0) {
      perror("listen failed");
      exit(3);
    }

    while (1) {

      /* now wait until we get a connection */
      printf("waiting for a connection...\n");
      clilen = sizeof(client_addr);
      conn = accept(sock, (struct sockaddr *)&client_addr, &clilen);

      if (conn < 0) {
        perror("accept failed");
        exit(4);
      }

      /* now client_addr contains the address of the client */
      printf("connection from %s\n", inet_ntoa(client_addr.sin_addr));

      printf("sending message\n");

      write(conn, MESSAGE, sizeof(MESSAGE));

      /* close connection */
      close(conn);
    }

    return 0;
}
```

A.2   TCP Client

This makes a TCP connection to the server and reads the message it sends:

- The client is somewhat simpler. We just use `connect` to connect a socket to a specified address and then we can use `read` and `write` as before.

```c
#include <stdio.h>
#include <unistd.h>
#include <stdlib.h>
#include <sys/types.h>
#include <sys/socket.h>
#include <netinet/in.h>
#include <arpa/inet.h>
#include <string.h>

#define PORT 12345
#define SERVADDR "127.0.0.1"

int main(void)
{
  int sock;
  struct sockaddr_in server_addr;
  char buffer[1024];

  /* create a STREAM (TCP) socket in the INET (IP) protocol */
  sock = socket(PF_INET, SOCK_STREAM, 0);

  if (sock < 0) {
    perror("creating socket");
    exit(1);
  }

  /* create server address: where we want to connect to */

  /* clear it out */
  memset(&server_addr, 0, sizeof(server_addr));

  /* it is an INET address */
  server_addr.sin_family = AF_INET;

  /* the server IP address, in network byte order */
  inet_aton(SERVADDR, &server_addr.sin_addr);

  /* the port we are going to send to, in network byte order */
  server_addr.sin_port = htons(PORT);
```

```
    /* now make the connection */
    if (connect(sock, (struct sockaddr *)&server_addr,
                sizeof(server_addr)) < 0) {
        perror("connect failed");
        exit(4);
    }

    printf("reading message\n");

    read(sock, buffer, 1024);

    printf("got '%s'\n", buffer);

    /* close connection */
    close(sock);

    return 0;
}
```

A.3   UDP Server

This waits on a UDP port for a datagram and returns a simple message. In contrast with TCP, which knows when a connection has been made, the only way UDP knows if data is going to arrive is when it arrives:

- A UDP socket is called a SOCK_DGRAM.

- Having no connection protocol, a UDP socket simply uses recvfrom to wait for data to arrive. This also returns the address of the client that sent the data.

- We use sendto to send a message, specifying the destination address.

```
#include <stdio.h>
#include <unistd.h>
#include <stdlib.h>
#include <sys/types.h>
#include <sys/socket.h>
#include <netinet/in.h>
#include <arpa/inet.h>
#include <string.h>

#define PORT 12345
#define MESSAGE "hello"

int main(void)
{
    int sock, clilen;
```

```c
struct sockaddr_in server_addr, client_addr;
char buffer[1024];

/* create a DGRAM (UDP) socket in the INET (IP) protocol */
sock = socket(PF_INET, SOCK_DGRAM, 0);

if (sock < 0) {
  perror("creating socket");
  exit(1);
}

/* create server address: this will say where we will be
   willing to accept datagrams from */

/* clear it out */
memset(&server_addr, 0, sizeof(server_addr));

/* it is an INET address */
server_addr.sin_family = AF_INET;

/* the client IP address, in network byte order */
/* in this example we accept datagrams from ANYwhere */
server_addr.sin_addr.s_addr = htonl(INADDR_ANY);

/* the port we are going to listen on, in network byte order */
server_addr.sin_port = htons(PORT);

/* associate the socket with the address and port */
if (bind(sock, (struct sockaddr *)&server_addr,
  sizeof(server_addr)) < 0) {
  perror("bind failed");
  exit(2);
}

while (1) {

  /* now wait until we get a datagram */
  printf("waiting for a datagram...\n");
  clilen = sizeof(client_addr);
  if (recvfrom(sock, buffer, 1024, 0,
    (struct sockaddr *)&client_addr,
    &clilen) < 0) {
    perror("recvfrom failed");
    exit(4);
  }

  /* now client_addr contains the address of the client */
  printf("got '%s' from %s\n", buffer,
    inet_ntoa(client_addr.sin_addr));
```

```
        printf("sending message back\n");

        if (sendto(sock, MESSAGE, sizeof(MESSAGE), 0,
                (struct sockaddr *)&client_addr,
            sizeof(client_addr)) < 0) {
            perror("sendto failed");
            exit(5);
        }

    }

    return 0;
}
```

A.4   UDP Client

This sends a datagram to the server and reads the message it returns:

- The client needs to do very little, just use `sendto` on some data and the server address and `recvfrom` to get the reply. Note that some other host could send data to this socket before the server had a chance to reply: if we are being careful we should check that the address and port number are what we expect since anyone could be sending data to us, not just the server. If the address and port are not who we want we should discard the data and repeat the `recvfrom`.

```
#include <stdio.h>
#include <unistd.h>
#include <stdlib.h>
#include <sys/types.h>
#include <sys/socket.h>
#include <netinet/in.h>
#include <arpa/inet.h>
#include <string.h>

#define PORT 12345
#define MESSAGE "hi there"
#define SERVADDR "127.0.0.1"

int main(void)
{
    int sock, clilen;
    struct sockaddr_in server_addr, client_addr;
    char buffer[1024];

    /* create a DGRAM (UDP) socket in the INET (IP) protocol */
```

```
sock = socket(PF_INET, SOCK_DGRAM, 0);

if (sock < 0) {
  perror("creating socket");
  exit(1);
}

/* create server address: where we want to send to */

/* clear it out */
memset(&server_addr, 0, sizeof(server_addr));

/* it is an INET address */
server_addr.sin_family = AF_INET;

/* the server IP address, in network byte order */
inet_aton(SERVADDR, &server_addr.sin_addr);

/* the port we are going to send to, in network byte order */
server_addr.sin_port = htons(PORT);

/* now send a datagram */
if (sendto(sock, MESSAGE, sizeof(MESSAGE), 0,
        (struct sockaddr *)&server_addr,
     sizeof(server_addr)) < 0) {
     perror("sendto failed");
     exit(4);
}

printf("waiting for a reply...\n");
clilen = sizeof(client_addr);
if (recvfrom(sock, buffer, 1024, 0,
     (struct sockaddr *)&client_addr,
        &clilen) < 0) {
     perror("recvfrom failed");
     exit(4);
}

printf("got '%s' from %s\n", buffer,
inet_ntoa(client_addr.sin_addr));
/* close socket */
close(sock);

return 0;
}
```

B

RESOURCES

Assigned Numbers (RFC1700)	`http://www.iana.org/numbers.htm`

ISO 3166 country codes	`http://www.iso.org/iso/en/prods-services/`
	`iso3166ma/02iso-3166-code-lists/`
	`index.html`

AfriNIC	`http://www.afrinic.org`
APNIC	`http://www.apnic.net`
ARIN	`http://www.arin.net`
ETSI	`http://www.etsi.org`
IAB	`http://www.iab.org`
IANA	`http://www.iana.org`
ICANN	`http://www.icann.org`
IEEE 802.11	`http://standards.ieee.org/getieee802`
IETF	`http://www.ietf.org`
IRTF	`http://www.irtf.org`
ISO	`http://www.iso.ch`
ISOC	`http://www.isoc.org`
ITU	`http://www.itu.int`
JANET	`http://www.ja.net`
LACNIC	`http://lacnic.net`
OASIS	`http://www.oasis-open.org`
RIPE	`http://www.ripe.net`
UKERNA	`http://www.ukerna.ac.uk`
W3C	`http://www.w3c.org`
RFC	`http://www.rfc.net` `http://www.rfc-editor.org`
RFC search	`http://www.rfc-editor.org/rfcsearch.html`
xml.org	`http://www.xml.org`
ccTLDs	`http://www.iana.org/cctld/` `cctld-whois.htm`
USENET archive	`http://groups.google.com`
Internet timeline	`http://www.zakon.org/robert/internet/` `timeline/`

ACRONYMS

C

1G	First Generation Cellular
2G	Second Generation Cellular
2.5G	Enhanced Second Generation Cellular
21CN	21st Century Network
3G	Third Generation Cellular
3GSM	Third Generation GSM
6bone	IPv6 backbone
AAL	ATM Adaption Layer
ACK	Acknowledgement
ADSL	Asymmetric Digital Subscriber Line
AES	Advanced Encryption Algorithm
AfriNIC	African Regional Network Information Centre
AFS	Andrew Filing System
AH	Authentication Header
AM	Amplitude Modulation
AML	Astronomical Markup Language
AO/DI	Always On/Dynamic ISDN
AoE	ATA over Ethernet
AP	Access Point
API	Application Programming Interface
APNIC	Asia Pacific Network Information Centre
ARIN	American Registry for Internet Numbers
ARP	Address Resolution Protocol
ARPA	Advanced Research Projects Agency
AS	Autonomous System
ASO	Address Supporting Organization
ASCII	American Standard Code for Information Interchange
ATM	Asynchronous Transfer Mode
AUI	Attachment Unit Interface

BGP	Border Gateway Protocol
BNC	British Naval Connector/Bayonet Neill Concelman
BONDING	Bandwidth on Demand Interopability Network Group
BOOTP	Boot Protocol
BRI	Basic Rate Interface
BSS	Basic Service Set
BT	British Telecommunications plc
CAN	Community Area Network
CAP	Carrierless Amplitude Phase
CATV	Cable TV
CBC	Ciplier Block Chaining
CCITT	International Telephone and Telegraph Consultative Committee
CCMP	Counter-Mode/CBC-MAC
CCK	Complementary Code Keying
ccNSO	Country-Code Names Supporting Organization
ccTLD	Country Code TLD
CDMA	Code Division Multiple Access
CE	Congestion Experienced
CERT	Computer Emergency Response Team
CIDR	Classless InterDomain Routing
CIFS	Common Internet File System
CIPE	Crypto IP Encapsulation
CNAME	DNS Canonical Name
CRC	Cyclic Redundancy Check
CSD	Circuit Switched Data
CSLIP	Compressed SLIP
CSMA/CA	Carrier Sense, Multiple Access, Collision Avoidance
CSMA/CD	Carrier Sense, Multiple Access, Collision Detection
CSS	Cascading Style Sheets
CTS	Clear To Send
CWR	Congestion Window Reduced
DAMA-TDMA	Demand Assignment Multiple Access–Time Division Multiple Access
DARPA	Defense Advanced Research Projects Agency
DAS	Direct Attached Storage
DBPSK	Differential Binary Phase Shift Keying
DDNS	Dynamic DNS
DDOS	Distributed Denial of Service
DF	Don't Fragment
DFS	Dynamic Frequency Selection
DHCP	Dynamic Host Configuration Protocol
DMT	Discrete Multi Tone
DNS	Domain Name System

DOCSIS	Data Over Cable Service Interface Specifications
DQPSK	Differential Quadrature Phase Shift Keying
DRM	Digital Rights Management
DS	Differentiated Services
DSCP	Differentiated Services Code Point
DSL	Digital Subscriber Line
DSLAM	Digital Subscriber Line Access Multiplexer
DSSS	Direct Sequence Spread Spectrum
DTD	Document Type Definition
DWDM	Dense Wave Division Multiplexing
EAP	Extensible Authentication Protocol
EBCDIC	Extended Binary-Coded Decimal Interchange Code
ECE	ECN-Echo
ECN	Explicit Congestion Notification
ECT	ECN-capable Transport
EDGE	Enhanced Data rates for GSM Evolution
EGP	Exterior Gateway Protocol
ENUM	Electronic Numbering
ESP	Encapsulating Security Payload
ESS	Extended Service Set
ETSI	European Telecommunications Standards Institute
FC	Fibre Channel
FCC	Federal Communications Commission
FCIP	Fibre Channel over IP
FDDI	Fiber Distributed Data Interface
FEC	Forwarding Equivalence Class
FHSS	Frequency Hopping Spread Spectrum
FM	Frequency Modulation
FQDN	Fully Qualified Domain Name
FTP	File Transfer Protocol
FTTC	Fibre to the Cabinet
FTTH	Fibre to the Home
FTTK	Fibre to the Kerb
FTTN	Fibre to the Node
FTTP	Fibre to the Premises
GNSO	Generic Names Supporting Organization
GPRS	General Packet Radio Service
GRE	Generic Routing Encapsulation
GSM	Global System for Mobile Communications
HBA	Host Bus Adaptor
HD	High Definition
HDLC	High-Level Data Link Control
HDSL	High Rate DSL
HSCSD	High-Speed Circuit Switched Data

HTML	HyperText Markup Language
HTTP	HyperText Transfer Protocol
HTTPS	Secure HTTP
IAB	Internet Architecture Board
IANA	Internet Assigned Number Authority
IBSS	Independent Basic Service Set
ICANN	Internet Corporation for Assigned Names and Numbers
ICMP	Internet Control Message Protocol
IDSL	ISDN DSL
IEC	International Electrotechnical Commission
IEEE	Institute of Electrical and Electronics Engineers
IESG	Internet Engineering Steering Group
IETF	Internet Engineering Task Force
iFCP	Internet Fibre Channel Protocol
IGMP	Internet Group Management Protocol
IGP	Interior Gateway Protocol
IKE	Internet Key Exchange
IMAP	Internet Message Access Protocol
IMAPS	Secure IMAP
IMP	Interface Message Processor
IP	Internet Protocol
IPComp	IP Payload Compression Protocol
IPSec	Secure IP
IPTV	Internet Protocol Television
IRSG	Internet Research Steering Group
IRTF	Internet Research Task Force
ISAKMP	Internet Security Association and Key Management Protocol
iSCSI	Internet SCSI
ISDN	Integrated Services Digital Network
ISM	Industrial, Scientific and Medical
ISN	Initial Sequence Number
ISO	International Organization for Standardization
ISOC	Internet Society
ISODE	ISO Development Environment
ISP	Internet Service Provider
ITU	International Telecommunications Union
ITU-T	ITU, Telecommunications Standardization
IV	Initialization Vector
JANET	Joint Academic Network
L2F	Layer Two Forwarding
L2TP	Layer Two Tunneling Protocol

LACNIC	Latin American and Caribbean Network Information Centre
LAN	Local Area Network
LCP	Link Control Protocol
LDAP	Lightweight Directory Access Protocol
LFN	Long Fat Network
LI-XML	Lawful Intercept XML
LLC	Logical Link Control
LOGML	Log Markup Language
MAA	Mail Access Agent
MAC	Media Access Control
MAN	Metropolitan Area Network
MAPS	Mail Abuse Prevention System
MathML	Mathematical Markup Language
MBONE	Multicast Backbone
MBWA	Mobile Broadband Wireless Access
MDA	Mail Delivery Agent
MIME	Multipurpose Internet Mail Extension
MIMO	Multiple Input Multiple Output
MLD	Multicast Listener Discovery
MNP	Microcom Networking Protocol
MP	Multilink PPP
MPEG	Motion Picture Experts Group
MPI	Message Passing Interface
MPLS	Multiprotocol Label Switching
MPPE	Microsoft Point-to-Point Encryption
MRU	Maximum Receive Unit
MSL	Maximum Segment Lifetime
MSS	Maximum Segment Size
MTA	Mail Transport Agent
MTU	Maximum Transmission Unit
MUA	Mail User Agent
NACK	Negative Acknowledgement
NAPT	Network Address Port Translation
NAPTR	Naming Authority Pointer
NAS	Network Attached Storage
NAT	Network Address Translation
NCP	Network Control Protocol
NFS	Network File System
NIC	Network Information Centre
NNTP	Network News Transfer Protocol
NSF	National Science Foundation
NTP	Network Time Protocol

OASIS	Organization for the Advancement of Structured Information Standards
OC	Optical Carrier level
OFDM	Orthogonal Frequency Division Multiplexing
OFX	Open Financial Exchange
OML	Open Mobile Alliance
OS	Operating System
OSI	Open Systems Interconnection
OSPF	Open Shortest Path First
PAN	Personal Area Network
PAT	Port Address Translation
PAWS	Protection Against Wrapped Sequence Numbers
PCS	Physical Coding Sublayer
PDML	Product Data Markup Language
PGP	Pretty Good Privacy
PHY	Physical Layer
PLCP	Physical Layer Convergence Procedure
PM	Phase Modulation
PMD	Physical Media Dependent
POP	Post Office Protocol
POTS	Plain Old Telephone Service
PPI	Payload Protocol Identifier
PPP	Point-to-Point Protocol
PPPoA	PPP over ATM
PPPoE	PPP over Ethernet
PPTP	Point-to-Point Tunneling Protocol
PRI	Primary Rate Interface
PTR	DNS Pointer Record
PVM	Parallel Virtual Machine
QAM	Quadrature Amplitude Modulation
QoS	Quality of Service
QPSK	Quadrature Phase Shift Keying
RADIUS	Remote Authentication Dial In User Service
RADSL	Rate Adaptive Digital Subscriber Line
RARP	Reverse ARP
RBL	Realtime Blackhole List
RDF	Resource Description Framework
RED	Random Early Detection
RIP	Routing Information Protocol
RIPA	Regulation of Investigatory Powers Act
RIPE	Réseaux IP Européens
RPC	Remote Procedure Call
RR	Resource Record

RSS	RDF Site Summary
RTP	Real-time Transport Protocol
RTS	Request to Send
RTSP	Real Time Streaming Protocol
RTT	Round Trip-Time
SACK	Selective Acknowledgement
SAML	Security Assertion Markup Language
SAN	Storage Area Network
SCSI	Small Computer System Interface
SCTP	Stream Control Transmission Protocol
SDH	Synchronous Digital Hierarchy
SDSL	Symmetric DSL
SGML	Standard Generalized Markup Language
SHTTP	Secure HTTP
SID	Stream ID
SIMAP	Secure IMAP
SIP	Session Initiation Protocol
SLIP	Serial Line IP
SMB	Server Message Block
SMDS	Switched Multimegabit Data Service
SMIL	Synchronized Multimedia Integration Language
SMTP	Simple Mail Transfer Protocol
SMTPS	Secure SMTP
SNA	Systems Network Architecture
SOA	Start of Authority
SOAP	Simple Object Access Protocol
SOHO	Small Office/Home Office
SONET	Synchronous Optical Network
SPF	Sender Policy Framework/Sender Permitted From
SPOP	Secure POP
SSL	Secure Socket Layer
SSMTP	Secure SMTP
SSN	Stream Sequence Number
ST	Internet Stream Protocol
STM	Synchronous Transport Module
STS	Synchronous Transport Signal
STUN	Simple Traversal of UDP through Network Address Translators
SVG	Scalable Vector Graphics
SWAP	Shared Wireless Access Protocol
SWS	Silly Window Syndrome
TCM	Trellis-Coded Modulation
TCP	Transmission Control Protocol

TDMA	Time Division Multiple Access
TKIP	Temporal Key Integrity Protocol
TLA	Three Letter Acronym
TLD	Top Level Domain
TLS	Transport Layer Security
TOE	TCP/IP Offload Engine
TOS	Type of Service
TPC	Transmit Power Control
TSN	Transmission Sequence Number
T/TCP	TCP for Transactions
TTL	Time to Live
UCS	Universal Character Set
UDP	User Datagram Protocol
UKERNA	United Kingdom Education and Research Networking Association
UMTS	Universal Mobile Telephone System
UNII	Unlicensed National Information Infrastructure
UPnP	Universal Plug'n'Play
USB	Universal Serial Bus
USENET	User Network
UTF	UCS Transformation Format
UTP	Unshielded Twisted Pair
UWB	Ultra-Wideband
VDSL	Very High Rate DSL
VID	virtual LAN identifier
VLAN	Virtual LAN
VoiceXML	Voice Extensible Markup Language
VoIP	Voice over IP
VPN	Virtual Private Network
W3C	World Wide Web Consortium
WAN	Wide Area Network
WAP	Wireless Application Protocol
WCDMA	Wideband-CDMA
WDSL	Web Services Description Language
WECA	Wireless Ethernet Compatibility Alliance
WEP	Wired Equivalent Privacy
Wi-Fi	Wireless Fidelity
WiMAX	World Interoperability for Microwave Access
WLAN	Wireless Local Area Network
WML	Wireless Markup Language
WMM	Wi-Fi Multimedia, 802.11e
WPA	Wi-Fi Protected Access
WPA2	Wi-Fi Protected Access, 802.11i

WPAN	Wireless Personal Area Network
WRAN	Wireless Regional Network
WUSB	Wireless USB
WWAN	Wireless Wide Area Network
WWW	World Wide Web
XAUI	10Gb Attachment Unit Interface
XDR	External Data Representation
xDSL	Any or all of the DSL standards
XHTML	Extensible HyperText Markup Language
XML	Extensible Markup Language
XMPP	Extensible Messaging and Presence Protocol
XSL	Extensible Style Language
XSLT	XSL Transformations
XUL	XML User-interface Language

INDEX

XMPP, *see* Extensible Messaging and Presence
  Protocol
XSL, *see* Extensible Style Language
XSL Transformations (XSLT), 224
XSLT, *see* XSL Transformations
XUL, *see* XML User-interface Language

zero configuration IP networking, 148
Zeroconf, 148
Zigbee, 72
zone, 140
  transfer, 140
zowie, 31